SHOWING
THE
SPIRIT

SHOWING THE SPIRIT

A Theological Exposition of
1 Corinthians 12–14

D.A.Carson

Baker Books

A Division of Baker Book House Co.
Grand Rapids, Michigan 49516

©1987 by Baker Book House Company

Published by Baker Books
a division of Baker Book House Company
P.O. Box 6287, Grand Rapids, MI 49516-6287

Fifth printing, November 1996

Printed in the United States of America

Library of Congress Cataloging-in-Publication Data

Carson, D. A.
  Showing the Spirit: a theological exposition of 1 Corinthians
12–14 / D. A. Carson
    p. cm.
  "Moore College lectures of September 1985"—Pref.
  Bibliography: p.
  Includes indexes.
  ISBN 0-8010-2521-4
  1. Bible. N.T. Corinthians. 1st, XII–XIV—Criticism,
interpretation, etc. 2. Gifts, Spiritual—Biblical teaching. I. Title. II. Title: Moore
College lectures.
  BS2675.2.C38 1987
  227'.026—dc19
                                                           87-21457

For information about academic books, resources for Christian leaders, and all new releases available from Baker Book House, visit our web site:
http://www.bakerbooks.com/

To the principal, faculty, staff, and students of Moore College,
Sydney, on the occasion of my first trip to Australia,
September 1985

Contents

Preface

The pages of this book were first prepared for oral delivery as the Moore College Lectures of September 1985. I am very grateful to the former principal, Dr. Broughton Knox, for issuing the invitation, and to the current principal, Dr. Peter Jensen, and his faculty for the warm welcome they accorded me. I cannot speak too highly of the many kindnesses shown me, far beyond mere courtesy. The two happy weeks I spent "down under" brought renewed friendships with Rev. Allan and Pamela Blanch, Rev. Phillip and Helen Jensen, and Dr. Peter and Mary O'Brien, and a host of new friends and acquaintances too numerous to mention. But one very special friend was a three-year-old charmer, Anne Woodhouse.

The invitation to give the lectures became the spur to put into print some material I had been thinking about and teaching for some years. Without that incentive, it would still be formless. Because the issues are so complex and widely disputed both in academic circles and in the church at large, I have included fairly extensive notes and bibliography for the more advanced student, while retaining the style of the lectures in the body of the text.

One does not reach conclusions like those put forth in these pages without extensive interaction with many people. I am reluctant to begin a list of names; but in addition to the help I received from the largely technical sources mentioned in the notes, I am particularly indebted to three people: Dr. Max Turner of Aberdeen University, whose long conversations with me more than ten years ago helped to sharpen my thinking; Dr. Roy Clements, pastor of Eden Baptist Church in Cambridge, England, whose expository series on this epistle was a great and stimulating delight; and Dr. Kenneth S. Kantzer, who kindly provided me with extensive class notes from a course he has been teaching for years. I am sure I have borrowed from these men without always realizing it. None of them will agree with everything I have written; but that probably means I have much more to learn.

Because the debate over the "charismatic movement" is far from being of merely academic interest, I have included in the bibliography and notes, as well as in the topics discussed, a representative number of more popular treatments along with the technical studies. Otherwise, I fear these lectures would have scratched where only a few fellow academics itch. My graduate assistant, Mr. Mark Reasoner, was indefatigable in tracking down obscure articles and books; and the staff of Rolfing Library, invariably helpful and courteous, must nevertheless be grateful the project has come to an end. One or two works in the bibliography, in particular the book by P. Benoit et al., arrived too late to be used—except for one essay by James D. G. Dunn, an offprint of which was kindly loaned me by Dr. Scot McKnight. I am grateful as well for the work of Rev. Dan Estes and Rev. Bruce Winter, who compiled the indexes for me at an extraordinarily busy juncture of my life.

The series was delivered in slightly abbreviated form at Mennonite Brethren Biblical Seminary in Fresno, California, and at Canadian Theological Seminary in Regina, Saskatchewan, in the autumn of 1985, providing me with further opportunities for reflection and revision. I am grateful for the many kindnesses shown me on those occasions.

Soli Deo gloria.

D. A. Carson
Trinity Evangelical Divinity School

Introduction

In the entire range of contemporary Christian theology and personal experience, few topics are currently more important than those associated with what is now commonly called "the charismatic movement." The label itself, as we shall see, is in the light of the biblical usage of χάρισμα *(charisma)* somewhat misleading; but because it is the common term, I shall continue to use it. What makes the subject difficult in any case is not so much the label as the substance. The movement embraces not only the traditional "Pentecostal" denominations but substantial minorities in most of the denominations of Christendom; and in some parts of the world—South America for instance—it is simultaneously the major Protestant voice and a successful invader of the Roman Catholic Church. Whatever their theological commitments, young clergy will wrestle with questions raised by the charismatic movement as frequently and in some instances as painfully as anything else that comes their way.

As the charismatic movement has grown, so also has it become more diversified, thereby rendering many generalizations about it remarkably reductionistic. But it is probably fair to say that both charismatics and noncharismatics (if I may continue to use those terms in nonbiblical ways) often cherish neat stereotypes of the other party. As judged by the charismatics, noncharismatics tend to be stodgy traditionalists who do not really believe the Bible and who are not really hungry for the Lord. They are afraid of profound spiritual experience, too proud to give themselves wholeheartedly to God, more concerned for ritual than for reality, and more in love with propositional truth than with the truth incarnate. They are better at writing theological tomes than at evangelism; they are defeatist in outlook, defensive in stance, dull in worship, and devoid of the Spirit's power in their personal experience. The noncharismatics themselves, of course, tend to see things a little differently. The charismatics, they think, have succumbed to the modern love of "experience," even at the expense of truth. Charismatics are thought to be profoundly unbiblical, especially when they elevate their experience of tongues to the level of theological and spiritual shibboleth. If they are growing, no small part of their strength can be ascribed to their raw triumphalism, their populist elitism, their promise of short cuts to holiness and power. They are better at splitting churches and stealing sheep than they are at evangelism, more accomplished in spiritual one-upmanship before other believers than in faithful, humble service. They are imperialistic in outlook (only they have the "full gospel"), abrasive in stance, uncontrolled in worship, and devoid of any real grasp of the Bible that goes beyond mere proof-texting.

Of course, both sides concede that the caricatures I have drawn admit notable exceptions; but the profound suspicions on both sides make genuine dialogue extremely difficult. This is especially painful, indeed embarrassing, in the light of the commitment made by most believers on both sides to the Bible's authority. The stereotyped positions of the two sides are so antithetical, even though both claim to be biblical, that we must conclude one of three things: one side or the other is right in its interpretation of Scripture on these points, and the other is correspondingly wrong; both sides are to some degree wrong, and some better way of understanding Scripture must be found; or the Bible simply does not speak clearly and univocally to these issues, and both sides of the dispute have extrapolated the Bible's teachings to entrenched positions not themselves defensible in Scripture.

We must in any case return to Scripture. That is the rationale for this series. I have no delusions that what I say is particularly innovative or will prove thoroughly convincing to everyone who has thought about these issues; and the narrowness of the primary focus—only three chapters from one New Testament document—necessarily circumscribes my conclusions. Nevertheless, I hope my concluding chapter will integrate enough other biblical material, especially from the Book of Acts, that the conclusions will not appear distorted. Moreover, although most of my attention will be devoted to the text of 1 Corinthians 12–14, my concern to make this a *theological* exposition (as the subtitle stipulates) will force me to interact a little with some other Christian doctrines, as well as with the findings of linguists, social anthropologists, historians, and the practical and popular beliefs of the contemporary church, even where such considerations range outside the domain of the student of the New Testament; for I am persuaded that if the church is to have peace on these issues, we must evenhandedly attempt to weigh all the relevant evidence even while we insist that the authority of Scripture must prevail. That authority, of course, should not be transferred to me, as the interpreter; and so I shall from time to time indicate the degree of certainty with which I make interpretative judgments, so that even if we cannot agree on all the details, perhaps most of us can come to agreement on the most central matters.

List of Abbreviations

BAG   Arndt, William F., and Gingrich, F. Wilbur, trans. *A Greek-English Lexicon of the New Testament and Other Early Christian Literature* by Walter Bauer, 4th ed. Chicago and London: University of Chicago Press, 1957.

BAGD   Gingrich, F. W., and Danker, F. W., trans. *A Greek-English Lexicon of the New Testament and Other Early Christian Literature,* by W. Bauer, 2d ed. Chicago and London: University of Chicago Press, 1979.

BDF   Blass, F., and Debrunner, A., *A Greek Grammar of the New Testament and Other Early Christian Literature,* trans. and rev. Robert W. Funk. Chicago and London: University of Chicago Press, 1961.

TDNT   Bromiley, G. W., trans. and ed., *Theological Dictionary of the New Testament,* 10 vols. (Original German work ed. G. Kittel.) Grand Rapids: Eerdmans, 1964–76.

1

The Unity of the Body and the Diversity of Gifts (12:1–30)

Reflections on the Background of the Argument in 1 Corinthians 12–14

Modern opinion on the background has been cataloged not only in commentaries but also in several recent studies, and need not be repeated here.[1] I shall merely summarize my own conclusions. From

1. E.g., John C. Hurd, *The Origin of 1 Corinthians* (New York: Seabury, 1965), 186–87; K. S. Hemphill, "The Pauline Concept of Charisma: A Situational and Developmental Approach" (Ph.D. diss., Cambridge University, 1976), 45ff.; and see A. C. Thiselton, "Realized Eschatology at Corinth," *New Testament Studies* 24 (1978): 510–26.

chapter 7 on, Paul appears to be answering a series of questions put to him in a letter from the Corinthians: "Now for the matters you wrote about," he begins (7:1). That explains why the topics change so radically: at one point Paul is dealing with relations between the sexes (chap. 7), at another with meat offered to idols (8:1ff.). He can move from women praying and prophesying in the congregation (11:2–16), to the Lord's Supper (11:17–34), to grace-gifts and love (chaps. 12–14), to the resurrection (chap. 15). Sometimes (as here in 12:1) he opens a new subject with a set expression, Περὶ δέ (*peri de*, now concerning . . .). But three features in his argument stand out.

First, one of the common denominators in the problems at Corinth was overrealized eschatology.[2] It is a commonplace that Paul places the church in dynamic tension between an "already" view of what God has done, and a "not yet" view of what he is still to do. Already the kingdom has dawned and the Messiah is reigning, already the crucial victory has been won, already the final resurrection of the dead has begun in the resurrection of Jesus, already the Holy Spirit has been poured out on the church as the down payment of the promised inheritance and the first fruits of the eschatological harvest of blessings. Nevertheless, the kingdom has not yet come in its consummated fullness, death still exercises formidable powers, sin must be overcome, and opposing powers of darkness war against us with savage ferocity. The new heaven and the new earth have not yet put in an appearance. Maintaining this balance is crucial to the church's maturity. If we think only in terms of what is still to come (i.e., if we focus on futurist eschatology), we may not only play endless speculative games but we may also depreciate the climactic nature of the incarnation, cross-work, and resurrection of Jesus that have *already* taken place. We may so pine for the future that we neglect to serve God with enthusiastic gratitude for what he has done in the past. On the other hand, if we think only in terms of what Christ has already accomplished (i.e., if we focus on realized eschatology), we fall into the errors that characterized many of the believers in Corinth. We may feel that as children of the king we have the *right* to unqualified blessings; we may go so far as to let this stance transform our belief structure until we insist that the crucial experiences of grace we have enjoyed constitute the true "resurrection," and that no other awaits us. That is why one recent commentator on chapters 12–14 includes a study of chapter 15 as well.[3] The Corinthian eschatology was probably rein-

    2. See especially Thiselton, ibid.
    3. Ralph P. Martin, *The Spirit and the Congregation: Studies in 1 Corinthians 12–15* (Grand Rapids: Eerdmans, 1984).

forced by some brand of Hellenistic dualism that took a dim view of present bodily existence while vastly misunderstanding the nature of spiritual vitality. Perhaps nowhere does the overrealized eschatology of Corinth surface more strongly than in chapter 4: "Already you have all you want!" writes Paul with considerable heat and not a little sarcasm. "Already you have become rich! You have become kings— and that without us! How I wish that you really had become kings so that we might be kings with you!" (4:8). The apostles, Paul goes on to say, are treated like scum; the Corinthians are above the dirt and delight to think how full of knowledge and wisdom they are. This overrealized eschatology, it can be argued, stands behind many of the pastoral questions Paul faces in Corinth, and is related to the theme of chapters 12–14.

Second, the church in Corinth is a divided church. This is seen not only in the party labels reported at 1:12 ("What I mean is this: One of you says, 'I follow Paul'; another, 'I follow Apollos'; another, 'I follow Cephas'; still another, 'I follow Christ.' ") and treated in the first four chapters of the book, but also in a style of argumentation that pervades much of chapters 7–12. It might be called the "yes—but" form of argument. If people in the church take different sides of an issue, Paul's aim is not only to present his apostolic judgment on the matter but also to reconcile the warring factions. To do this, he tips his head to each faction in turn, and says in effect, "Yes, yes, you have something of the truth on your side, I largely agree with you—*but.* . . ." To those more ascetically inclined, he writes, "It is good for a man not to touch a woman" (7:1);[4] *but*, he goes on to say, marriage helps reduce promiscuity and in any case it is also a good gift from God (7:2–7). In chapter 8, he acknowledges that Christians know an idol has no real power and constitutes no evil in itself, and therefore food that has been offered to it cannot have undergone some kind of poisonous transformation that makes it dangerous for the Christian (8:1–6). *"But,"* he goes on to say, "not everyone knows this" (8:7), by which he is referring to other Christians in the Corinthian church; and on this basis he works out some mediating principles.

Not every "but" in 1 Corinthians is traceable to Paul's concern to unite warring factions; and in one or two instances the apostle sets his stance in diametric opposition to the church (e.g., "In the following directives I have no praise for you" [11:17]). Nevertheless the feature is common enough that we must ask what stands behind it when it

---

4. The translation of the NIV, "It is good for a man not to marry," is incorrect: see Gordon D. Fee, "1 Corinthians 7:1 in the NIV," *Journal of the Evangelical Theological Society* 23 (1980): 307–14.

occurs. "I would like every one of you to speak in tongues, *but* I would rather have you prophesy. . . . I thank God that I speak in tongues more than all of you. *But* in the church I would rather speak five intelligible words to instruct others than ten thousand words in a tongue" (14:5a, 18–19).[5] Few doubt that Paul's primary interest in these chapters is to curtail somewhat the excesses of certain tongues-speakers; but in these texts he first aligns himself with the tongues-speakers. Are there also hints in these chapters of those who do *not* speak in tongues?

I think there are, although nowhere do they appear behind an analogous "yes—but" argument. At the end of his discussion, Paul can write, "Do not forbid speaking in tongues" (14:39)—which surely suggests that is what some would have preferred. They cannot be the tongues-speakers themselves, since not only would tongues-speakers have a vested interest the other way, but also nothing Paul has said up to that point demands abolition of this gift.[6] Again, in the metaphor of chapter 12, some seem to be threatened by the gifts of others, and are therefore withdrawing in some form (12:14ff.). In the context of these two chapters, the only threatening gift is the gift of tongues.[7]

These reflections turn out to be important, for some scholars have argued that Paul's concerns for divisions within the church have come to an end with chapter 4.[8] The letter from Corinth that occupies Paul from chapter 7 on must have come from the *whole* church, they say, not some faction within it; Paul's responses suggest that the Corinthian church was more divided *against Paul* than internally. I remain unconvinced. In the first place, this seems to divorce chapters 7–16 from the factionalism we know about from chapters 1–4. Second, a letter may come from an entire church, and with a belligerent tone, while asking questions that betray difference of opinion *within* the church. After all, if the church were unified on the points that it raises, it is

5. The varied forms of adversative (e.g., ἀλλά, μᾶλλον δέ) are no impediment to the observation, since the argument turns on the logical relationship of a pair of clauses within a context, not to a purely lexical feature.

6. The "but" that immediately succeeds 14:39 does not belong to the "yes—but" form of argument, since it is immediately preceded by a prohibition.

7. See Mattie Elizabeth Hart, "Speaking in Tongues and Prophecy as Understood by Paul and at Corinth, with Reference to Early Christian Usage" (Ph.D. diss., University of Durham, 1975), whose primary ambition is to demonstrate that there were both "procharismatic" and "anticharismatic" forces at Corinth, while Paul adopts a stance that is open to every work of the Spirit yet critical of much of what he observes at Corinth.

8. E.g., Hurd, *Origin of 1 Corinthians*, 193–95; Gordon D. Fee, "Tongues—Least of the Gifts? Some Exegetical Observations on 1 Corinthians 12–14," *Pneuma* 2/2 (1980): 4–7.

not at all clear why the Corinthians would have questions to raise (except perhaps purely theoretical ones). Third, the central chapter of the three under scrutiny emphasizes love so strongly that it is not hard to believe that the Corinthian church was singularly lacking in this commodity, again doubtless owing to factionalism.

Third, the dominant focus of these chapters is the conduct of the church as it is assembled together. That is equally true, of course, of chapter 11; but the observation becomes especially important when we try to integrate this stance into the flow of the argument at several crucial points (e.g., "in the church," 14:19, "when you come together," 14:26).

These reflections set the stage for the exegesis, to which we must now turn.

The Bearing of Christianity's Central Confession on What It Means to Be Spiritual (12:1–3)

The principal turning points in these verses are five.

Paul's Use of χάρισμα (charisma)

In the New Testament, the term is found sixteen times in the Pauline writings, and once in Peter (1 Peter 4:10). Clearly cognate with χάρις (grace), at its simplest it refers to something grace has bestowed, a "grace-gift" if you will. It is not that Paul coined the term: that is most likely going too far, although admittedly pre-Pauline occurrences are textually uncertain.[9] But for the apostle who so delights to discuss grace, it is eminently appropriate that he should devote attention to the things of grace, to the concretizations of grace, to grace-gifts.

Of more importance is what the word refers to. Outside 1 Corinthians 12–14, Paul uses it to refer to the "spiritual gift" he wishes to impart to the Romans when he sees them, in the context of a mutual encouragement of faith (Rom. 1:11); to the "gift" that generates life over against the trespass of Adam that generated death (Rom. 5:15–16, where the word is also in parallel with δώρημα [gift]); to the gift of

---

9. E.g., in Ecclus. 7:33, the correct word is probably χάρις, not χάρισμα; and in 38:34[30] the original may be χρῖσμα: see Archibald Robertson and Alfred Plummer, *A Critical and Exegetical Commentary on the First Epistle of St Paul to the Corinthians*, 2d ed. (Edinburgh: T. and T. Clark, 1914). There is no textually certain pre-Pauline example: see Siegfried Schulz, "Die Charismenlehre des Paulus: Bilanz der Probleme und Ergebnisse," in *Rechtfertigung: Festschrift für Ernst Käsemann*, ed. Johannes Friedrich, Wolfgang Pöhlmann, and Peter Stuhlmacher (Tübingen: J. C. B. Mohr; Göttingen: Vandenhoeck und Ruprecht, 1976), 445–46; U. Brockhaus, *Charisma und Amt*, 2d ed. (Wuppertal: Brockhaus, 1975), 128–29.

God, eternal life in Christ Jesus, that alone can offset the wages of sin, which is death (Rom. 6:23); to the election of Israel, since God's "gifts" and call are irrevocable (Rom. 11:29); to the list of "gifts" presented in Romans 12:6–7: prophesying, serving, teaching, encouraging, contributing to the needs of others, leadership, and showing mercy. That accounts for the uses in Romans. In 2 Corinthians 1:11, χάρισμα (*charisma*) refers to "the gracious favor" granted to Paul in response to the prayers of many—presumably deliverance from an unspecified "deadly peril." There are two occurrences in the pastoral Epistles. In 1 Timothy 4:14 Timothy is told not to neglect the "gift" that was given him through a prophetic message when the elders laid their hands on him; but the gift itself is not further specified. Similarly in 2 Timothy 1:6 he is told to "fan into flame the gift of God" that is in him through the laying on of Paul's hands. Perhaps we may deduce from these two contexts that the gift was the ministry to which he was called, in danger of being curtailed by timidity and insufficient self-discipline. The usage in 1 Peter 4:10 tightly ties "grace-gift" to "grace": each believer is to use whatever gift (χάρισμα, *charisma*) he has received to serve others, thereby administering God's grace (χάρις, *charis*) in its various forms.

We have now scanned every instance of the noun in the New Testament, except for those in 1 Corinthians. In the first chapter, Paul assures the Corinthians that they do not lack any "spiritual gift" as they wait for the Lord's return (although one wonders if the reference to the Lord's return is a not-too-subtle reminder that even such spiritual wealth is nothing compared with the glory that is to come [1:7]). In one of the most intriguing occurrences, Paul tells his readers that each person has a particular gift from God—one this, and another that—in a context where "this" and "that" refer to marriage and celibacy (1 Cor. 7:7). Presumably, one cannot enjoy both of these χαρίσματα (*charismata*) simultaneously! The remaining five instances are all found in 1 Corinthians 12. The word stands behind the different kinds of "gifts" in 12:4, and behind the word *gifts* in 12:31a (rendered in the NIV, "But eagerly desire the greater gifts."). Finally, it is found three times in the plural expression *gifts of healing* (12:9, 28, 30). The word χάρισμα (*charisma*) does *not* stand behind what the New International Version calls "spiritual gifts" in 12:1, 14:1, and elsewhere.

So much for the raw data. What shall we make of them? Dealing first with the superficial, it is very clear that the term is not a technical one for Paul that refers only to a select set of supranormal gifts like healing and tongues. Not only can it embrace gifts like encouraging and generous giving, but it can be used repeatedly for the gift of salvation itself—not to mention the gift of celibacy and the gift of marriage. In that sense, therefore, every Christian is a charismatic. Moreover, if the term can extend to celibacy and marriage, every person, Christian or not, is a charismatic; that is, every person has received gracious gifts from God. It is for this reason that I do not like to talk about the "charismatic movement" unless I am given space to define terms: it seems like a terrible reduction of the manifold grace of God. Having clarified what Paul's range of referents is under this term, however, I shall bow to popular coinage and speak of the "charismatic movement."

But if χάρισμα (charisma) should not be turned into a technical term by the charismatic movement, neither should it receive such treatment from other voices in the field. Grau, Käsemann, and Dunn have made attempts;[10] but these attempts cannot be judged successful.[11] It is reductionistic to think the word refers only to the fundamental gift of salvation, or only to specific acts or events immediately imparted by the Spirit but having no underlay in the individual's "natural" gifts. On the one hand, the χάρισμα (charisma) of Romans 6:23 ("the gift of God is eternal life") must not be made to stand as the source of all the other χαρίσματα (charismata); for although the referent of the word in Romans 6:23 (i.e., eternal life) may be the source of all the other χαρίσματα (charismata), nevertheless "it is a blunder in the realm of lexical semantics to confuse the referent of a predicate (in a referring expression) with its sense, and it leads to forced interpretation of Romans 1:11; 1 Corinthians 7:7; 2 Corinthians 1:11; Romans 5:15 and 11:29."[12] On the other hand, it is not clear that the word acquires a semitechnical force in 1 Corinthians 12–14, meaning concrete events or actions, specific events or occasions of leadership, prophecy, teaching, and the like. Dunn uses this distinction to apply the term charismatic only to specific acts or events, refusing to apply it to gifts of grace that might be latent or temporarily hidden.[13] The term simply cannot have that force outside 1 Corinthians 12–14; and even here, as Hemphill remarks, if Paul thought of the χαρίσματα (charismata) primarily as Spirit-given events or acts, he could have curtailed much of the Corinthian boasting by pointing out that no one

10. F. Grau, "Der neutestamentliche Begriff χάρισμα" (Ph.D. diss., Tübingen University, 1946 [I have not been able to secure a copy; I know of this work only from secondary sources]); Ernst Käsemann, Essays on New Testament Themes, trans. W. J. Montague (Philadelphia: Fortress, 1982), 64–65; James D. G. Dunn, Jesus and the Spirit (Philadelphia: Westminster, 1975), 209.

11. For excellent discussion, see M. M. B. Turner, "Spiritual Gifts Then and Now," Vox Evangelica 15 (1985): 30–31.

12. Ibid., 30.

13. Dunn, Jesus and the Spirit, 209.

can in fact *possess* or *have* such gifts. In fact he freely speaks of people *having* certain gifts, and gives instructions on the *use* of the gift one has.[14]

What is clear, then, is that the particular "spiritual gifts" Paul wishes to discuss in these chapters are gifts of God's grace. To say more than that,[15] we must extend the discussion first to another word for spiritual gift, and then to the relationship between these two words.

The Meaning of πνευματικῶν *(pneumatikōn)*

When Paul opens the chapter with the words *now about spiritual gifts, brothers* (12:1), he is setting the agenda of the ensuing three chapters. Clearly, then, the word rendered "spiritual gifts" is important; but in fact it hides a difficult ambiguity. In Pauline usage it can be taken as masculine and refer to "spiritual people" (see 2:15; 3:1; 14:37), or as neuter and refer to "spiritual things" (i.e., "spiritual gifts"; see 9:11; 14:1; 15:46). Which is the meaning here? Both interpretations have been strongly defended; and the fact that these chapters close with the personal use (14:37) might be taken as a point in favor of the masculine. In that case Paul is dealing less with the nature of spiritual gifts than with the nature of spiritual people, although obviously the two are in some way related. There would also be an immediate effect on the way the first three verses (12:1–3) are interpreted. Nevertheless, the word is probably to be taken as a neuter. After all, if it occurs in 14:37 as a reference to spiritual people, it also occurs in 14:1 as a reference to spiritual gifts. More important, the word is conceptually parallel in certain respects to χαρίσματα *(charismata)*, and the latter never refers to persons.

The crucial point to recognize is that in 12:1 Paul is bringing up a point in the Corinthians' letter. What question were they posing to him to generate so ambiguous a response? For reasons that will become clear in a moment, I suggest that at least one of the questions being put to him ran something like this: "Is it really true that spiritual manifestations (πνευματικά, *pneumatika*) constitute unfailing evidence of spiritual people (πνευματικοί, *pneumatikoi*)?" This question, I shall suggest, had opposing barbs. As phrased by the Corinthian "pneu-

14. Hemphill, "Pauline Concept of Charisma," 78 n. 92.
15. As many do: e.g., John Howard Schütz, *Paul and the Anatomy of Apostolic Authority* (Cambridge: Cambridge University Press, 1975), 277, argues that Paul's authority rests precisely in his ability to help his readers experience the same "charismatic" power he enjoys; and John Koenig, "From Mystery to Ministry: Paul as Interpreter of Charismatic Gifts," *Union Seminary Quarterly Review* 33 (1978): 167–74, associates χάρισμα and μυστήριον to argue that the ultimate concern behind even the "mysteries" to which Paul as a charismatic has access is ministry.

matics" it was shaped like this: "Is it not true that . . . ?" As shaped by the "non-pneumatics" it sounded more like this: "Surely it isn't true that . . . ?" Paul responds with a reference to their discussion of "the question of spirituals" (περὶ δὲ τῶν πνευματικῶν, peri de tōn pneumatikōn), knowing that his readers will recognize thereby the subject he is about to broach.

The Relationship Between χάρισμα (charisma) and πνευματικόν (pneumatikon)

It is widely recognized that the introductory formula of 12:1 means that Paul is introducing the subject in the terms preferred by his Corinthian readers (πνευματικόν, pneumatikon),[16] and that at least through chapter 12 he then proceeds to use the term he himself prefers (χάρισμα, charisma). But what does he intend to achieve by this change?

An easy guess, and almost certainly right in itself, is that Paul wants to remind his readers that whatever might truly be considered "spiritual" is better thought of as a gracious gift from God. The quest for an individualizing and self-centered form of "spirituality" was in danger of denying the source of all true spiritual gifts, the unbounded grace of God. This does not mean Paul depreciates the term πνευματικόν (pneumatikon); for elsewhere in his epistle, with only one possible exception (14:37, and in my judgment that possibility is not a real exception), Paul always uses the word with positive overtones of spiritual maturity. The apostle who so persistently insists that God's πνεῦμα (pneuma) is the down payment of the age to come is in no position to despise any πνευματικόν (pneumatikon). Still, in this context the switch to χάρισμα (charisma) serves to lay emphasis on grace. But are there sharper lines to be drawn between these two words?

One way of proceeding has become especially popular. Some have argued that πνευματικόν (pneumatikon) should be restricted to prophecy or to prophecy and tongues.[17] This interpretation is usually tied

16. E.g., Käsemann, Essays on New Testament Themes, 66; Brockhaus, Charisma und Amt, 150ff.; D. Moody Smith, "Glossolalia and Other Spiritual Gifts in a New Testament Perspective," Interpretation 28 (1974): 311; Birger Albert Pearson, The Pneumatikos-Psychikos Terminology (Missoula, Mont.: Scholars, 1973), 44.

17. E.g., Pearson, Pneumatikos-Psychikos Terminology, argues that the reference is to prophecy alone; Max-Alain Chevallier, Esprit de Dieu, Paroles d'Hommes (Neuchâtel: Delachaux et Niestlé, 1966), followed by David L. Baker, "The Interpretation of 1 Cor 12–14," Evangelical Quarterly 46 (1974): 224–34, argues for both prophecy and tongues. See also D. W. B. Robinson, "Charismata versus Pneumatika: Paul's Method of Discussion," Reformed Theological Review 31 (1972): 49–55, who draws attention to the parallel between 14:1 and 14:5, both with μᾶλλον δέ. But this does not mean that the only πνευματικά in the Corinthians' mind were prophecy and tongues, but only that

in with an attempt to make prophecy at Corinth ecstatic; and Paul's aim in effect is to replace the emphasis on the ecstatic by the broader category of gracious gift that results in service. But outside these three chapters the word certainly does not have that meaning. If then someone argues that what is important here is what the *Corinthians* mean by the word, not Paul, since he is quoting their correspondence, we still face two difficulties: (1) If Paul knows that the Corinthians use the word in a special sense, it is surprising to find him using it three times earlier in this epistle in his normal way (2:15; 3:1; 9:11), and then switching here without warning to *their* meaning. (2) A specialized meaning in 12:1 such as "concerning persons whom you designate 'spiritually gifted' " makes a poor heading to a chapter where Paul is repeatedly concerned to show that *all* Christians are spiritually gifted, unless he takes explicit pains to point out their faulty *category* and not just their distorted *theology.*[18]

These first three points have not drawn us into the flow of the passage; but they had to be discussed, for the results come back to bless us (or haunt us) in what ensues. My main point so far is that a number of studies have overspecified what can be learned from a few individual words.

The Flow of the Argument in 12:1–3

The statement "brothers, I do not want you to be ignorant" (12:1), or its near equivalent, is a Pauline expression (cf. 10:1; Rom. 1:13; 11:25; 2 Cor. 1:8; 1 Thess. 4:13) by which the apostle assures his readers that what he is passing on is part of the heritage of central Christian truth; and sometimes it introduces content that cannot be more than a reminder of material previously taught. In the dominant interpretation of 12:1–3, it is presupposed that the truth of which the apostle does not wish the Corinthians to remain ignorant is found in verses 2 and 3. This has the effect of tying those two verses tightly together, reinforced by the strong "therefore" (διό) at the beginning of verse 3; that is, *because* you were led away to serve dumb idols when you were pagans (v. 2), *therefore* (v. 3) I am telling you that no one who speaks by the Spirit of God can say "Jesus is anathema," and no one can say "Jesus is Lord" except by the Holy Spirit. By forging so tight a link

the gift of tongues was the principal focus of abuse, and the gift of prophecy was the foil Paul used to show how ideally spiritual gifts should serve others. The particular use of the disjunction made by Martin, *The Spirit and the Congregation*, is compounded by his retrieval of quotes from the Corinthians' letter—a point that will be discussed later.

18. See especially Wayne Grudem, *The Gift of Prophecy in 1 Corinthians* (Washington, D.C.: University Press of America, 1982), 157–62.

between verses 2 and 3, this interpretation has two important consequences. First, it entices the interpreter to look for clues in verse 2 that
suggest the Corinthians had been heavily involved in ecstatic frenzies
connected with their pagan worship before they became Christians;
and this pagan worship offered, perhaps, instances in which Jesus
might well have been cursed. Second, the pagan ecstatic frenzy presupposed under this interpretation is in certain respects compared
with the work of the Spirit (v. 3); and the conclusion is drawn that the
proper test or criterion for appropriate inspiration is the acknowledg-
ment of Christ as Lord. So, for example, Professor Bruce:

> In classical literature, Apollo was particularly renowned as the source
> of ecstatic utterances, as on the lips of Cassander of Troy, the priestess
> of Delphi or the Sibyl of Cumae (whose frenzy as she prophesied under
> the god's control is vividly described by Virgil); at a humbler level the
> fortune-telling slave girl of Ac. 16:16 was dominated by the same kind
> of 'pythonic' spirit. Paul does not suggest that any prophecy or glosso-
> lalia at Corinth proceeded from such a source; he simply reminds his
> readers that there are 'inspired' utterances [not from] the Spirit of God.[19]

But this line of reasoning is not very compelling. First, there is
nothing in verse 2 itself that testifies to a background in pagan ecstasy.
For instance, the verbs themselves (NIV "influenced and led astray"),
despite many statements to the contrary, do not conjure up visions of
demonic force.[20] And second, quite apart from such questions as
whether the Pythia used unintelligible language truly parallel to the
Corinthian Christians' glossolalia,[21] it seems very difficult to imagine
a Paul who could forbid any fellowship with demons (10:21) now
drawing an ambiguous comparison between pagan "inspiration" and
Christian "inspiration" with the sole difference being the resulting
confession. True, Paul knows that not everything from the spirit world
is the Holy Spirit; but the antitheses he draws in this arena are normally sharp.

19. F. F. Bruce, *1 and 2 Corinthians*, New Century Bible (London: Marshall, Morgan
and Scott, 1971), ad loc.
20. See especially Grudem, *Gift of Prophecy*, 162–64; C. Senft, *La première épître de
saint Paul aux Corinthiens* (Neuchâtel: Delachaux et Niestlé, 1979); contra C. Wolff,
Der erste Brief des Paulus an die Korinther. Zweiter Teil: Auslegung der Kapitel 9–16
(Berlin: Evangelische Verlagsanstalt, 1982); K. Maly, "1 Kor. 12,1–3: Ein Regel zur
Unterscheidung der Geister?" *Biblische Zeitschrift* 10 (1966): 82–95, prefers to draw
a distinction between the *dumb* idols (v. 2) and the Spirit-impelled *talking* believers
in v. 3, and thus necessarily avoids detecting ecstatic pagan cults in v. 2.
21. See David E. Aune, "Magic in Early Christianity," in *Aufstieg und Niedergang
der römischen Welt* II.2 (Berlin: de Gruyter, 1980), 1549–51; and J. Fontenrose, *The
Delphic Oracle* (Berkeley: University of California, 1978), 212–24.

In fact, de Broglie and Mehat have pointed to a better way to under-stand the flow.[22] It is better, they argue, to take verse 2 with verse 1, as an expansion on the theme of the Corinthians' ignorance. After all, elsewhere when Paul uses the formula "I do not want you to be ig-norant," he can insert some kind of explanatory or parenthetical aside before he turns to the content he wishes to convey (cf. 1 Cor. 8:1–4; 15:1–4; 1 Thess. 4:13–15; and then he always introduces the content with a ὅτι (hoti). But no ὅτι (hoti) is found at the beginning of verse 2. For that we turn to verse 3, where Paul uses γνωρίζω (gnōrizō, lit., I make known) in a resumptive fashion. The connective διό (dio; NIV's "therefore") connects verse 3 not with verse 2 but with verses 1 and 2. In short, the flow runs like this: I do not want you to be ignorant of certain central truths (v. 1). You know of course that when you were pagans your ignorance on such matters was profound (v. 2). Now (since I do not want you to be ignorant in these matters, vv. 1–2) I am making them known to you (v. 3).

This means we no longer have to interpret verse 3 in the light of verse 2, and vice versa. That link broken, we shall be less inclined to detect pagan ecstasy behind the words of verse 2; and we are freer to explore how verse 3 ties in with the rest of the chapter, and especially with verses 4ff. These latter verses insist on the diversity of the gifts, but the oneness of the source. This suggests that Paul's correspondents were at least partly made up of charismatics (in the modern sense of the term) who wanted to elevate their gifts to the place where they could give exclusive authentication for spiritual life and who wanted Paul to approve this judgment; and partly they were made up of non-charismatics (again in the modern sense) who were profoundly skep-tical of the claims of the charismatics, and wanted Paul to correct them. Their skepticism, it may be, arose from their own pagan backgrounds (for nothing that I have said denies that the majority of Corinthian believers emerged from paganism, but only that pagan ecstasy is in view in 12:2), just as the pagan backgrounds of certain people made them uneasy about eating food that had been offered to idols (see 1 Cor. 8). Mehat prefers the latter group;[23] I see no reason why both groups could not have been among Paul's correspondents in Corinth, reflecting different factions in the church. To both parties, Paul offers a telling rebuttal: your horizons are too narrow, he says, for partici-

---

22. G. de Broglie, "Le texte fondamentale de Saint Paul contre la foi naturelle," *Recherches de Science Religieuse* 39 (1951): 253–66; André Mehat, "L'Enseignement sur 'les choses de l'Esprit' (1 Corinthiens 12,1–3)," *Revue d'Histoire et de Philosophie Religieuses* 63 (1983): 395–415. Mehat also points out that this interpretation was favored by some older commentators, e.g., Cajetan and Bisping.
23. Mehat, ibid., 410–15.

pation in the things of the Holy Spirit is attested by *all* who truly confess Jesus as Lord. Both parties must expand their horizons: the charismatics should not feel they have some exclusive claim on the Spirit, and the noncharismatics should not be writing them off.

This interpretation, I suggest, makes much better sense than those which see in "Jesus is Lord" a sufficient criterion for distinguishing the true from the false in all prophetic utterances. After all, taken as such a criterion it is disturbingly broad and undiscriminating: for instance, it is quite helpless in the face of the false spirits confronting John (1 John 4:1–6). There the problem lay with those who denied Jesus was the Christ. But if 1 Corinthians 12:3 offers a criterion *not* to establish true and false ecstatic utterance but to establish whether or not any particular spiritual manifestation may be used to authenticate the powerful presence of the Holy Spirit, then Paul's answer is in line with the entire New Testament. To be able to confess that the Jesus of the incarnation, cross, and resurrection is truly the Lord, especially in the face of a society that has lords aplenty, already attests the powerful, transforming work of the Holy Spirit. To put the matter another way, "But if anyone does not have the Spirit of Christ, he does not belong to Him" (Rom. 8:9 NASB). Both to those who want to exalt spiritual manifestations as the infallible criterion of the Holy Spirit's powerful presence, and to those who want to question the genuineness of the spirituality attested by such manifestations, Paul provides a profoundly christological focus. As Schweizer puts it (perhaps too simply): "The Holy Spirit makes us receptive to Jesus."[24] In short, the purpose of 12:1–3 is *not* to provide a confessional test to enable Christians to distinguish true from false spirits, but to provide a sufficient test to establish who has the Holy Spirit at all.

Moreover, this interpretation offers a smooth transition to 12.4–6, for here Paul's point has nothing to do with the way true and false spiritual manifestations may be detected, but with the diversity of spiritual manifestations from the Triune God. But before turning our attention there, I must say something about another point.

The Significance of the Blasphemy "Jesus Be [or Is]²⁵ Cursed"

What shall we make of this foul curse? As long as verses 2–3 are understood to provide a criterion to distinguish true spiritual mani-

---

24. Eduard Schweizer, *The Holy Spirit*, trans. Reginald and Ilse Fuller (Philadelphia: Fortress, 1978), 126.

25. Since there is no verb, it is uncertain whether Paul means εἴη or ἐστίν; but by analogy with "Jesus is Lord" (equally without a verb, but with an unambiguous meaning), the latter is marginally more likely.

festations from false manifestations *in the church,* we are forced to scramble around to find some situation in which this might actually be said *in a Corinthian assembly,* a situation where Paul's criterion would have some force.

Many suggestions have been put forward, none of them convincing. The more important ones are the following.

It has been argued that some Christians had been dragged before a court and forced to deny Jesus (see Pliny *Epistles* 10.96) and then, once released, had returned to the Christian congregation and attempted to justify their actions by appealing to the Spirit's leading. Paul's words then serve to remove their defense. But this reconstruction not only "presupposes the circumstances of a later date";[26] it also provides a test that must be judged needless. Would any first-century church have entertained much doubt as to whether the Holy Spirit had prompted the blasphemy in such cases?

Many suggest that Paul is thinking of some specific pagan worship setting. Appeal is often made, among others, to Origen's statement (*Celsus* 6.28) that initiates into the Ophite sect were required to say that Jesus is anathema.[27] But the parallels are not convincing; and even the Ophites may not have cursed Jesus in so many words, but cursed him de facto by equating him with the serpent.[28] Moreover, Origen is a late witness for sixth-decade Corinth; and in any case Paul is dealing with *Christian* worship, not pagan utterances.

Many envisage some sort of background in the Jewish synagogue. People in that environment would after all remember that Jesus had died on a cross, a cursed man; and believing that God's Spirit was with them, they might well have uttered "Jesus is anathema!" while claiming to be led by the Spirit.[29] Again, however, this fails to recognize that Paul is dealing with a *Christian* context; and there is too little emphasis in the surrounding context on the Judaizing controversy to believe that he is taking a general swipe at the local synagogue as a kind of foil to the proper confession, "Jesus is Lord." In any case, the expression ἀνάθεμα *(anathema)* makes the association with the

---

26. C. K. Barrett, *The First Epistle to the Corinthians,* 2d ed. (London: Black, 1971).

27. See Ceslaus Spicq, *Agapé dans le Nouveau Testament,* 3 vols. (Paris: Gabalda, 1958–59), ad loc.

28. The question is extremely difficult: cf. the relevant text from Origen cited and discussed in Hans Conzelmann, *First Corinthians: A Critical and Historical Commentary on the Bible,* ed. George W. MacRae, trans. James W. Leitch, Hermeneia series (Philadelphia: Fortress, 1974), 204 n. 10, with a contrary position taken by Grudem, *Gift of Prophecy,* 168–69.

29. Adolf Schlatter, *Paulus—Der Bote Jesu: Eine Deutung seiner Briefe an die Korinther,* 3d ed. (Stuttgart: Calwer, 1962), 333.

synagogue less likely than would have been the case if other expressions had been used.[30] Some have tried to sidestep one or more of these difficulties by ingenious speculation. Derrett, for example, proposes that a synagogue ruler may have actually tutored a would-be Jewish Christian in this curse, in order to help him save his membership in the synagogue.[31] The ingenuity of this proposal is not helped by the fact that such a breach would be so outrageous the Corinthians would surely not have needed Paul to set up an appropriate test. More believably, Bassler suggests this is an oblique *self*-description of the apostle. He is making reference to his own pre-Christian days as a foil for the basic Christian confession.[32] Even so, it is surprising that a self-reference can be so obscure that it has taken almost twenty centuries to find it. Was it not similarly opaque to the Corinthians? Van Unnik suggests there were "Christians" who believed that Jesus died on the cross as a curse to bear our sin, but did not believe he rose from the dead and therefore could not confess him as Lord.[33] But I know of no evidence for such a hybrid; it is not clear how such people might have been accepted as Christians in the first place; and in any case ἀνάθεμα *(anathema)* is never used in a sin-bearing context.[34]

Still others detect a docetic Gnosticism in the background.[35] Adopting a radical dualism that elevates spirit and associates flesh with evil, they might well (it is argued) prove their commitment to Gnostic insight by loudly proclaiming that Jesus the man is cursed. Paul's desire is to exclude such people from the church. This proposal might make sense of verse 3 in isolation. Indeed, much of the best criticism of this position has come from those who see verses 2 and 3 tightly linked together[36]—a position I have already rejected. But the position is weak

---

30. Schlatter draws special attention to inter alia Deut. 21:23; but for the Masoretic Text's קִלְלַת אֱלֹהִים (cursed of God) the Septuagint offers κεκατηραμένος, and Paul elsewhere uses ἐπικατάρατος (cf. Gal. 3:13); so it is unclear that a passage like Deut. 21:23 would have suggested itself to the reader. On the bearing of 1QpNah 1.7–8, see Conzelmann, *First Corinthians*.

31. J. Duncan M. Derrett, "Cursing Jesus (1 Cor. XII.3): The Jews as Religious 'Persecutors,' " *New Testament Studies* 21 (1974–75): 544–54.

32. J. M. Bassler, "1 Cor 12:3—Curse and Confession in Context," *Journal of Biblical Literature* 101 (1982): 415–18.

33. W. C. van Unnik, "Jesus: Anathema or Kyrios (I Cor. 12:3)," in *Christ and Spirit in the New Testament: Studies in Honour of C. F. D. Moule,* ed. Barnabas Lindars and Stephen S. Smalley (Cambridge: Cambridge University Press, 1973), 113–26.

34. Cf. Grudem, *Gift of Prophecy,* 170–71 n. 93.

35. E.g., Walther Schmithals, *Gnosticism in Corinth: An Investigation of the Letters to the Corinthians,* trans. John E. Steely (Nashville: Abingdon, 1971); Norbert Brox, "ΑΝΑΘΕΜΑ ΊΗΣΟΥΣ (1 Kor 12,3)," *Biblische Zeitschrift* 12 (1968): 103–11; R. H. Fuller, "Tongues in the New Testament," *American Church Quarterly* 3 (1963): 162–68.

36. See especially Pearson, *Pneumatikos-Psychikos Terminology,* 48–49.

even if verse 2 is more tightly tied to verse 1 than to verse 3; for quite apart from the difficult question regarding the date of full-blown Gnosticism's rise, it remains unclear why Paul should introduce a test for Gnostics in the context of these chapters.

Albright and Mann find the question so difficult that they propose to emend the text in favor of an Aramaic construction they detect behind *Didache*. Textual emendations should be the court of last appeal; and as we shall see, there is an easier solution.[37]

Several commentators suggest that Paul is referring to Christian ecstatics who are *resisting* a Spirit-given trance or ecstasy as it comes on them by resorting to blasphemous utterances.[38] Parallels are drawn to the Sibyl who foamed as she resisted being possessed, or to Cassander who cursed Apollo in Aeschylus's *Agamemnon*. But I know of no parallel in which a *Christian* is so committed to resisting the Spirit's power as to utter christological blasphemies in an attempt to ward the Spirit off—assuming in any case the Holy Spirit manifested himself to the Corinthian believers by taking them up into some sort of ecstatic trance, even though the evidence suggesting that ecstatic trances constituted a major part of the Corinthians' spiritual experience is extremely thin on the ground.

And finally, not a few commentators propose that the curse part of verse 3 is a Pauline creation, cut out of whole cloth to stand in savage juxtaposition to the true Christian confession, a kind of shock treatment to tell the Corinthians to recognize that not all that is spiritual is divine.[39] But if the warning is entirely hypothetical (i.e., without any instance in the life of the Corinthian church where someone was actually crying out, "Jesus is cursed!"), it is hard to see why the Corinthians should not dismiss this part of the verse as a bit of overblown rhetoric.

There are other attempts at solutions, of course;[40] but most of them

---

37. W. F. Albright and C. S. Mann, "Two Texts in I Corinthians," *New Testament Studies* 16 (1969–70): 271–76.

38. E.g., Barrett, *First Epistle to the Corinthians*, following E.-B. Allo, *Première épître aux Corinthiens*, 2d ed. (Paris: Gabalda, 1956).

39. E.g., Bruce, *1 and 2 Corinthians*; de Broglie, "Le texte fondamentale"; David E. Aune, *Prophecy in Early Christianity and the Ancient Mediterranean World* (Grand Rapids: Eerdmans, 1983), 256–57.

40. E.g., F. W. Grosheide (*Commentary on the First Epistle to the Corinthians* [Grand Rapids: Eerdmans, 1953]) suggests that some Corinthian believers were worried that some of the utterances spoken in unintelligible tongues might actually be blasphemous statements, possibly unrecognized even by the speakers; and Paul reassures them by saying that no one who has the Spirit of God could possibly say such things. But it is difficult to see how this fits with the second part of the verse. H. D. Seyer, *The Stew-*

depend heavily on the presupposition that Paul is attempting to provide a quick if rough criterion to enable his hearers to distinguish between true and false "spiritual gifts." If we free ourselves from that presupposition and perceive that Paul's interest lies rather in establishing who truly has the Holy Spirit, then the pressure to identify a precise and believable background is reduced. If Paul is not wielding the curse language of verse 3a as a test for detecting false prophets *in the church*, then the objections raised against several of the backgrounds just listed disappear. It is no longer necessary to hold that "Jesus is cursed" was actually ever uttered in a Corinthian church meeting: Paul's point is to draw a sharp contrast between what those who have the Holy Spirit (i.e., Christians) say about Jesus, and what those who do not have the Holy Spirit say about Jesus. The latter group might include Jews and Gentiles, whether within cultic contexts or not. Paul's concern is quite simply to establish an essentially christological focus to the question of who is spiritual, who has the Holy Spirit.

The Bountiful Diversity of the Grace-Gifts (12:4–11)

As in Ephesians 4:1–16, so here: Paul first sets a foundation in unity, in the one confession prompted by the Holy Spirit, and then introduces the diversity.[41] The connecting δέ *(de)* is probably adversative: I want you to know that all who truly confess Jesus as Lord do so by the Holy Spirit, and thus attest his presence in their lives; *but* that does not mean there are no distinctions to be made among them. Paul's concern

---

ardship of Spiritual Gifts: A Study of First Corinthians, Chapters Twelve, Thirteen, and Fourteen, and the Charismatic Movement (Madison: Fleetwood, 1974), 7–8, casting around for a modern instance in which tongues-speaking led to blasphemy, urges the example of Edward Irving, who (he claims) became enmeshed in tongues and thereby became so distorted in his Christology that he was eventually deposed from the ministry. But the parallel is both inappropriate and historically distorted: inappropriate because there is no suggestion that tongues were the vehicle of blasphemy, and historically distorted because Irving's root christological deviations antedated his tongues-speaking experiences (most recently, see Arnold Dallimore, *Forerunner of the Charismatic Movement: The Life of Edward Irving* [Chicago: Moody, 1983]).

41. The parallel to Eph. 4:1–16 has been strenuously denied by Rudolf Schnackenburg, "Christus, Geist und Gemeinde (Eph. 4:1–16)" in *Christ and Spirit in the New Testament: Studies in Honour of C. F. D. Moule*, ed. Barnabas Lindars and Stephen S. Smalley (Cambridge: Cambridge University Press, 1973), 279–96, especially 290–91, who argues that the "each" in Eph. 4:7 introduces a change of subject and refers to official office-bearers in the church, thus apparently breaking the flow from the stress on unity (4:1–6) to the stress on diversity (4:7–16). He has been decisively rebutted by Ronald Y. K. Fung, "Ministry in the New Testament," in *The Church in the Bible and the World*, ed. D. A. Carson (Exeter: Paternoster, 1987), especially n. 28.

now is not so much with unity as with diversity.[42] The Triune God loves diversity—so much so, as someone has remarked, that when he sends a snowstorm he makes each flake different. We manufacture ice cubes. Doubtless the church is in some sense like a mighty army, but that does not mean we should think of ourselves as undifferentiated khaki. We should be more like an orchestra: each part making its own unique contribution to the symphonic harmony. Dictators of the right and the left seek to establish their brand of harmony by forcefully imposing monotonous sameness, by seeking to limit differentiation. God establishes his brand of harmony by a lavish grant of highly diverse gifts, each contributing to the body as a whole.

The word rendered "different kinds" in the New International Version (διαίρεσις, *diairesis*), judging from usage in the Septuagint (as the word does not occur in the New Testament outside this chapter), might mean either "varieties" (i.e., "different kinds") or "distributions." Because the cognate verb (διαιροῦν, *diairoun*) in verse 11 unambiguously bears the latter sense, probably the noun should here be taken in the same way: there are *distributions* of gifts. Of course, that implies variety; but it does more. As in Ephesians 4:7ff., we are reminded that God himself is the one who apportions grace; the diversity of gifts is grounded in his distribution of gifts.

The parallelism of verses 4–6 is remarkable. Paul tells us that there are different distributions:

of *gifts* (χαρίσματα, *charismata*), but the same *Spirit;*
of *service* (διακονίαι, *diakoniai*), but the same *Lord;*
of *working* (ἐνεργήματα, *energēmata*), but the same *God.*

There are some, of course, who cannot detect here or elsewhere in the New Testament any trinitarian thought;[43] but this appears to me to owe more to a doctrinaire reconstruction of early historical theology than to exegesis. I am not even sure that it is entirely adequate to say that the trinitarian consciousness in these verses is "the more impressive because it seems to be artless and unconscious."[44] Despite some prestigious opinion to the contrary, it appears exegetically certain that New Testament writers can on occasion *self-consciously* mark out the

<hr>

42. See the exchange between Joachim Gnilka, "Geistliches Amt und Gemeinde nach Paulus," in *Foi et Salut selon S. Paul,* ed. D. G. B. Franzoni et al., Analecta Biblica, vol. 42 (Rome: Pontifical Biblical Institute, 1970), 233–53; and in the same volume, the discussion of the article by C. F. Evans.

43. E.g., Conzelmann, *First Corinthians;* Johannes Weiss, *Der erste Korintherbrief,* 10th ed. (Göttingen: Vandenhoeck und Ruprecht, 1897).

44. Barrett, *The First Epistle to the Corinthians.*

Holy Spirit as "person." For instance, the *understanding* of the New Testament writers seems to be a necessary presupposition when, for instance, with only one exception "Holy Spirit" is anarthrous in passages that stress power, and articular in contexts where "the Holy Spirit" is treated as a personality.[45]

Be that as it may, two errors are to be avoided in attempting to understand the relationship between, on the one hand, gifts, service, and working, and, on the other, Spirit, Lord, and God. First, it would be wrong to think that the connections are exclusive: as if the Spirit gives only distributions of gifts, the Lord Jesus gives only distributions of service, and so forth; for (1) verses 4–6 do not so much suggest that the Spirit *gives* gifts, the Lord *gives* forms of service, and God *gives* "workings," as that diversity of distributions of these "gifts," for want of a more generic term, goes hand in glove with one Spirit, one Lord, one God; and (2) in the ensuing verses in this chapter, everything is ascribed to the Spirit (though still not so much as the giver of the gifts as the one who distributes them and "energizes" them [12:11]).[46] We are inevitably reminded of the Farewell Discourse (John 14–16), where Jesus promises that the coming "Paraclete," the Holy Spirit, will make his abode in Christ's disciples (14:17), and then goes on to say that both he himself and the Father will make their home in the believer (14:23), apparently through the agency of the Holy Spirit. Yet it would be equally wrong to think that the parallelism of 1 Corinthians 12:4–6 is nothing but arbitrary rhetoric.[47] Because the word χαρίσματα (*charismata*, gifts), as we have seen, is largely parallel to πνευματικά (*pneumatika*), it is not surprising that "gifts" should be associated with the πνεῦμα (*pneuma*, Spirit). "Service" goes well with "Lord"; and "workings" nicely fits "God," as the last clause of verse 6 shows: this God is the one who "works" (ὁ ἐνεργῶν, *ho energōn*) all things[48] in all men.

What is clear from this sequence is that Paul is not concerned to define "spiritual gift" too narrowly. We have already noted the considerable range of χαρίσματα (*charismata*). The two parallel terms are if anything even broader. The "service" of verse 5 (διακονία, *diakonia*) is a general term used in secular Greek for all kinds of work—waiting on tables, the civil service, a collection for the poor (2 Cor. 8:4–5). Precisely because of its range, Josephus can occasionally use it of

45. See D. Pitt Francis, "The Holy Spirit: A Statistical Inquiry," *The Expository Times* 96 (1985): 136–37.

46. Robinson, "Charismata versus Pneumatika," 54.

47. So Hans Lietzmann and Werner Georg Kümmel, *An die Korinther I. II*, Handbuch zum Neuen Testament, vol. 9 (Tübingen: J. C. B. Mohr, 1969).

48. Because τὰ πάντα is articular, it is better to take it as a substantive than as adverbial ("in every way"), contra Martin, *The Spirit and the Congregation*, 5.

priestly service, even though there is no clerical notion intrinsic to the use of the term. In this context, the New Testament diaconate is not in view.[49] The point is that even everyday acts of service must be included under this rubric. Similarly, ἐνέργημα (*energēma*, working) simply hints at the ἐνέργεια (*energeia*, energy or power) of God that is operating. "Workings" are merely "ways in which the divine power is applied";[50] "it is almost co-extensive with χαρίσματα [*charismata*], but it gives prominence to the idea of power rather than that of endowment."[51]

The parallelism does not of course make the words strictly synonymous, any more than Spirit, Lord, and God are strictly synonymous; but because none of the three terms can be associated with only certain spiritual gifts and not with others, it is clear that Paul uses the three terms to describe the full range of what we might call spiritual-gift phenomena. One conclusion is unavoidable: Paul tends to flatten distinctions between "charismatic" gifts and "noncharismatic" gifts in the modern sense of those terms.

Verse 7 is transitional. It glances back to the preceding verses by embracing gifts, service, and working alike under the one expression *the manifestation of the Spirit.* All of these manifest the Spirit; they show the Spirit (if the genitive is objective).[52] But the verse makes two new points.

First, *each* believer is given some manifestation of the Spirit; and at least in this text, "there is no warrant for saying that one gift manifests his presence more than another,"[53] even if some manifestations are more spectacular or more useful than others. To take the "each one" as a reference to each specially endowed charismatic, as some do,[54] not only misunderstands the flow of the argument so far, in which Paul's principal aim has been to display the full breadth of the Christian, Holy-Spirit-endued communion, but also flies in the face of verses 12–30.

Second, these gifts are not for personal aggrandizement, but "for

49. Cf. Eduard Schweizer, *Church Order in the New Testament*, trans. Frank Clarke, Studies in Biblical Theology, vol. 32 (London: SCM, 1971), 173–76.

50. Barrett, *The First Epistle to the Corinthians.*

51. Robertson and Plummer, *Corinthians.*

52. So inter alios Robertson and Plummer, *Corinthians.* C. F. G. Heinrici holds the genitive is subjective, "the manifestation that the Spirit gives." There is no syntactical clue that clarifies the meaning. But there are some interesting parallels (ἡ φανέρωσις τῆς ἀληθείας [2 Cor. 4:2] is clearly objective); and more important, nowhere do these chapters explicitly make the Spirit the giver of the spiritual gifts (cf. discussion, supra).

53. Bruce, *1 and 2 Corinthians.*

54. Cf. the list in Brockhaus, *Charisma und Amt*, 204 n. 3.

the common good." The peculiar expression that is used[55] might be literally rendered "with a view to profiting," not in itself making it clear whether the profit is for the individual or the group. The broader context makes it clear that the latter is in view (see especially chap. 14). Even so, this clearly stated purpose of "spiritual gifts" (if I may continue to use that term for the full range of the manifestations of the Spirit that Paul envisages) must not be brought to bear on the broader discussion in a heavy-handed way. As we shall see, some wish to rule out the legitimacy of any *private* use of tongues on the basis of this and similar texts: What possible benefit for the entire community is there, they ask, in such *private* tongues-speaking? Clearly there is no *direct* benefit: no one but God is hearing what is being said. But Paul was granted extraordinary visions and revelations that were designed *only* for his *immediate* benefit (2 Cor. 12:1–10); yet surely the church received *indirect* profit insofar as those visions and revelations, not to mention the ensuing thorn in his flesh, better equipped him for proclamation and ministry. In the same way, it is hard to see how verse 7 of this chapter renders illegitimate a private use of tongues if the result is a better person, a more spiritually minded Christian: the church may thereby receive indirect benefit. The verse rules out using any χάρισμα *(charisma)* for personal aggrandizement or *merely* for self-satisfaction; it does not rule out all benefit for the individual (just as marriage, one of the χαρίσματα [*charismata*] according to 1 Cor. 7:7, may benefit the individual), providing that the resulting matrix is for the common good. The context demands no more.

These two new points from verse 7 are then further expanded in verses 8–11 and verses 12–30 respectively.

The list of spiritual gifts in verses 8–11 is worth setting out in parallel with other similar New Testament lists (see table 1). One might also add the list of rhetorical questions in 1 Corinthians 12:29–30, but I shall omit it here. Comparison of these lists makes several things obvious.

First, no list, including the one immediately before us in 1 Corinthians 12:8–11, is meant to be exhaustive. This should already have been expected from Paul's discussion in verses 4–6, which suggests that not even the addition of all twenty or twenty-one[56] entries from the five lists should be taken as exhaustive.

Second, the order of the gifts varies considerably. It cannot be assumed that the entries are in order of importance when prophecy is sixth in the first list, second in the second list, and first in the third.

---

55. πρὸς τὸ συμφέρον in the best texts.
56. Some link the last two in Ephesians.

Table 1 **New Testament Lists of Spiritual Gifts**

1 Cor. 12:8–11	1 Cor. 12:28	Rom. 12:6–8	Eph. 4:11	1 Peter 4:11
word of wisdom	apostles	prophecy	apostles	speaking
word of knowledge	prophets	service	prophets	service
faith	teachers	teaching	evangelists	
gifts of healings	workers	exhortation	pastors	
working of miracles	of miracles	giving	teachers	
prophecy	helps	leadership		
distinguishing	administration	showing of		
of spirits	kinds of tongues	mercy		
kinds of tongues				
interpretation				
of tongues				

The second list enumerates the first three entries (first, second, third) and uses personal categories for them (apostles, prophets, teachers); but thereafter the list is not enumerated, and changes from persons to functional ministries. In this second part of the list, Paul appears to select two from the first list (but inverts their order!), adds two more not from the first list, and ends up with tongues (from the first list), while omitting the interpretation of tongues.[57] From this it has been strenuously argued that there is no warrant in these chapters to think of tongues as the least of the χαρίσματα *(charismata)*.[58] I agree that the point has been overplayed by some noncharismatics; but perhaps it is not entirely without force. In the first two lists, as well as in the list of rhetorical questions in verses 29–30, the gift of tongues (and its correlative, the gift of interpretation of tongues, where it is present) is always last. When I compare the New Testament lists of the apostles, I cannot help but notice that although there is some reordering of the entries from list to list, Judas Iscariot is always last (except of course in Acts 1:13, where he is simply omitted).[59] In light of the sustained downplaying of tongues in chapter 14, the least that can be said is that even if Paul does not consider tongues to be the least of the spiritual gifts on some absolute scale, it is highly likely he makes it the last entry in each list in 1 Corinthians because his readers were far too prone to exalt this one gift.

57. Cf. Charles E. Hummel, *Fire in the Fireplace: Contemporary Charismatic Renewal* (Downers Grove: Inter-Varsity, 1978), 243–46.

58. E.g., Fee, "Tongues," 9–11.

59. See Matt. 10:2–4; Mark 3:16–19; Luke 6:13–16; and discussion in D. A. Carson, "Matthew," in *The Expositor's Bible Commentary,* ed. Frank E. Gaebelein, 12 vols. (Grand Rapids: Zondervan, 1984), 8:237.

Third, the lists as a whole contain an impressive mixture of what some might label "natural" and "supernatural" endowments, or "spectacular" and "more ordinary" gifts. This is in line with what we have gleaned from Paul's argument in 12:1–7. The intriguing thing is that Paul himself makes no such distinctions: it is the same God who works all things in all men. Paul's overarching doctrine of divine sovereignty is precisely what can prompt him to ask the Corinthians elsewhere: "For who makes you different from anyone else? What do you have that you did not receive? And if you did receive it, why do you boast as though you did not?" (1 Cor. 4:7). This suggests in turn that Paul would not have been uncomfortable with spiritual gifts made up of some mix of so-called natural talent—what he would consider still to be God's gift—and of specific, Spirit-energized endowment.

Turning to the list in 12:8–11, three preliminary things must be said.

Attempts at classifying the entries in the list are numerous.[60] If any such classification is warranted by features in the text itself, it is the one that notes the variation in the Greek terms for "another." Sometimes Paul maintains a distinction between these two terms ἄλλος (allos) and ἕτερος (heteros)—for example, in Galatians 1:6–7—and sometimes he does not. If the distinction is maintained here, some argue, an intelligible result is achieved: when ἕτερος (heteros) appears, a new division in the list is intended.[61] This issues in the following division: the word of wisdom and the word of knowledge lie in the intellectual arena; faith, healing, miracles, prophecy, and distinguishing of spirits are grouped separately, perhaps linked with special faith, the lead item in this division; and tongues and the interpretation of tongues, in a category by itself. The division is possible; but there is enough overlap between the first two categories to make the theory less than convincing. Does not prophecy, in the second division, also produce intellectual results (first division)? Is faith more characteristic of distinguishing spirits (second division) than of uttering a word of wisdom (first division)? On balance, it is best to treat the gifts one by one.

For similar reasons, it is not clear to me that Paul is making profound points when he changes the prepositions he uses with "Spirit": διά (dia), strictly "through the Spirit" (v. 8a); κατά (kata), strictly "according to the Spirit" (v. 8b); ἐν (en), strictly "in the Spirit" and related expression (v. 9, bis). He may have felt it was more appropriate to use one preposition or another with particular gifts; but there is no evi-

60. See Martin, The Spirit and the Congregation, 11–12.
61. Robertson and Plummer adduce an example from Homer Iliad 13.730–32.

dence that he intended thereby to designate distinct operations of the
Spirit.

I must offer some brief remarks on the particular χαρίσματα *(charismata)* discussed in this chapter. For the time being, I shall say nothing about prophecy, tongues, or the interpretation of tongues, or, from
the second list, apostles and teachers, relegating this discussion to the
third chapter.

The message of wisdom and *the message of knowledge.* The emphasis
is not exactly on wisdom but on the messages (the λόγος, *logos*, word,
as in 1:18) that issue from wisdom and knowledge. It is not entirely
clear how or even whether these two gifts differ from one another. Old
Testament usage might have dictated that the message of wisdom was
more practical, telling believers how to live their lives under the fear
of God, while the message of knowledge was more theoretical or doctrinal. The problem with such a breakdown is that usage of "wisdom"
and "knowledge" in this epistle recognizes no such dichotomy. In light
of 2:6ff., "wisdom" can be essentially doctrinal, and the word of wisdom can be the fundamental message of Christianity; in light of
8:10–11, knowledge can be immensely practical. Perhaps a distinction
was clearer to the first readers than it is to us; but even so, it is unlikely
to have been more than a distinction in shading, in emphasis.

Probably those who were endowed with these gifts enjoyed a special
experience of the Spirit by which a message came to them that they
transmitted to the congregation; but it is not clear that the content of
such messages was invariably what could not have been known any
other way. Montague suggests that a message of knowledge was expected when Jesus was blindfolded and beaten, the soldiers shouting,
"Prophesy! Who hit you?"[62] Perhaps, but knowledge is so regularly
related by Paul to knowing God and his will that the example
seems a bit strained. And interestingly, the soldiers apparently would
have labeled the result a "prophecy"—more evidence of overlapping
categories.

Faith. Neither here nor in 13:2 is this saving faith; for saving faith
all Christians must possess. This rather is faith to perform some extraordinary work,[63] the kind of faith, in Jesus' terms, that can move
mountains (whether Paul is dependent on Jesus' teaching or not).[64]

---

62. George T. Montague, *The Holy Spirit: Growth of a Biblical Tradition* (New York:
Paulist, 1976), 151.

63. Oda Wischmeyer, *Der höchste Weg. Das 13. Kapitel des 1. Korintherbriefes* (Gütersloh: Gerd Mohn, 1981), 73, helpfully distinguishes between *Kerygmaglaube* and
Wunderglaube. Presumably this faith is tied to action rather than knowledge. Robertson and Plummer cite Chrysostom: πίστιν οὐ τὴν τῶν δογμάτων, ἀλλὰ τὴν τῶν σημείων.

64. The issues are extremely complex: see C. M. Tuckett, "1 Corinthians and Q,"
Journal of Biblical Literature 102 (1983): 607–19.

Saving faith is ultimately grounded in God's gracious and public self-disclosure in Christ Jesus and in the Scriptures; even though the work of the Holy Spirit is required for such faith, faith's object lies in revelatory events and words that are in the public arena. This special faith, however, enables a believer to trust God to bring about certain things for which he or she cannot claim some divine promise recorded in Scripture, or some state of affairs grounded in the very structure of the gospel. One thinks, for instance, of George Müller of Bristol.[65] The suggestion of Conzelmann, that this is not faith at all "but apparently the ability to work miracles,"[66] is worse than mere pedantry: it reflects a view of faith without certain object, a view of faith unknown to Paul, however appealing to contemporary existentialism.

Gifts of [lit.] *healings*. It is immensely reductionistic to say that the gift of healing "consisted of a natural gift of sympathy or empathy combined with a capacity of knowing the right thing to do in any individual situation and with any individual patient. This intuitive knowledge was sharpened and made more sensitive by the operation of the Holy Spirit."[67] There can be little doubt that Paul understands these healings to be as miraculous as those of the Lord Jesus himself.

The theological and eschatological significance of such miracles I shall briefly explore in the last chapter. For now it is sufficient to note these remarkable plurals: *gifts of healings* in all three occurrences in this chapter (cf. vv. 28, 29). This strongly suggests that there were *different* gifts of healings: not everyone was getting healed by one person, and perhaps certain persons with *one* of these gifts of healing could by the Lord's grace heal certain diseases or heal a variety of diseases but only at certain times. Perhaps, then, one of the things that our own generation needs to avoid is the institutionalizing of gifts. If a Christian has been granted the χάρισμα *(charisma)* to heal one partic-

65. The gift of faith here and in 13:2, as I have expounded it, is rather different from what is often meant by "the prayer of faith" in some Reformed circles. The latter is a prayer grounded in the promises of God in Scripture: the wavering believer petitions God for help on the basis of, say, John 10:28 and Phil. 1:6, just as Moses interceded with God on behalf of the Israelites on the basis of antecedent divine promises (Exod. 32:11–14). Such "prayers of faith" are principially open to every believer, for the promises, the bases of such faith, are in the public arena. But the gift of faith in 1 Cor. 12:9; 13:2 is amongst the χαρίσματα *(charismata)* that are *not* universally distributed to the church (12:12–31). It appears to be the God-given ability, without fakery or platitudinous exhortations to believe what you do not really believe, to trust God for a certain blessing *not* promised in Scripture—exactly as in the well-known case of George Müller of Bristol.

66. Conzelmann, *First Corinthians*, citing Rudolf Bultmann, "πίστις, etc.," *TDNT*, 6:206; but in fact Bultmann does not go so far.

67. John Wilkinson, *Health and Healing: Studies in New Testament Principles and Practice* (Edinburgh: Handsel, 1980), 109.

ular individual of one particular disease at one time, that Christian should not presume to think that *the* gift of healing has been bestowed on him or her, prompting the founding of "a healing ministry." But I shall say a little more about healing, and especially about the so-called third-wave movement, the "signs-and-wonders" movement, in the last chapter.

Miraculous powers. Literally "workings of powers": the first word was introduced in verse 6. The plurals are again noteworthy, and probably signal the same sort of diversity as in the previous gift. Presumably all healings are demonstrations of miraculous powers, but not all miraculous powers are healings: they may include exorcisms, nature miracles, and other displays of divine energy. The close relationship among the gifts of faith, healings, and miracles again suggests that the entries on the list are not quantum packages, each discrete from the others. Rather, there is considerable overlap.

The ability to distinguish between spirits. The Greek διαϰρίσεις πνευμάτων *(diakriseis pneumatōn)* is understood by Dautzenberg to refer to the gift of "interpreting the revelations of the Spirit" (i.e., the prophecies themselves);[68] but he has been decisively refuted by Grudem.[69] Spectacular displays often attest the power of the spirit world; they do not in themselves attest the power of the *Holy* Spirit. Moses discovered that Egyptian sorcerers could duplicate many of the miracles God enabled him to do; and Jesus warned that there would arise people who would perform miracles and cast out demons in his name, even though they would never be recognized by Christ as his own (see especially Matt. 7:21–23). There is ever a need to distinguish demonic forces from the Holy Spirit. This gift is apparently designed to meet that need. The insight needed may be granted by some special endue-ment; or, if 1 John 4:1–6 is anything to go by, the outworking of this gift may on occasion be the by-product of profound doctrinal discernment.

Gifts of support and *gifts of direction.*[70] These are the two new gifts introduced into the second part of the second list (12:28), rendered in the New International Version "those able to help others" and "those with gifts of administration" respectively.[71] The first word (ἀντιλήμψεις, *antilēmpseis*) is used only here in the New Testament; but judging from

68. Gerhard Dautzenberg, "Zum religionsgeschichtlichen Hintergrund der διάϰρισις πνευμάτων (1 Kor 12,10)," *Biblische Zeitschrift* 15 (1971): 93–104.

69. Wayne A. Grudem, "A Response to Gerhard Dautzenberg on 1 Cor. 12:10," *Biblische Zeitschrift* 22 (1978): 253–70.

70. The rendering here is that of Barrett.

71. Apparently the NIV translators decided to make the list consistent by casting all its entries in personal terms, instead of the first three only.

its widely distributed use elsewhere, it is a very general term for all kinds of assistance. The cognate verb is found at Luke 1:54; Acts 20:35; 1 Timothy 6:2. The second word (κυβερνήσεις, *kybernēseis*) is primarily used for the piloting or steering of a ship: its use is metaphorical here. Some have suggested that these two gifts represent the spiritual enduement necessary for the offices of deacon and bishop respectively. Doubtless that much is true; but there is nothing to suggest that these gifts are restricted to people serving in these offices. It is at any rate very clear that these spiritual gifts are not among those frequently regarded today as "charismatic," even though Paul is happy to think of them that way.

Paul ends the section by reminding his readers that all these spiritual gifts "are the work of one and the same Spirit." This emphasis on the one Spirit prepares us for the one body Paul is about to introduce into the discussion. These gifts, we are further reminded, are distributed to *each man:* no one is giftless, for the Spirit works with individuals. But a new thought is articulated: not only does the Spirit distribute these gifts to each individual, he does so "just as he determines."

This clause is taken by some interpreters to entail the conclusion that Paul cannot possibly be exhorting believers in 12:31 and 14:1 to be pursuing the best gifts, since their distribution is bound up with the Spirit's sovereign determination. The Greek in those verses, it is argued, must therefore not be imperative but indicative: "You eagerly desire . . . ," not "Eagerly desire. . . ." The same clause is used by noncharismatics to speak against *seeking* any gift, whether tongues or any other. Both conclusions are premature. They fail to recognize the ways in which God's sovereignty and human responsibility function side by side in the Scriptures, where philosophical compatibilism is not a problem but a presupposition.[72] In Paul's thought, after all, salvation itself is a χάρισμα *(charisma);* and if it is sovereignly given in line with God's elective purposes, it is equally to be sought and gained. This does not evacuate 1 Corinthians 12:11 of all meaning. Paul's aim is not to discourage Christians from pursuing what is best, but to prevent them from making any one gift the sine qua non, the sign without which one might legitimately call in question whether the Holy Spirit was present and active.[73] Christians may pursue what is best of the χαρίσματα *(charismata);* but they have no right to any particular one,

72. See D. A. Carson, *Divine Sovereignty and Human Responsibility: Biblical Perspectives in Tension* (Atlanta: John Knox, 1981).
73. Cf. Hemphill, "Pauline Concept of Charisma," 124.

and must ultimately trust the wisdom of their heavenly Father's gracious distribution through the mediation of his Holy Spirit.

The Baptism in the Holy Spirit and the Body Metaphor: The Mutual Dependence of Believers on One Another (12:12–26)

This section flows quite naturally out of the argument to this point. Indeed, Paul begins verse 12 with the logical γάρ (*gar*, for): there is a diversity of gifts and graces given to the church for the common good, *for* the body is a unit with many parts contributing to the organic whole.

The body metaphor that opens this final section of the chapter has plenty of antecedents in the ancient world that need not concern us. They tend to refer to the entire human race.[74] One of the most interesting potential backgrounds is the excavated Asclepion, whose remains include a "huge number of terracotta ex-votos, representing heads, hands and feet, arms and legs, breasts and genitals, eyes and ears. . . . These represented the afflicted members cured by a god. . . . Against this background Paul would have seen the dismembered limbs displayed in the Asclepion as symbols of everything that Christians should *not* be: 'dead,' divided, unloving and unloved."[75]

Whatever the background, the metaphor takes a strange twist at the end of the verse. We might have expected "so also is *the church*"; instead, we have "so also is *Christ*." The intervening logical step, of course, is that the church is the body of Christ. Paul probably first began to understand such language on the Damascus road, when the exalted Christ did not call out, "Saul, Saul, why do you persecute my church?" but "Saul, Saul, why do you persecute me?" (Acts 9:4),[76] Understandably, this has generated considerable debate as to whether Paul's language in this passage is best thought of as metaphor or as

74. See Barrett, *The First Epistle to the Corinthians;* Conzelmann, *First Corinthians.*

75. J. Murphy-O'Connor, *St. Paul's Corinth: Texts and Archaeology* (Wilmington: Glazier, 1983), 165, 167. See also Mabel Lang, *Cure and Cult in Ancient Corinth: A Guide to the Asklepion* (Princeton: American School of Classical Studies of Athens, 1977); Andrew E. Hill, "The Temple of Asclepius: An Alternate Source for Paul's Body Theology," *Journal of Biblical Literature* 99 (1980): 437–39; G. G. Garner, "The Temple of Asklepius at Corinth and Paul's Teaching," *Buried History* (Melbourne) 18 (1982): 52–58.

76. See John A. T. Robinson, *The Body* (London: SCM, 1952), 58–59; and especially Seyoon Kim, *The Origin of Paul's Gospel* (Tübingen: J. C. B. Mohr; Grand Rapids: Eerdmans, 1981); Paul S. Minear, *Images of the Church in the New Testament* (Philadelphia: Westminster, 1960), 190–95.

a description of a profound ontological reality.[77] Such discussions need not detain us; for if we sidestep the difficult questions about the nature of metaphor, we can still perceive what the *functional result* of Paul's step will be. It is this: we are not talking about the human race as a human body in which each member plays a part; nor are we talking about the interrelatedness of the cosmos; still less are we concerned with the body politic. We are talking about something far more important, far more enduring, far more expensive than any of these: we are talking about the church, the body of Christ. For all who truly love Christ, that must be immensely sobering.

Another "for" (γάρ, *gar*) joins verse 12 to verse 13: that Christians constitute one body, the body of Christ, is established on this truth, that all of them were baptized in (or "by" or "with": we shall return to that in a moment) one Spirit into one body. All of us belong to that body, Paul tells the Corinthian believers, *for* all of us[78] were baptized into it.

Almost every word and syntactical unit in this verse is disputed, and it would take a very long discussion to weigh all the options. I must here restrict myself to a few remarks.

Scholars from mainline denominations tend to focus attention on the relation between Spirit baptism and such rites as water baptism, the Lord's Supper, and confirmation. Most of the arguments are admittedly speculative because all must concede that Paul does not write these words with the purpose of sorting such matters out. The connection between Spirit baptism and water baptism is in my judgment neatly summarized by Bruce:

> Faith-union with Christ brought his people into membership of the Spirit-baptized community, procuring for them the benefits of the once-for-all outpouring of the Spirit at the dawn of the new age, while baptism in water was retained as the outward and visible sign of their incorporation 'into Christ' (cf. Gal. 3:27). And as it was in *one Spirit* that they *were all baptized*, therefore it was *into one body* that they were all baptized.[79]

Those who find the Lord's Supper in verse 13 find it in the second part

---

77. See inter alios Conzelmann, *First Corinthians;* Ernst Käsemann, *Leib und Leib Christi* (Tübingen: J. C. B. Mohr, 1933); Colin G. Kruse, *New Testament Models for Ministry: Jesus and Paul* (Nashville: Nelson, 1983), 116–18; J. Havet, "Christ collectif ou Christ individuel en I Cor., XII,12?" *Ephemerides Theologicae Lovaniensis* 23 (1947): 499–529; and especially Edmund P. Clowney, "Interpreting the Biblical Models of the Church: A Hermeneutical Deepening of Ecclesiology," in *Biblical Interpretation and the Church: Text and Context*, ed. D. A. Carson (Exeter: Paternoster, 1984), 64–109.

78. The ἡμεῖς πάντες pair is emphatic, regardless of debates over its referent.

79. Bruce, *1 and 2 Corinthians*, ad loc.

of the verse: baptism in the first part, the Lord's Supper in the second.[80] Neither the verb nor the tense behind the expression "we were all given one Spirit to drink"[81] is particularly congenial to that interpretation,[82] any more than to the interpretation that finds confirmation in verse 13b.[83] But these debates do alert us to the fact that there is a long tradition of reading one's particular ecclesiastical tradition into the text; and one must wonder if history is repeating itself in contemporary debates over the charismatic movement, even though it is a rather different tradition that is now being found there.

Lengthy debate has been waged as to whether this baptism *brings about* this body,[84] or incorporates people into a body that is already preexistent.[85] The latter is surely correct—not, with Conzelmann, because this view corresponds with prevailing Hellenistic notions of space, but because the church exists as an entity before the Corinthians are incorporated into it. In other words, the answer turns on the Corinthians' concrete historical experience, not on speculative notions of space. If then we push the question farther back and ask if the *first* Christian was baptized into a church that already existed, or was somehow by his baptism establishing the church, we must return to Pentecost and ask questions about the relationship between the post-Pentecost church and the people of God before Pentecost. That subject I shall reserve for the last chapter, for it does not concern Paul here.

Speaking of Pentecost, a certain reading of Acts 2 governs the interpretation of this text in 1 Corinthians among an older generation of Pentecostalists, especially at the popular level. This baptism in the Spirit is in their view a postconversion experience in line with the dominant Pentecostalist and neo-Pentecostalist interpretation of the Book of Acts. The first "we . . . all" of verse 13 does not embrace all Christians, but only those who have enjoyed this postconversion enduement. This interpretation is supported in various ways. For instance, some have argued that εἰς ἕν σῶμα *(eis hen sōma)* should not be rendered "into one body" but something like "for the body." This

---

80. E.g. Käsemann, *Leib und Leib Christi*, 176; Schlatter, *Paulus;* Heinz-Dietrich Wendland, *Die Briefe an die Korinther*, Das Neue Testament Deutsch, vol. 7, 13th ed. (1936; reprint ed., Göttingen: Vandenhoeck und Ruprecht, 1972).

81. ἐποτίσθημεν.

82. Cf. Rudolf Schnackenburg, *Baptism in the Thought of St. Paul: A Study in Pauline Theology*, trans. G. R. Beasley-Murray (New York: Herder and Herder, 1964), 84.

83. Contra Joseph Hanimann, "Nous avons été abreuvés d'un seul Esprit," *Nouvelle Revue Théologique* 94 (1972): 400–405.

84. So Franz Mussner, *Christus, das All und die Kirche im Epheserbrief* (Trier: Paulinus, 1955), 125ff.; Lucien Cerfaux, *The Church in the Theology of Saint Paul*, trans. Geoffrey Webb and Adrian Walker (New York: Herder and Herder, 1959), 270–77.

85. Conzelmann, *First Corinthians*.

means that the Spirit-baptism in this verse does not incorporate its beneficiaries "into one body" (which would clearly embrace *all* believers and therefore rule out any view that assigns this baptism to only a subset of believers), but simply prepares *some* believers *for* the body (i.e., for service in the body).[86] But these and similar arguments have been so soundly refuted[87] that nowadays an increasing number of charismatics acknowledge the point.[88] Perhaps the most startling weakness of the entire theory lies in its insensitivity to the context. The flow, including the initial "for," demands that Paul be talking about the incorporation of *all* believers into the one body that constitutes the theme of the verse preceding verse 13 and of the verses succeeding it.

Contemporary charismatics cannot be categorized as easily as their Pentecostal forebears. Roman Catholic charismatics, for instance, tend to play down interpretations of the baptism of the Spirit that form part of a larger "second-blessing" theology; most Protestant charismatics retain some form of that tradition. So far as this verse is concerned, however, the evidence for this position is now less frequently drawn from verse 13a than previously; appeal is made instead to verse 13b.[89] If we concede that the baptism in the Spirit in verse 13a is related to conversion, they say in effect, we still believe there are strong reasons to think that "we were all given the one Spirit to drink" (v. 13b)—or however the Greek be translated—refers to a *second* work of the Spirit. After all, writes one charismatic author, "the imagery of drinking one's way into the body is more than a curious mixing of metaphors."[90] But of course that is not what Paul says. The idea of being given to drink of one Spirit, in the noncharismatic view, does

86. By contrast, some early charismatic writers (e.g., Ralph M. Riggs, *The Holy Spirit Himself* [Springfield, Mo.: Gospel Publishing, 1949], 58) held to the view that the baptism in the Spirit in v. 13a is to be connected with conversion, leaving the second work of grace for v. 13b.

87. See inter alios James D. G. Dunn, *Baptism in the Holy Spirit*, Studies in Biblical Theology, vol. 15 (London: SCM, 1970), 127ff.; John R. W. Stott, *The Baptism and Fullness of the Holy Spirit* (Chicago: Inter-Varsity, 1964), 23; Frederick Dale Bruner, *A Theology of the Holy Spirit: The Pentecostal Experience and the New Testament* (Grand Rapids: Eerdmans, 1970), 291ff.

88. This does not mean that charismatic writers willingly accept all the arguments of noncharismatics on 12:13a, but only that the main point is now largely conceded: that the Spirit baptism in v. 13a is to be linked with conversion. The charismatic focus then switches to v. 13b: for the argument and bibliography, see infra.

89. E.g., Howard M. Ervin, *Conversion-Initiation and the Baptism of the Holy Spirit: A Critique of James D. G. Dunn, "Baptism in the Holy Spirit"* (Peabody, Mass.: Hendrickson, 1984), 98–102; Harold D. Hunter, *Spirit-Baptism: A Pentecostal Alternative* (Lanham, Md.: University Press of America, 1983), 39–42.

90. Ervin, *Conversion-Initiation*, 100.

not stand in parallel to "baptism in Spirit," but to "baptism in Spirit
into the one body." In other words, Paul adds one metaphor to another,
and expects his readers not to mix them. Another scholar in the charismatic tradition compares Galatians 3:27 and the pair "baptized into
Christ"/"clothed with Christ," and argues that since "clothed" language "is readily identifiable with the charismatic Spirit,"[91] a similar
move from initiation in 12:13a to charismatic enduement in 12:13b is
entirely defensible. But Galatians 3:27b speaks of being clothed *with
Christ*, not the Spirit; and there is simply no New Testament tie that
connects this "being clothed" language with charismatic (in the modern sense) enduement.

I think the verb ποτίζω *(potizō)*, which often means "I make to
drink," here bears another common meaning, "I flood" or "I pour out"
as in irrigation. The connection between this verb and Spirit is found
in only one other biblical passage (Isa. 29:10 [LXX]) where it bears
this meaning. The sense of the passive form ἐποτίσθημεν *(epotisthēmen)*
in this passage, then, should be rendered "we were all drenched" or
"we were all flooded" in one Spirit.[92] But who are the "we . . . all"?
Are they not exactly the same people embraced by the same words in
verse 13a? One charismatic writer tries to escape this difficulty by
suggesting that "we . . . all" refers to all the believers in Corinth, not
all Christians everywhere. It could not be said of all Christians everywhere that they have received this second enduement; but it could be
said of the Corinthian believers.[93] This sounds too much like special
pleading. Why did not Paul then write "*you* . . . all" to make his point
clearer? At the beginning of this chapter we noticed some evidence
that we shall have occasion to weigh more thoroughly in the fourth
chapter: these chapters betray the fact that there was a *non*-tongues-
speaking party at Corinth. More important, how does the introduction
of a second work of the Spirit contribute to the flow of the argument?
As Packer puts it, "Reference to a second blessing has to be read into
the text; it cannot be read out of it."[94]

Finally, I should say something about ἐν ἑνὶ πνεύματι *(en heni pneu-
mati)*, "in one Spirit" or "by one Spirit" or "with one Spirit." It has

91. Hunter, *Spirit-Baptism*, 41.

92. This rendering is increasingly recognized by charismatics and noncharismatics
alike; but other options are often set forth: e.g., G. J. Cuming, "ἐποτίσθημεν (I Corinthians
12,13)," *New Testament Studies* 27 (1981): 283–85; E. R. Rogers, "ΕΠΟΤΙΣΘΗΜΕΝ
Again," *New Testament Studies* 29 (1983): 139–42.

93. R. E. Cottle, "All Were Baptized," *Journal of the Evangelical Theological Society*
17 (1974): 75–80.

94. J. I. Packer, *Keep in Step with the Spirit* (Leicester: Inter-Varsity; Old Tappan,
N.J.: Revell, 1984), 203.

sometimes been argued that if we render the Greek phrase by "in one Spirit," the combination of "*in* one Spirit *into* one body" is so harsh as to be unacceptable. Therefore the phrase in question must be instrumental: "we were all baptized *by* one Spirit into one body."[95] On this basis, some have argued that although this baptism *with* or *by* the Spirit is coincidental with conversion, in the Gospels and Acts the baptism *in* the Spirit is something different: a postconversion experience. If so, this would be the only place in the New Testament where the Spirit is the agent of the baptism. In the other six instances, related to the prophecy of John the Baptist, Christ as the agent does the baptizing, and the Holy Spirit is the medium or sphere *in* which we are baptized. Moreover whenever the verb *baptize* is used in the New Testament, it is the *medium* of the baptism—water, fire, cloud, and so forth—that is expressed using this preposition ἐν *(en)*, not the *agent*. Although "*in* one Spirit *into* one body" sounds harsh in English, it is not at all clear that it is harsh in Greek, partly because the English paronomasia is absent. Indeed, the combination of Greek phrases nicely stresses exactly the point that Paul is trying to make: *all* Christians have been baptized in *one* Spirit; *all* Christians have been baptized into *one* body. So much attention has been centered on the prepositions that we have neglected Paul's repetition of the adjective *one*. Paul is setting the stage to demonstrate, in the words of MacGorman, "There are no one-member churches, nor are there any every-member gifts."[96] Whatever one finally decides about the disputed phrase, however, it is important to recognize that nothing crucial hangs on the outcome: charismatics and noncharismatics alike have held both sides on the issue.[97]

The oneness of the body, the church, predicated on the fact that *all* its members have been baptized in one spirit into this body, is now applied to the problems in Corinth.[98] Whenever an elitist group claims to have an inside track or a "full" gospel not recognized by others, then quite apart from the merits of the claim certain divisive forces come into play. The claims generate a kind of inner-ring syndrome: the insiders feel secure but dangerously smug, and the outsiders feel threatened and put upon. Some of the latter group may also in time

---

95. So, for instance, Michael Green, *I Believe in the Holy Spirit* (Grand Rapids: Eerdmans, 1975), 141.

96. Jack W. MacGorman, *The Gifts of the Spirit: An Exposition of 1 Corinthians 12–14* (Nashville: Broadman, 1974), 394.

97. E.g., Robert L. Thomas, *Understanding Spiritual Gifts: The Christian's Special Gifts in the Light of 1 Corinthians 12–14* (Chicago: Moody, 1978), 186–87, a noncharismatic, favors taking the preposition in an instrumental sense.

98. The connecting Καὶ γάρ should be rendered "for indeed" (Conzelmann).

stoop to feelings of superiority: *they* are not arrogant and smug like those misguided elitists!

Paul deals with both groups in turn. In verses 14–19, he tells the outsiders that, precisely because of the diversity of gifts God has distributed in the church, the member that seems inferior cannot reasonably say it does not belong, or threaten to leave. In each pair Paul mentions (foot/hand, ear/eye), it is the part that seems inferior that is making its case, in a kind of self-pitying fashion.[99] But it can bemoan its limitations all it likes: it does not on their account[100] stop being a member of the body. Indeed, a body consisting of a single organ—a giant eyeball, perhaps, or one single, massive toenail or knee—would be grotesque. The body requires the contribution of each member. So it is silly, for instance, for a Christian with the χάρισμα (charisma) of encouragement or of giving to feel hopelessly threatened by someone with the χάρισμα (charisma) of tongues.

Whatever the rights and wrongs of the doctrines of the charismatic movement, we are forced to reflect on the many Christians whom charismatics have *dis*couraged. I could provide a long list of Christian university groups and local churches where, once the charismatic movement became dominant with strong pressure to speak in tongues as the decisive proof of Spirit baptism, other Christians gradually walked away and drifted to other groups or churches. Doubtless if they did so they displayed little grasp of these verses; doubtless the charismatics whose views prompted the withdrawal displayed little grasp of this chapter. The fact of the matter is that "God has arranged the parts in the body, every one of them, just as he wanted them to be" (12:18)—a repetition of the thought of verse 11, focusing here on God and not the Spirit per se.

Paul now turns to the elitists themselves (vv. 20–26). No longer in this extended metaphor do the members speak to themselves from a position of inferiority, as in the preceding verses; here the members speak to those they judge inferior, in wretched, condescending tones. Few barbs hurt more than a blistering "I don't need you!" At this point the elitists may be either the so-called charismatics or those who oppose them: it is their attitude that Paul excoriates. The Christian who has any particular gift, whether tongues or anything else, has no right to dismiss in any sense that fellow believer who has some other gift. Thiessen offers a sociological interpretation of the more honorable and

99. See Robertson and Plummer; Weiss, contra Conzelmann, who thinks vv. 14–15 are directed against enthusiastic individuals whose sense of superiority is prompting them to withdraw.

100. For discussion of this rendering of παρὰ τοῦτο, see Thomas, *Understanding Spiritual Gifts*, 190–91.

the less honorable, and so forth;[101] but I suspect he is missing the point. At the level of the metaphor, Paul is still dealing with the body, and the less presentable or less honorable parts are probably sexual organs, judging by the "shame" language. At the level of the church, Paul is not here interested in the varied social strata that made up the Corinthian church, but in the perceived stratification of the χαρίσματα (*charismata*). God's intent is to honor what others dishonor. Applied to the church, it becomes our collective responsibility to honor gifts given little thought or prominence.

As in a body, the pain of one member is the pain of all. If you smash your finger with a hammer, you may exclaim with equal appropriateness, "I hurt my finger!" or "I hurt myself!" The same principle holds when some member is honored. Can we think of Placido Domingo's voice apart from the man? We do not honor his voice alone; we honor him. "If one part suffers, every part suffers with it; if one part is honored, every part rejoices with it" (12:26). So must it be in the church. No Christian is to think in individualistic terms, but in terms of the body. Where this attitude dominates the believers, there can no longer be any place for spiritual one-upmanship, self-promotion, or an unbalanced stress on select gifts.

Conclusion (12:27–30)

As if the metaphor were not already clear enough, Paul spells it out yet once more: "Now you are the body of Christ, and each one of you is a part of it." "You" and "body of Christ" are the equivalents of "church," indeed, in this context the *Corinthian* church. In the New Testament, characteristically each local church is not a part of the whole church, but simply the church — the outcropping of the church or the exemplar of the church in any particular place. So also with Paul's language about the body. Paul does not mean that each congregation is a part of the body of Christ, or a body of Christ. Each congregation, each church, is *the* body of Christ. Each local church, if I may put it this way, is the exemplification of the church. The people of God in any place *are* the people of God, the church, not simply a part of the people of God.[102] And it is in the church that God has appointed various spiritual gifts. This does not mean therefore that

101. Gerd Thiessen, *The Social Setting of Pauline Christianity: Essays on Corinth* (Philadelphia: Fortress, 1982), 56, 72.
102. For thoughtful discussion, see Peter T. O'Brien, "The Church as a Heavenly and Eschatological Entity," in *The Church in the Bible and the World*, ed. D. A. Carson (Exeter: Paternoster, 1987). Anarthrous σῶμα Χριστοῦ must not be taken to mean "a body of Christ."

each local congregation must have apostles on site; for there is a sense in which if God gives apostles to his church, his people, then of course they are apostles of any particular outcropping of the church, of what we may call the local church. Paul's purpose at this juncture is not to establish ecclesiastical order but to stress the rich diversity of God's good gifts poured out on the church.

This list (v. 28) was partly discussed in connection with verses 8–11. I shall say more about "apostles," "prophets," and "teachers" in the third chapter. The main purpose of the list in this context, however, is to lead up to the concluding rhetorical questions, whose form in Greek indicates that Paul expects a firm negative after each one: "Are all apostles? *No!* Are all prophets? *No!* Are all teachers? *No!* Do all work miracles? *No!* Do all have gifts of healing? *No!* Do all speak in tongues? *No!* Do all interpret? *No!*"

We have not yet considered other passages in the New Testament, of course; but on the basis of this chapter, at least, and its concluding rhetorical questions, how dare we make any one χάρισμα *(charisma)* the criterion of a certain enduement of the Spirit? How dare we make tongues the test of the Spirit's baptism?

It would be premature to try to draw together many theological and practical strands; moreover, I have not yet attempted to identify the admirable features in the charismatic movement. But I must offer at least one suggestion. If the charismatic movement would firmly renounce, on biblical grounds, not the gift of tongues but the idea that tongues constitute a special sign of a second blessing, a very substantial part of the wall between charismatics and noncharismatics would come crashing down. Does 1 Corinthians 12 demand any less?

Thank God that, beyond all the χαρίσματα *(charismata)*, there remains a more excellent way.

2

The Most Excellent Way; or, When Does Perfection Come? (12:31–13:13)

As a youth I was frequently advised that a text without a context becomes a pretext for a prooftext. That is not always true, of course: an aphorism can often be wielded with great and hermeneutically proper effect even when no attention is paid to its original context. Although the text before us cannot be called an aphorism, certainly many fine studies and expositions of it have devoted little or no attention to chapters 12 and 14. In one sense that is both understandable and commendable, for its theme is so exalted and so central to Christian living that it crops up in many contexts and can be theologically related to the very heart of the gospel itself. The chapter is a masterpiece even when cut loose from its literary context. Nevertheless, the first readers of this epistle read the chapter in the framework of what comes before and after; and similarly, I shall devote most attention to the contribution this chapter makes to the flow of the argument through these three chapters. Before turning to the three sections of the chapter in turn, therefore, I shall begin by commenting on the literary and thematic connections that bind the chapter to its context.

The Setting of Chapter 13

A considerable proportion of scholarly interest has been focused on the form and structure of this chapter, the majority classifying it as a hymn and the minority preferring to think of it as Christian paraenesis.[1] The parallels that are often adduced are of mixed quality: the best offers praise not to love but to truth.[2] I shall largely avoid such discussions here, along with technical treatments of the structure of the chapter[3] (except of course for the major divisions).

Many scholars are quite certain Paul has inserted this "hymn" (if I may call it that) into this context from some other source, whether composed by him or not. In addition to linguistic arguments put forward in favor of this view, the two most important reasons are these: the chapter, it is argued, does not fit well into the context, because the logic from the end of chapter 12 to the beginning of chapter 14 (omitting chap. 13) develops criteria for *ranking* spiritual gifts, whereas the emphasis within chapter 13 *depreciates* spiritual gifts in favor of love; and the sudden introduction of faith and hope in 13:13 introduces themes irrelevant to the flow of the argument in chapters 12 and 14. Neither of these reasons is very persuasive. It is true that chapter 13 does not make the *same* argument as chapter 14: the former deals with a perspective that transcends the spiritual gifts and therefore puts them into perspective, while the latter sets out principles by which to

1. See Jack T. Sanders, "First Corinthians 13," *Interpretation* 20 (1966): 159–87, for a fine summary of the interpretation of this chapter since World War I. For discussion of the literary genre and useful bibliography, see Hans Conzelmann, *First Corinthians: A Critical and Historical Commentary on the Bible*, ed. George W. MacRae, trans. James W. Leitch, Hermeneia series (Philadelphia: Fortress, 1974). The most influential voices asserting this chapter is paraenesis and not a hymn are Ceslaus Spicq, *Agapé dans le Nouveau Testament*, 3 vols. (Paris: Gabalda, 1959), 2:53–120, and Ernst Hoffmann, "Pauli Hymnus auf die Liebe," *Deutsche Vierteljahrsschrift für Literaturwissenschaft und Geistesgeschichte* 4 (1926): 58–73.

2. 3 Ezra 4:34–40. For convenient access to the most important parallels, see Conzelmann, *First Corinthians*.

3. On which see especially Nils Lund, "The Literary Structure of Paul's Hymn to Love," *Journal of Biblical Literature* 50 (1931): 266–76.

rank spiritual gifts according to their potential for building up the church. These two arguments, however, are not antithetical, but complementary; and in the historical context, so far as we can discern it, both were necessary. Moreover, although it is true that the faith and hope of 13:13 seem out of place among the concerns dominant in chapters 12 and 14, a first reading also suggests they are out of place even in chapter 13; and therefore they can scarcely be used to justify the secondary character of chapter 13. Of course there is nothing principially objectionable about the suggestion that Paul pieced this chapter into the argument by drawing it from another source, whether his own or someone else's. Source-critical questions are inevitable in Chronicles, the synoptic Gospels and elsewhere. But chapter 13, as we shall see, is an integral part of Paul's argument; and if he did not have the piece ready to hand, he would have had to compose something very much like it.[4] The chapter not only draws comparisons between love and such gifts as prophecy and tongues—obviously of concern to chapter 14—but it appears that even in the central section of the hymn, verses 4–7, the description of what love is and is not like seems to be cast in categories designed to combat specific problems in the Corinthian church.

The one question regarding the setting that we cannot avoid discussing in detail, however, is the meaning of 12:31. The proposed interpretations cluster in two groups.

Interpretations That Take ζηλοῦτε *(zēloute) as an Indicative*

This approach has many forms. Iber and Bittlinger have done their best to put the basic proposal on a solid footing.[5] In the wake of 12:11, 18, where the Spirit or God distributes the gifts sovereignly, how, these scholars ask, could Paul have been *commanding* his readers to desire the greater gifts? "As far as [Paul] could see it was their childish immaturity that had made them want the 'greatest' gifts."[6] In this light 12:31a is a rebuke, and its connecting δέ (*de*, but) is strongly adversative: that is, after the series of questions anticipating negative answers (12:29–30—e.g., Do all speak in tongues? *No!* Do all interpret? *No!*), Paul goes on in a somewhat exasperated or sardonic tone, "But you eagerly desire the greater gifts!" In this view "greater gifts" refers to every spiritual gift that the Corinthians highly prized. By contrast,

4. See F. F. Bruce, *1 and 2 Corinthians*, New Century Bible (London: Marshall, Morgan and Scott, 1971).

5. Gerhard Iber, "Zum Verständnis von I Cor. 12:31," *Zeitschrift für die neutestamentliche Wissenschaft* 54 (1963): 43–52; A. Bittlinger, *Gifts and Graces: A Commentary on 1 Cor 12–14*, trans. H. Klassen (Grand Rapids: Eerdmans, 1968).

6. Bittlinger, *Gifts and Graces*, 73.

what he will show them is the most excellent way (12:31b). Further, Bittlinger appeals to 14:12 as an important parallel: here Paul refers to the Corinthians' zeal for spiritual gifts as a simple statement of fact, but in a cognate term that allows no possibility of an imperatival interpretation.[7]

The immediate weakness with this interpretation that several have noted is the apparently imperatival use in 14:1 of exactly the same verbal form as in 12:31a: ζηλοῦτε (zēloute) in 14:1 means "eagerly desire spiritual gifts," and it appears to be resumptive of the thought in 12:31a. Iber tries to dampen the force of this criticism by pointing out that at least in 14:1 the direct object is different: in 12:31 it is "the greater gifts," and in 14:1 it is simply "spiritual gifts." The force of this rebuttal dissipates completely, however, when we remember that in 14:12 (in the cognate construction that simply affirms the Corinthians desire spiritual gifts) the direct object is the same as in 14:1, not 12:31a! Equally damaging to their case is their need to take the opening conjunction of 12:31b (καί, kai) as a strong adversative "but." The New International Version renders it "and now"; but consistent with Iber's and Bittlinger's interpretation of the first part of the verse, however, they must envisage the flow something like this: "So, you eagerly desire the greater gifts [this part sardonically]. *But* I will show you the most excellent way." The trouble is that although this Greek conjunction is used nine thousand times in the New Testament, only very rarely does it take on any adversative force—and then usually for stylistic reasons. Why did Paul not use some clearer adversative, if that were his point?

Other scholars have expanded on this interpretation in order to alleviate one or two of the perceived difficulties. Baker,[8] drawing on Chevallier,[9] integrates the thesis we looked at in the last chapter that draws a distinction between χαρίσματα (charismata) and πνευματικά (pneumatika), and takes the following two steps: he suggests that in 12:31 Paul is actually quoting a Corinthian slogan; and he further suggests that this Corinthian slogan used the word πνευματικά (pneumatika), but Paul purposely changes it in 12:31a to χαρίσματα (charismata). Martin adopts the same approach, and also turns 12:31a into a question (the Greek, of course, could be read affirmatively or interrogatively): "You are seeking, then, the great[est] gifts, are you? Well,

7. ἐπεὶ ζηλωταί ἐστε.

8. David L. Baker, "The Interpretation of 1 Cor 12–14," *Evangelical Quarterly* 46 (1974): 224–34.

9. Max-Alain Chevallier, *Esprit de Dieu, Paroles d'Hommes* (Neuchâtel: Delachaux et Niestlé, 1966).

I will [or I intend to] show you a still better way."[10] And then, to remove the objection that the verb ζηλοῦτε *(zēloute)* in 14:1 is in the imperative mood, Martin suggests that it too can be taken in the indicative provided we detect yet another quotation from the Corinthian letter. He renders 14:1 as follows: "Make love your goal: yet 'you are striving for spiritual gifts,' but [I say] rather that you should all prophesy."[11] He adopts a similar tactic in 14:39, the only other place where the same verbal form appears in these chapters. He renders verses 39 and 40 as follows: "So then, my brothers, 'you are striving to prophesy and you are not forbidding speaking in tongues' [Good]; let everything (you do) be done in a seemly manner and in good order."[12]

To avoid its built-in difficulties, we must frankly recognize that this theory appears to be adding implausibility to speculation. In both 14:1 and 14:39–40, Martin must add words to the text to make his interpretation work out. Greek of course often omits words that English requires; thus, so-called additions are often nothing more than recognizing that the receptor language requires words whose semantic contribution is *presupposed* by the Greek. But that does not constitute a license to add words in support of interpretations that are already based on a fair bit of speculation—in this instance the speculation that Paul is quoting the Corinthian letter. During the last decade, one notable trend in Corinthian studies has been to postulate that Paul is quoting the Corinthians in more and more places. That he does so occasionally no one disputes (see, e.g., 6:12; 7:1b; 8:1b). But the instances that are almost universally recognized have certain characteristics: they are short, they are usually followed by sustained qualification, and the Pauline response is unambiguous and does not require the addition of words or phrases to make sense of the text. Only the first criterion is met in Martin's two reconstructions; and even so his interpretation remains dependent on an extremely improbable rendering of the conjunction in 12:31b.[13]

In short, the interpretation of 12:31a that takes the verb as an indicative, although growing in popularity, has not received adequate justification. But another cluster of interpretations is possible.

---

10. Ralph P. Martin, *The Spirit and the Congregation: Studies in 1 Corinthians 12–15* (Grand Rapids: Eerdmans, 1984), 35.

11. Ibid., 57.

12. Ibid., 75.

13. It is inadequate for Martin, *The Spirit and the Congregation*, 35, to refer to Wischmeyer, *Der höchste Weg. Das 13. Kapitel des 1. Korintherbriefes* (Gütersloh: Gerd Mohn, 1981), 32, and remark that she has shown that καί can have the adversative sense. One must also ask if that sense is intrinsically probable, frequent, or infrequent. As we have seen, it is both improbable and infrequent.

Interpretations That Take ζηλοῦτε (zēloute) as an Imperative

One interpretation in this cluster is not very attractive. It harks back to the preceding verses and says that Paul is commanding his readers to look over the lists already given and mark those gifts the apostle judges most important. These they should pursue, not the gift of tongues, which Paul places last.[14] This probably places too much weight on the order of the lists of gifts, as I indicated in the first chapter.

But another form of this cluster stands up to close scrutiny. The opening adversative of 12:31a is rather mild: not all prophesy, speak in tongues, and so on (12:30), *but* you must earnestly desire the greater gifts. What these gifts are cannot easily be deduced from what Paul has said so far (although he has hinted at stances he will adopt in chapter 14 by a passage like 12:7); but that is precisely why he is about to write chapter 14. Before taking up the point, however, he recognizes that given the Corinthian triumphalism and over-realized eschatology, he must do more than simply urge the believers to seek the greater gifts. He must point out that the supreme fruit of the Spirit, love, might somehow get shunted aside even when believers start scrambling for the best gifts; and so, after commanding them to pursue the greater χαρίσματα *(charismata)*, he adds: "And I will show you a yet more excellent way." The conjunction "and" (καί, *kai*) is now treated normally; the difficulties of textual variant and translation in the rest of the clause do not too greatly affect the flow.[15] Paul's point is that the love he is about to discuss cannot be classed with the χαρίσματα *(charismata):* it is not one χάρισμα *(charisma)* of many, but an entire "way" of life,[16] an overarching, all-embracing style of life that utterly

14. So inter alios W. Harold Mare, "1 Corinthians," in *The Expositor's Bible Commentary,* ed. Frank E. Gaebelein, 12 vols. (Grand Rapids: Zondervan, 1976), vol. 10.

15. The difficulties are as follows: (1) In P[46] and D*, ἔτι is replaced by εἴ τι, a reading preferred by many, including BDF §272: "If there is anything beyond, I show you a way." If this reading were correct, one might have expected the article with ὁδόν. Moreover, G. Zuntz, *The Text of the Epistles: A Disquisition upon the Corpus Paulinum* (London: British Academy, 1953), 90, reports that P[46] is in fact damaged here, making us unsure of the reading; and it is "unwise to commit oneself to the Western text" by itself. (2) I have followed Barrett in taking ἔτι καθ᾽ὑπερβολήν adjectivally, "a yet better way" or "a yet more excellent way." But the expression could be taken adverbially: "beyond all this [that I have said so far], I show you a way." This seems to make love a means toward an end; the rendering I have preferred makes love itself the "way." See Conzelmann, *First Corinthians;* Robert L. Thomas, *Understanding Spiritual Gifts: The Christian's Special Gifts in the Light of 1 Corinthians 12–14* (Chicago: Moody, 1978).

16. The ὁδός language derives from wisdom literature, and in this context neatly sets up a sharp contrast between love as an entire way of life, and χαρίσματα. See especially Stanislas Lyonnet, "Agape et charismes selon 1 Co 12,31," in *Paul de Tarse: apôtre de notre temps,* ed. L. De Lorenzi (Rome: Abbaye de S. Paul h.l.m., 1979), 509–27.

transcends in importance the claims of this or that χάρισμα (cha-risma). That does *not* mean, of course, that Paul is saying the χαρίσματα (charismata) are *not* important; it means, rather, that if too much attention is paid to them, believers may overlook the absolutely cru-cial importance of the entire way of life that ought to characterize *every* believer, *every* person who has been baptized in the Holy Spirit. Then, after the chapter on love, which is integral to Paul's overall strategy but not to the question of the ranking of spiritual gifts, the latter is resumed in 14:1ff.—and thus the verb ζηλοῦτε (zēloute) bears imperative force there as well, as also in 14:39.

Love, then, is not a χάρισμα (charisma)[17] but an entire way of life without which, as we shall see, all χαρίσματα (charismata) must be judged utterly worthless. It is this way of life that gives meaning and depth to any spiritual gift God grants, but it can always be distin-guished from them—as in 14:1, "Follow the way of love and eagerly desire spiritual gifts." In Paul's epistle to the Galatians (5:22–23), love heads the list of virtues he calls "the fruit of the Spirit"—that "har-mony of nine graces which make up a mature Christian character and provide conclusive evidence of the Spirit's indwelling presence."[18]

Three objections are commonly raised against this interpretation of 12:31 and 14:1 and the place of the love chapter between the two texts. First, it would be inconsistent for Paul to exhort the Corinthians to desire spiritual gifts after his firm insistence that spiritual gifts are distributed according to the Spirit's sovereign determination (12:11), according to God's own arrangement (12:18). But I argued in the first chapter that these two verses, 12:11, 18, cannot be pressed so far. The objection is without foundation. Second, it is pointed out that in 14:12, the Corinthians are actually said to be eager to have spiritual gifts (refer to earlier discussions about the cognate construction); and there-fore there is presumptive evidence that the ambiguous cognate verb in 12:31 and 14:1 should be taken the same way. But this essentially linguistic argument cannot be separated from the situation the inter-preter understands Paul is addressing. All must agree that Paul ap-preciates that the Corinthian church is well endowed with spiritual gifts (1:7), so the restatement of that fact in 14:12 comes as no surprise. The question then is whether he encourages this spiritual wealth while simultaneously pointing out the inherent limitations of the "spiritual gifts" and the transcendent importance of love as an entire way of life that alone can validate any particular gift. If so, there can be no ob-jection to reading the three instances of ζηλοῦτε (zēloute) imperatively,

17. Contra Hans Lietzmann and Werner Georg Kümmel, *An die Korinther I. II*, Handbuch Zum Neuen Testament, vol. 9 (Tübingen: J. C. B. Mohr, 1969).
18. Bruce, *1 and 2 Corinthians*.

"earnestly desire" (12:31; 14:1, 39). Third, it is sometimes argued that the verb is more frequently used in a bad sense in the New Testament, "to be jealous of" something or someone, or "to desire" in some wicked way; and this negative sense should have the benefit of the doubt, and better fits the view that makes Paul out to be *describing* what he finds in the Corinthians' attitude toward spiritual gifts. The ratio of good uses to bad uses, however, can have little force when there are only eleven occurrences in the entire New Testament, with positive examples other than these three under dispute (e.g., 2 Cor. 11:2). In any case, this argument serves to work against Martin's theory that in 14:1, 39 Paul is quoting the Corinthians; for they would certainly not be describing their own desire for spiritual gifts as something wicked. In short, this objection can cut both ways, and in any case is rather insubstantial.

And so we turn to chapter 13, whose three divisions may be summarized under the next three points.

The Indispensability of Love (13:1–3)[19]

Partly out of pastoral empathy, partly because he himself speaks in tongues (see 14:18), Paul casts this section in the first person. The construction of the first clause[20] probably signals intensity toward the end: "If I speak in the tongues of men and *even* of angels. . . ." It is not clear whether either Paul or his readers thought their gifts of tongues were the dialects of angels. A few interesting Jewish parallels make this possible;[21] but Paul may be writing hyperbolically to draw as sharp a contrast as possible with love. I suppose a pedant might argue that they cannot be the tongues of angels, because in that case it would be silly for tongues to cease when perfection comes since that is precisely when we are more likely to encounter angels! But I shall leave

19. In addition to standard commentaries and specialized studies, one should not overlook the treatments of this chapter by Karl Barth, *Church Dogmatics* (Edinburgh: T. and T. Clark, 1961), 4/2: 824–40; by Leon Morris, *Testaments of Love* (Grand Rapids: Eerdmans, 1981), 238–59; and by Heinrich Schlier, *Nun aber bleiben diese Drei: Grundriss des christlichen Lebensvollzuges*, 2d ed. (Einseideln: Johannes Verlag, 1972), 186–93.

20. Spicq, *Agapé*, 2:66–67, followed by Conzelmann, *First Corinthians*, points to the location of λαλῶ between τῶν ἀνθρώπων and καὶ τῶν ἀγγέλων, instead of either before or after both of these expressions. This construction (a noun modified by two other nouns joined by καί yet interrupted by a finite verb) a GRAMCORD computer check shows to be found only here in the Greek New Testament.

21. Some cite Rev. 14:2–3; H. L. Strack and P. Billerbeck, *Kommentar zum Neuen Testament aus Talmud und Midrasch*, 5 vols. (München: Beck, 1922–28), 3:449–50; Ascension of Isaiah 7:15–37. But the most impressive parallel is Testament of Job 48–50, where Job's daughters speak in the dialects of various classes of angels.

the question as to what language or languages we shall speak in the new heaven and on the new earth to those more gifted in speculation than I. Paul's point is relatively simple. No matter how exalted my gift of tongues, without love I am nothing more than a resounding gong or a clanging cymbal.

This value judgment is meant to be shocking. Part of its power is that Paul does not merely say that under this condition—that is, under the condition of speaking in tongues but without love—it is not the gift of tongues that is only a resounding gong or a clanging cymbal, but I, myself. Even the perfect γέγονα (gegona) may be significant: not simply "*I am* only a resounding gong or a clanging cymbal," but (lit.) "*I have become* only a resounding gong or a clanging cymbal"—as if my action of speaking in tongues without love has left a permanent effect on me that has diminished my value and transformed me into something I should not be.[22]

Exactly what the resounding gong and clanging cymbal refer to is not clear. Parallels are so numerous that it is not easy to be certain what Paul had in mind.[23] The least he is saying is that under these conditions I become empty, meaningless noise. There is no spiritual significance to my gift of tongues. Because he may be referring to instruments used in pagan worship, some have suggested that he is saying the one who speaks in tongues without distinctively Christian love is indistinguishable from a pagan. That interpretation is possible, but only if Paul is mixing his metaphors a little: he is after all talking about *himself*, not his gift of *tongues*, becoming like a resounding gong or a clanging cymbal. If he had wanted to make the connection with paganism unambiguous, it might have been better to say either that the gift of tongues degenerates to pagan instruments or that the participant degenerates to the level of the worshiper at a pagan cult.

Certainly verse 2 finds Paul playing with hypothetical superlatives. He himself does not think that any prophet "can fathom all mysteries

22. But most scholars, if they comment at all, would approve Barrett's remark: " 'I have become' would be pedantic."

23. In addition to the commentators (especially Archibald Robertson and Alfred Plummer, *A Critical and Exegetical Commentary on the First Epistle of St. Paul to the Corinthians*, 2d ed. [Edinburgh: T. and T. Clark, 1914]; C. K. Barrett, *The First Epistle to the Corinthians*, 2d ed. [London: Black, 1971]; Conzelmann, *First Corinthians;* William Barclay, *The Letters to the Corinthians* [Philadelphia: Westminster, 1956]; and M. E. Thrall, *I and II Corinthians* [Cambridge: Cambridge University Press, 1965]), see K. L. Schmidt, "κύμβαλον," *TDNT*, 3:1037–39; Hans Dieter Betz, *Lukian von Samosata und das Neue Testament: Religionsgeschichtliche und Paränetische Parallelen*, Texte und Untersuchen zur Geschichte der altchristlichen Literatur, vol. 76 (Berlin: Akademie-Verlag, 1961); W. Harris, " 'Sounding Brass' and Hellenistic Technology," *Biblical Archaeology Review* 9 (1982): 38–41.

and all knowledge," since he goes on to say that at present "we know in part and we prophesy in part" (13:9). If there is a difference between "mysteries" and "knowledge" in this context, the former refers to the eschatological situation and the latter to the entire redemptive purpose of God; but Paul may not be making nice distinctions.[24] The point is that even the gift of prophecy, no matter how much reliable information comes from it, is intrinsically valueless if it operates without love. So also the gift of faith—as in 12:9, this refers not to saving faith but to something more specialized, such as the faith that can move mountains—has no intrinsic value. Again, however, Paul's conclusion is even more shattering: not only are the spiritual gifts exercised without love of no value, but, says Paul, "I am nothing"—"spiritually a cipher."[25]

But Paul is not content to draw examples only from the more spectacular or "miraculous" of the χαρίσματα (charismata). In verse 3 he goes on to incredibly self-sacrificing philanthropy[26] and even personal martyrdom by fiery ordeal (if that reading is adopted as correct),[27] like the martyrdom of Maccabean Jews[28] or the three heroes of Daniel 3:28. The result is the same: without love, I gain nothing. My deeds of philanthropy and my resolute determination to remain loyal to the truth even in the face of martyrdom cannot in themselves attest my high spiritual position or the superiority of my experiences with the Holy Spirit. In all of this, if there is no love, I gain nothing. In this divine mathematics, five minus one equals zero.

In the context of the three chapters, the point of Paul's argument in these verses is clear. He says, in effect: You who think that because you speak in tongues you are so spiritual, you who prove your large endowment from the Holy Spirit by exercising the gift of prophecy, you must understand that you have overlooked what is most important. By themselves, your spiritual gifts attest nothing spiritual about you. And you who prefer to attest your rich privilege in the Holy Spirit by works of philanthropy, you must learn that philanthropy apart

24. Cf. Barrett, *The First Epistle to the Corinthians.*

25. Robertson and Plummer, *Corinthians.*

26. The precise meaning of ψωμίσω is obscure. It customarily means "to feed" (cf. Rom. 12:20); but it may have the meaning *to divide in pieces,* i.e., "if I divide all my goods into pieces to feed the poor," or the like.

27. For the variants, see not only the commentators but also Zuntz, *Text of the Epistles,* 35ff.; J. K. Elliott, "In Favour of καυθήσομαι at I Corinthians 13³," *Zeitschrift für die neutestamentliche Wissenschaft* 62 (1971): 297–98; René Kieffer, " 'Afin que je sois brûlé' ou bien 'afin que j'en tire orgueil'? (1 Cor XIII.3)," *New Testament Studies* 22 (1975–76): 95–97.

28. Cf. H. Strathmann, "μάρτυς κτλ," *TDNT,* 4:486–89, and the primary literature there cited.

from Christian love says nothing about your experience with God. You remain spiritually bankrupt, a spiritual nothing, if love does not characterize your exercise of whatever grace-gift God has assigned you.

If Paul were addressing the modern church, perhaps he would extrapolate further: You Christians who prove your spirituality by the amount of theological information you can cram into your heads, I tell you that such knowledge by itself proves nothing. And you who affirm the Spirit's presence in your meetings because there is a certain style of worship (whether formal and stately or exuberant and spontaneous), if your worship patterns are not expressions of love, you are spiritually bankrupt. You who insist that speaking in tongues attests a second work of the Spirit, a baptism of the Spirit, I tell you that if love does not characterize your life, there is not evidence of even a first work of the Spirit.

In none of these instances does Paul depreciate spiritual gifts, but he refuses to recognize *any* positive assessment of *any* of them unless the gift is discharged in love. Principially, therefore, any particular gift is dispensable, so far as spiritual profit or attestation of the Spirit's presence is concerned; but love is indispensable.[29]

Some Characteristics of Love (13:4–7)[30]

In these verses, love is not so much defined as described; and even this description is not so much theoretical as practical. Not one element in this pithy list is sentimental; everything is behavioral. Paul shifts back and forth between saying what love is, and what it is not: the first pair of characteristics is positive, then come four pairs of negative characteristics (the last of which is restated positively), followed by two more pairs of positive characteristics. Throughout, love is personified: it is love itself that is kind, or does not boast, or the like, rather than the person who displays love, so powerfully does love take over in Paul's thought in this chapter.

29. This is not to say that Paul recognizes no other ultimate test of authentic Christianity. For instance, Gal. 1:8–9 makes it clear that Paul holds certain doctrines to be essential to Christianity. But in the disparate claims of love and of "charismatic" gifts, only the former is indispensable.

30. This part of the "hymn" is certainly modeled on Jewish paraenesis; Gerhard von Rad, "Die Vorgeschichte der Gattung von 1 Cor. 13,4–7," in *Geschichte und Altes Testament: Festschrift für A. Alt* (Tübingen: J. C. B. Mohr, 1953), 153–68, suggests it is based on a "negative confession" pattern. Some parallels (e.g., Testament of Issachar 4, adduced by Conzelmann, *First Corinthians*) have certain formal similarities to this chapter, but are about quite different subjects—in this instance, the simple-minded man.

When love is absent, what happens? Lovelessness breeds thousands of variations on inferiority complexes and superiority complexes. It almost seems as if verses 4–5 respond directly to such traits. Love is patient: the word usually suggests not merely willingness to wait a long time, or endurance of suffering without giving way, but endurance of injuries without retaliation.[31] Love is kind—not merely patient or long-suffering in the face of injury, but quick to pay back with kindness what it received in hurt.[32]

Negatively, love does not envy: the noncharismatics must learn that lesson. Nor does it boast: the charismatics must learn that lesson. The particular verb that Paul uses is found only here in the New Testament; but it is known from other sources, and it has overtones of ostentatious bragging.[33] More broadly, love is not proud (lit., "puffed up," a word Paul has had to apply to the Corinthians before [4:6, 18, 19; 5:2; 8:1]). Love is not rude; that is, it does not behave improperly toward others, as in 7:36 (where the same word is used) where a man would be acting improperly if he provoked a young woman's affections and then refused to marry her. It is well said that you can spot a gentleman not by the way he addresses his king but by the way he addresses his servants. The former may not be courtesy at all, but merely enlightened self-interest. More foundationally, love is not self-seeking: "Love not merely does not seek that which does not belong to it; it is prepared to give up for the sake of others even what it is entitled to."[34] In personal relationships, love is not easily angered; that is, it is not touchy, with a blistering temper barely hidden beneath the surface of a respectable facade, just waiting for an offense, real or imagined, at which to take umbrage.[35]

But suppose genuine injury has been done? What then? Paul's answer is that love "keeps no record of wrongs," a private file of personal grievances that can be consulted and nursed whenever there is possibility of some new slight. Its stance in the presence of genuine evil precludes such accounting; for at a very deep level, love cannot bear

---

31. I.e., μακροθυμεῖ. In the Septuagint the verb renders Hebrew אֶרֶךְ אַפַּיִם and related expressions; e.g., Prov. 19:11: "A man's wisdom *gives him patience;* it is his glory to overlook an offense."

32. The verb is χρηστεύεται, and is found only here in the New Testament; but the cognates χρηστότης and χρηστός are frequent in both the Septuagint and the New Testament, regularly characterizing God's dealings with people: e.g., Rom. 2:4; 11:22—here even under considerable provocation.

33. περπερεύεται. See H. Braun, "περπερεύομαι," *TDNT*, 6:93–95, who nicely relates its meaning to the situation Paul confronts in Corinth.

34. Barrett, *The First Epistle to the Corinthians.*

35. The word group is not always used negatively (cf. the use of the cognate in Heb. 10:24), but predominantly so.

to be censorious or hypocritical: love "does not delight in evil" (v. 6), like the fake self-righteousness that feigns moral indignation in the face of salaciousness, but secretly revels in the crudeness and vulgarity. It does not enjoy endless discussions about what is wrong with the churches and institutions we serve, and takes on such subjects only when competing demands of righteousness require it. If there is any report of something right or truthful going on, love will quickly rejoice over it, or, if the compound verb that is used is not merely intensive,[36] love *will join with others in rejoicing* over the truth. "Love does not seek to make itself distinctive by tracking down and pointing out what is wrong; it gladly sinks its own identity to rejoice with others at what is right."[37]

Verse 7 sums up, and is characterized by the word *always*.[38] Wischmeyer convincingly demonstrates that the repetition of the word (eight times in 13:1–7, and rendered "all" or "always") is polemical.[39] Paul is responding to the Corinthians' deep commitment to the overly realized eschatology mentioned in my first chapter. They take the view that "all things are permitted" (see 4:8; 6:12) since the eschatological reign has begun. But, responds Paul in 13:7, Christian love still *always* endures (probably a better rendering than NIV's "protects"), *always* trusts, *always* hopes, *always* perseveres: that is part of the voluntary curtailment of personal freedom love demands, already discussed by Paul earlier in this epistle (especially chaps. 8–9). Christian love always endures (or possibly "endures all things"); it always trusts— which does not mean it is gullible, but that it prefers to be generous in its openness and acceptance rather than suspicious or cynical. Love hopes for the best, even when disappointed by repeated personal abuse, hoping against hope and "always ready to give an offender a second chance and to forgive him 'seventy times seven' (Mt 18:22)."[40] Love perseveres: "When the evidence is adverse, [love] hopes for the best. And when hopes are repeatedly disappointed, it still courageously waits."[41]

36. συγχαίρει. See Barrett, *The First Epistle to the Corinthians*.
37. Ibid.
38. Taking the word πάντα adverbially.
39. Wischmeyer, *Der höchste Weg*, 105. If her interpretation is correct, the other possible ways to translate πάντα στέγει are ruled out.
40. Bruce, *1 and 2 Corinthians*.
41. Robertson and Plummer, *Corinthians*. By contrast, some have taken πάντα to mean "always": love *always* protects, trusts, hopes, and perseveres, perhaps with overtones of eschatological promise. Syntactically such an interpretation cannot be ruled out. But v. 7 reads more coherently with what precedes it than with what succeeds it; and if vv. 4–7 are read as a block, what is in focus in that paragraph is how Christian love acts *now*, not how long into the eschaton it will hold up.

Before going on, we must pause to ask what is distinctive about Christian love, and to recognize firmly that the meaning of love described in this chapter is not intrinsic to the noun ἀγάπη *(agapē)* or its cognate verb ἀγαπάω *(agapaō)*. Of course, this verdict is contrary to popular opinion, which often suggests that this word is chosen in the Scriptures over other words for "love" because only this word group captures the determined love of God that seeks the other's good. Linguistically that is not true: the development of the various terms for love has been well and amusingly chronicled by Joly,[42] and cannot be retraced here. In the Septuagint, if Amnon incestuously loves his half-sister Tamar, the verb can be ἀγαπάω *(agapaō;* 2 Sam. 13:1). In John's Gospel, we are twice told that the Father loves the Son: one passage using ἀγαπάω *(agapaō)* and the other φιλέω *(phileō;* John 3:35; 5:20 respectively). When he details that Demas has forsaken him because he *loved* this world, Paul does not think it inappropriate to use the verb ἀγαπάω *(agapaō;* 2 Tim. 4:10). These examples could be multiplied. My point is simply that there is nothing intrinsic to a particular word group that makes its version of love particularly divine.[43] On the other hand, that is far from saying that there is nothing distinctive about God's love or about Christian love. There is; but if we want to discover what that difference is, we shall find it less in a distinctive semantic range of a particular word group than in the descriptions and characteristics of love given in the Scriptures.

As far as this chapter of 1 Corinthians is concerned, the love it describes has provoked lengthy scholarly debates about whether love for God or love for man is in view—as if the Christian gospel Paul preached allowed you to choose between the two.[44] Another famous work pits this love against *eros:* this Christian love, it is concluded, is essentially God's love given to man, almost the equivalent of grace.[45] But the first three verses insistently speak of the love *you and I* are supposed to exercise. A wiser assessment runs like this: "Perhaps the real distinction in 1 Cor[inthians] 13 is between egocentric and altruistic love. The line is not drawn between love of God and love of man, but be-

---

42. Robert Joly, *Le vocabulaire chrétien de l'amour est-il originel?* Φιλεῖν et ᾿Αγαπᾶν *dans le grec antique* (Bruxelles: Presses Universitaires, 1968).

43. D. A. Carson, *Exegetical Fallacies* (Grand Rapids: Baker, 1984), especially 26–32.

44. Cf. Spicq, *Agapé,* 2:108–11. In terms of the emphasis, it appears love for other believers receives greater stress, judging by the cast of vv. 4–7; e.g., love "endures all things," or "always endures," not itself an appropriate way to speak of love for God. But theologically it is hard to separate those two meanings in any Christian framework. For a useful survey of interpretations, see A. G. Vella, "Agapé in I Corinthians XIII," *Melita Theologica* 18 (1966): 57–66.

45. Anders Nygren, *Agape and Eros: A Study of the Christian Idea of Love,* 3 vols. (London: SPCK, 1932–38), 1:98–107.

tween both of these and self-love. It is in this that Christianity consists; in the charity that conquers selfishness."[46] But even this is somewhat inadequate; for 13:3 can envisage that rare altruism that gives away all personal possessions, and even life itself, *without love being present!*

If I must say in few words what is distinctive about God's love for us, it is that it is self-originating.[47] When a young man reveals his heart with a passionate declaration, "I love you!" at least in part he means that he finds the woman he loves lovely. At least some of his love is elicited by the object of that love. But God loves what is un-lovely. If, as John 3:16 tells us, God loves the world, it is not because the world is so lovely God cannot help himself: judging by John's use of the term *world*, God loves the world only because of what *he* is. And derivatively, that is how Christians learn to love: they learn to love with love that is, like God's, self-originating. Of course, unlike God's love, ours is not *absolutely* self-originating; but it is self-originating in the sense that God's grace so transforms the believer that his or her responses of love emerge out of the matrix of Christian character, and are correspondingly less dependent on the loveliness of the object.

The point was all the more startling in the Greco-Roman world, where love, one of the "passions," was not regarded as a public virtue. Philanthropy was honored, but not love, for major voices in Greek thought acclaimed "apathy"—that is, a passionless, rational approach to life—the great ideal. But here we find the apostle Paul insisting that the indispensable proof of authentic Christianity is a life *characterized* by love, that is, by a "passionate" existence.

By now you may be wondering if I have forgotten what this volume is about. I might be better occupied wrestling with the nature of prophecy and tongues, rather than chasing themes through the Scriptures, however interesting such themes may be. In fact, the point is immediately relevant. If this is the character of the love described in this chapter, we immediately understand not only how love can serve as the "more excellent *way*," but also how the presence of *such* love is an infallible test of the Spirit's presence. The various spiritual gifts, as important as they are and as highly as Paul values them, can all be duplicated by pagans. This quality of love cannot be. That is why Jesus himself declares it to be the distinguishing characteristic of his follow-ers; for it is this quality of love he presupposes when he declares, "All men will know that you are my disciples if you love one another" (John 13:35). Whatever theological and exegetical chasms divide char-

46. James Brennan, "The Exegesis of I Corinthians 13," *Irish Theological Quarterly* 21 (1954): 270–78.

47. See especially Morris, *Testaments of Love.*

ismatic from noncharismatic, none of us can afford to ignore what is *central, characteristic, and irreplaceable* in biblical Christianity.

The Permanence of Love (13:8–13)

The connection between this section and what has immediately preceded is entirely natural. In the preceding verse (13:7), Paul concludes by saying that love "always perseveres"; in other words, "Love never fails" (13:8). But the connections are deeper. In the first three verses of this chapter, Paul draws a contrast between love and the χαρίσματα *(charismata)*. Now in verses 8–13, he picks up the contrast again, but with a new wrinkle. Here the contrast turns on the fact that love is permanent, while the χαρίσματα *(charismata)* terminate. That, too, demonstrates love's intrinsic superiority. Thus the statement *love never fails* also anticipates verse 13.[48] Unfortunately the powerful thrust of Paul's argument is sometimes lost under detailed debates as to when the χαρίσματα *(charismata)* cease; but those debates can be an impetus to tracing out the thought of the apostle. If we get the issue of cessation straight, we shall grasp the central points of this section.

The debates turn on the following exegetical points.

The Significance of the Verb παύσονται

In verse 8, the verb with prophecies and with knowledge is in the passive voice: prophecies and knowledge "will be destroyed," apparently in connection with the coming of "perfection" (v. 10). But the verb with "tongues," παύσονται *(pausontai)*, is in the middle; some take this to mean that tongues will cease *of themselves.* There is something intrinsic to their character that demands they cease—apparently independently of the cessation of prophecy and knowledge.[49] This view assumes without warrant that the switch to this verb is more than a stylistic variation. Worse, it interprets the middle voice irresponsibly. In Hellenistic Greek, the middle voice affects the meaning of the verb in a variety of ways; and not only in the future of some verbs, where middles are more common, but also in other tenses the middle *form* may be used while the active *force* is preserved. At such points the verb is deponent. One knows what force the middle voice has only by

48. Lietzmann and Kümmel, *An die Korinther I. II.*
49. So inter alios Thomas, *Understanding Spiritual Gifts*, 105; Robert L. Thomas, "Tongues Will Cease," *Journal of the Evangelical Theological Society* 17 (1974): 81–89; S. D. Toussaint, "First Corinthians Thirteen and the Tongues Question," *Bibliotheca Sacra* 120 (1963): 311–16; Robert G. Gromacki, *The Modern Tongues Movement* (Philadelphia: Presbyterian and Reformed, 1967): 128–29; J. Heading, *First Epistle to the Corinthians* (Kilmarnok: Ritchie, 1967).

careful inspection of all occurrences of the verb being studied. In the New Testament, this verb prefers the middle; but that does not mean the subject "stops" under its own power. For instance, when Jesus rebukes the wind and raging waters, the storm *stops* (same verb, middle voice in Luke 8:24)—and certainly not under its own power.

Edgar takes a slightly different line.[50] He argues that prophecies and knowledge are stopped (i.e., they are destroyed [passive voice]), whereas tongues simply *stop*. The passive voice in connection with the cessation of prophecies and knowledge shows, he argues, that some external event brings the cessation about—the arrival of "perfection." That is why, in verses 9–10, only prophecies and knowledge are mentioned, and not tongues. Tongues, he claims, are in a class by themselves, and are not touched by the arrival of "perfection." After all, only prophecies and knowledge are "partial": the partial-versus-complete argument does not apply to tongues. Their cessation must therefore happen *before* the arrival of "perfection."

Edgar is not the only writer who believes there is great significance in the fact that tongues are not mentioned in verses 9–10; but he is probably the most lucid and dogmatic. Nevertheless, against his proposal weigh the following factors. First, must Paul mention all three— prophecy, knowledge, and tongues—repeatedly throughout these verses? One might as easily argue that in verse 12, where Paul writes, "Now I know in part; then I shall know fully," that prophecy has so dropped from view that it too must be excluded from the discussion. Must Paul be a stylistic pedant? Second, what applies to the content of prophecy, including the partial-versus-complete contrast, surely applies to the content of tongues *once it is assumed that tongues are interpreted* (see especially 14:5).

In short, I do not think that very much can be made of the use of παύσονται *(pausontai)* in verse 8, any more than one can make much of other stylistic features that regularly escape detailed comment (e.g., prophecy and knowledge change their order when Paul moves from v. 8 to v. 9).

The Relation Between "Perfection" (τὸ τέλειον) and the "Imperfect" ([τὸ] ἐκ μέρους)

When "perfection" comes, the "imperfect" disappears: what is the connection between these two categories?

Some of the details are clear. What passes away, of course, is not knowledge per se, but the charismatic gift of knowledge (for knowledge

50. Thomas R. Edgar, *Miraculous Gifts: Are They for Today?* (Neptune, N.J.: Loizeau, 1983), 336–37.

itself will never pass away; and if it did, no one would know it); not the content of prophecy, but the individual prophesyings; and by extrapolation, Paul doubtless has in mind the entire charismatic panoply. The time of their passing is clearly related to the contrast between "perfection" and "the imperfect" (v. 10). The latter is a synthetic expression based on an adverbial prepositional phrase[51] found three times in these verses: "we know *in part*," "we prophesy *in part*" (both in v. 9), and again "I know *in part*" (v. 12): that is, our knowledge of things divine is partial, and our prophecies likewise produce at best partial information. This adverbial prepositional expression is then substantivized in verse 10 by the addition of an article,[52] and rendered (in the NIV) "the imperfect"—that is, the in-part-ness. The disappearance of this kind of "imperfection" or in-part-ness, is dependent on the arrival of "perfection" (v. 10),[53] which thus stands over against the "in-part-ness" nature of the charismatic gifts in Paul's day. That is made clear by verse 12b: "Now I know in part; then I shall know fully, even as I am fully known."

But when does this perfection come, and in what does it consist? There are three groups of theories.[54]

It has been strongly argued that "perfection" refers to the maturity of the church, or the maturity of individual believers.[55] The word in New Testament usage most frequently relates to some such Christian maturity; and so (it is argued) Paul purposely chooses the term here to keep the precise locus of maturity open-ended. If the Lord returned before Paul's death, that would have brought the promised "maturity" or "perfection"; if not, the completion of the canon and all the information the believer needs for spiritual maturity would bring about this "perfection."

It has also been strongly argued that the "perfection" is the completed canon itself.[56] Much of the impetus for this position stems from a profound concern for the finality of biblical truth. If the gift of prophecy, say, is being exercised with the same authority as it had in the

51. ἐκ μέρους.

52. τὸ ἐκ μέρους.

53. τὸ τέλειον.

54. In my judgment, the best three discussions of these issues are in K. S. Hemphill, "The Pauline Concept of Charisma: A Situational and Developmental Approach" (Ph.D. diss., Cambridge University, 1976), 113ff.; Wayne A. Grudem, *The Gift of Prophecy in 1 Corinthians* (Washington, D.C.: University Press of America, 1982); and M. M. B. Turner, "Spiritual Gifts Then and Now," *Vox Evangelica* 15 (1985): 39.

55. Especially by Thomas, *Understanding Spiritual Gifts*, 106ff.

56. See especially Douglas Judisch, *An Evaluation of Claims to the Charismatic Gifts* (Grand Rapids: Baker, 1978), but the view is very common among noncharismatic writers treating this subject.

hands of Isaiah, Jeremiah, or Amos, it is extremely difficult to see how, if the gift of prophecy still operates, one can avoid sliding into the stance of the cults.[57] Why should not such modern prophets write down their prophecies, which in turn should be accepted as "canon" by the church? Although I shall argue shortly that this interpretation is wrong, it must be said nevertheless that charismatics have not always grasped the complexities of this issue. In one recent review, for instance, a charismatic scholar rather acidly mocks the position of those who want to make a distinction between the way God dispenses his gifts before the completion of the inspired writings and after their completion, accusing them of forcing a dichotomy between a "pre-canon God" and a "postcanon God." There is some perception in the charge; but it does not address difficult questions about how we should think of the uniqueness of God's gracious self-disclosure in Jesus and the first generation of witnesses.

The third and majority interpretation is that "perfection" is related to the parousia (or presumably death if that should intervene and if the matter of "perfection" is looked at from a purely individual point of view rather than absolutely). I say "related to the parousia" rather than "parousia" itself, because some have objected that the word πα-ρουσία *(parousia)* is feminine, whereas the word for "perfection" is masculine. The objection is without merit, for "perfection" is not the parousia itself, but the state of affairs brought about by the arrival of the parousia.

The outcome of the debate over these positions is very important, because Paul writes that the imperfect disappears *when perfection*

---

57. For instance, even a scholar like Richard B. Gaffin, Jr., *Perspectives on Pentecost: New Testament Teaching on Gifts of the Holy Spirit* (Phillipsburg, N.J.: Presbyterian and Reformed, 1979), who recognizes that τὸ τέλειον is connected with the parousia, nevertheless argues that prophecy, tongues, and the like are modes of revelation, and inscripturation has ceased.

> And if that be granted, then it is gratuitous to insist that this passage teaches that the modes of revelation mentioned, prophecy and tongues, are to continue functioning until Christ's return. Paul is not intending to specify the time when any particular mode will cease. What he does affirm is the termination of the believer's present, fragmentary knowledge, based on likewise temporary modes of revelation, when "the perfect" comes. The time of the cessation of prophecy and tongues is an open question so far as this passage is concerned (p. 111).

In other words, Gaffin recognizes that this passage cannot be used to teach that prophecy and tongues ceased in the first or second century, so he tries to neutralize the connection with the parousia by saying that the exact time of cessation is not specified at all, which can then be dealt with on dogmatic rather than exegetical grounds. But Paul specifies that prophecy and other gifts will cease *when* perfection comes; and if with Gaffin that perfection is connected with the parousia, then his interpretation sees too little in the text.

comes. In other words, the gifts of prophecy, knowledge, and tongues (and presumably by extrapolation most[58] other charismatic gifts) will pass away at some point future to Paul's writing, designated by him "perfection." If this point can be located in the first or second century, then no putative gift of prophecy, knowledge, or tongues is valid today. Conversely, if this point is located at the parousia, then there is nothing in this passage to preclude a valid gift of tongues or prophecy today. This would not necessarily mean, of course, that each contemporary claim of a particular gift is valid. Nor would it necessarily mean that a charismatic gift or gifts could not have been withdrawn earlier than the parousia. But it does mean that Scripture offers no shelter to those who wish to rule out all claims to charismatic gifts today.

In my judgment, this third position has powerful evidence in its defense. Among the most important factors are these: (1) It is difficult to believe that Paul could have expected the Corinthians to think that by "perfection" he was alluding to the cessation of the writing of Scripture. (2) Most important is verse 12b. Perfection entails a state of affairs where my knowledge is in some ways comparable with God's present knowledge of me: "then I shall know fully, even as I am fully known [sc., by God]." This does not mean that Paul expects to be granted omniscience, but "that in the consummation he expects to be freed from the misconceptions and inabilities to understand (especially to understand God and his word) which are part of this present life. His knowledge will resemble God's present knowledge of him because it will contain no false impressions and will not be limited to what is able to be perceived in this age."[59] Paul's point is not that the charismatic gifts disappear because of their intrinsic weakness or failure. His argument is built rather "on the foundation of what is to come."[60] In Barth's memorable words, "because the sun rises, all lights go out."[61] When that wonderful knowledge of God becomes ours, the purpose of such gifts as prophecy, knowledge, and tongues will have disappeared: what possible service could they still render? (3) Scarcely

58. I say "most" because χάρισμα, as we saw in the first chapter, can refer to salvation itself, which presumably does not disappear (though even in this instance the incompleteness of its present realization will eventually disappear). Moreover the gift of apostleship (12:28) has certain peculiarities associated with it that I shall briefly mention in the next chapter.

59. Grudem, *Gift of Prophecy*, 213.

60. Günther Bornkamm, *Early Christian Experience*, trans. Paul L. Hammer (London: SCM, 1969), 184–85.

61. Karl Barth, *The Resurrection of the Dead*, trans. H. J. Stenning (New York: Arno, 1977), 81.

less important is verse 12a. Now we see "but a poor reflection": the expression suggests unclear or still indistinct divine revelation;[62] but then, when perfection comes, "we shall see face to face"—almost a formula in the Septuagint for a theophany,[63] and therefore almost certainly a reference to the new state brought about by the parousia. As Turner remarks, the reference to the parousia is "so sure that Calvin was able to say: 'It is stupid of people to make the whole of this discussion apply to the intervening time.' However much we respect the New Testament canon, Paul can only be accused of the wildest exaggeration in verse 12 if *that* is what he was talking about."[64] (4) The force of verse 12 similarly rules out the suggestion that "perfection" refers (as in Ephesians) to the joining together of Jews and Gentiles into one new and "perfect" man. That theme is irrelevant in the context of 1 Corinthians 13.[65] Indeed, *any* preparousia maturity simply trivializes the language of verse 12. (5) Verse 11 also draws a sharp contrast. Although the infant/adult contrast is a standard rhetorical device in the ancient world,[66] its specific application here demands a considerable leap forward from infancy to manhood. To argue that the spiritual experience and maturity of the early church before the canon's completion are to the experience of maturity of the postcanonical church just what the experience of an infant's talk and understanding is to that of an adult is historical nonsense. (6) If it is true that the word for "perfection" is nowhere else used for the entire state of affairs brought about by the parousia, it is also true that it almost always

---

62. The combination δι' ἐσόπτρου ἐν αἰνίγματι has provoked considerable discussion. It probably embraces an allusion to Num. 12:6–8 (see Grudem, *Gift of Prophecy*, 145–46 n. 53). Both from the inferior quality of mirrors in the ancient world, and from the angle of vision, mirrors can provide only an indirect and incomplete picture of reality. The second prepositional phrase probably does not mean the revelation already given is enigmatic, mysterious in that sense, utterly baffling, but simply indistinct. See inter alios Wilfrid L. Knox, *St Paul and the Church of the Gentiles* (Cambridge: Cambridge University Press, 1961), 121; Norbert Hugedé, *La Métaphore du Miroir dans les Epîtres de saint Paul aux Corinthiens* (Neuchâtel: Delachaux et Niestlé, 1957); David H. Gill, "Through a Glass Darkly: A Note on 1 Corinthians 13,12," *Catholic Biblical Quarterly* 25 (1963): 427–29; Frederick W. Danker, "Postscript on 1 Corinthians 13,12," *Catholic Biblical Quarterly* 26 (1964): 248; Grudem, *Gift of Prophecy*, 144–47. Contra R. Seaford, "1 Corinthians XIII.12," *Journal of Theological Studies* 35 (1984): 117–20, it is not at all clear that there is a direct allusion to the mystery religions.

63. The words πρόσωπον πρός (or κατὰ) πρόσωπον are not found in the New Testament, but in the Septuagint in the following passages (only): Gen. 32:30; Deut. 5:4; 34:10; Judg. 6:22; Ezek. 20:35; cf. Exod. 33:11; and Grudem, *Gift of Prophecy*, 213.

64. Turner, "Spiritual Gifts Then and Now," 39.

65. Contra J. R. McRay, "To Teleion in 1 Cor 13:10," *Restoration Quarterly* 14 (1971):, 168–83.

66. See Conzelmann, *First Corinthians*.

occurs as an adjective. Only here is it a neuter, articular substantive, probably created precisely to serve as a contrast to "the partial" or "the imperfect." (7) The view that Paul is referring to the closing of the canon depends on understanding New Testament prophecy and related gifts as having the same revelatory and authoritative significance as inscripturated prophecy. If that presupposition can be challenged—and I shall attempt to challenge it in the next chapter—then there is considerably less *theological* pressure to adopt that stance.

None of this, of course, suggests Paul is interested in establishing the ideal relative frequency of prophecy in the church; nor have we yet mentioned historical objections that argue the gifts of prophecy and tongues actually did cease. At the moment, such matters are irrelevant. In these verses Paul establishes the end of the age as the time when these gifts must finally be abolished.

The Determination of What Remains into Eternity in 13:13

There are basically three positions.

1) Many understand the words *and now* (Νυνὶ δέ, *Nuni de*) temporally: now, during this age, only three virtues remain, faith, hope, and love; but if the greatest of these is love, presumably it outstrips the others because it alone goes into eternity. This, it is argued, is supported by the fact that faith and sight can be contrasted (2 Cor. 5:7): now we walk by faith, then we shall walk by sight. Further, hope is swallowed up in realization (Rom. 8:24–25). So love alone is permanent. That in turn suggests that if faith and hope terminate at the parousia (while nevertheless serving as the contrasting virtues to prophecy, tongues, and knowledge) then prophecy, tongues, and knowledge must cease *before* the parousia; and this in turn casts back onto what "perfection" seems to mean.[67]

2) It has also been argued that the words *these three* collectively sum up the triad of faith, hope, and love, so that collectively they serve as a standard of comparison for something new: greater than this collective entity is the love (sc., of God).[68] Whether *our* faith and hope

---

67. See inter alios Judisch, *An Evaluation of Claims to the Charismatic Gifts;* Thomas, *Understanding Spiritual Gifts,* 113–15; Vernon Moss, "I Corinthians xiii.13," *Expository Times* 73 (1962): 93; but see the response by John Moss, "I Corinthians xiii.13," *Expository Times* 73 (1962): 253; François Dreyfus, "Maintenant la foi, l'espérance et la charité demeurent toutes les trois (1 Cor 13,13)," *Studiorum Paulinorum,* 2 vols., Analecta Biblica, vols. 17–18 (Rome: Pontifical Biblical Institute, 1963), 1:403–12 (who also nicely categorizes the uses of νυνὶ δέ in the New Testament); Georg Eichholz, *Tradition und Interpretation: Studien zum Neuen Testament und zur Hermeneutik* (München: Chr. Kaiser, 1965), 121–37.

68. Wischmeyer, *Der höchste Weg,* 62ff.; Martin, *The Spirit and the Congregation,* 54ff.; idem, "A Suggested Exegesis of I Corinthians 13:13," *Expository Times* 82 (1970–71): 119–20.

and love carry on into eternity is a matter of relative indifference; the ultimate value we must recognize is God's love for us.

3) The opening words *and now* (Νυνὶ δέ, *Nuni de*) should not be taken temporally to refer to this age, but logically: "now in fact" or the like, "over against all the transient qualities and activities mentioned."[69] In this view all three virtues carry into eternity; but of these three, the greatest is love, for a reason unspecified but presumably because God himself displays love but neither faith nor hope.[70] Since all three virtues are eternal and permanent, under this interpretation there is no reason why gifts such as prophecy and tongues cannot be thought to continue in principle until the parousia.

In my view, the third interpretation is largely right and may be supported and slightly modified by the following considerations.

(1) There is no obvious way to determine whether the words *and now* (Νυνὶ δέ, *Nuni de*) should be taken temporally or logically. Both uses are found in the New Testament, but one cannot help noticing that if Paul had been trying to stress the temporality of the "now," he would have been less ambiguous if he had written ἄρτι *(arti)* for "now" instead of νῦν or νυνί *(nun or nuni)*. In other words, if Paul had wanted to stipulate the first view unambiguously, he chose a strange way of doing it.

(2) In connection with the second view, it is true that μείζων *(meizōn, greater)* is formally a comparative, not a superlative; and superficially that might be taken to support the position that Paul is comparing only two things, the triad on the one hand, and the love of God on the other. But it is common knowledge that comparative forms regularly serve as superlatives in Hellenistic Greek, and this is common in the New Testament (e.g., "Who is the greatest [μείζων, *meizōn*] in the kingdom of heaven?") Indeed, the *formal* superlative, μέγιστος *(megistos)*, is rare in Hellenistic Greek, and is found in the New Testament only once (2 Peter 1:4). This does not mean that the second interpretation is necessarily wrong, but it does mean that it can hang no weight on the form of μείζων *(meizōn)*.

(3) There is no other instance in the New Testament where the article followed by a number and a demonstrative pronoun/adjective suggests the rendering *these the three* or *these the [well-known] triad* or the like.[71]

(4) Irreparably damaging to the second position is the plural number of the pronoun τούτων *(toutōn, of these)*. In the interpretation I espouse, the plural number is no problem: the genitive is partitive,

69. Barrett, *The First Epistle to the Corinthians*.
70. See 1 John 4:19.
71. Based on the GRAMCORD computer retrieval system for Greek syntax.

and love is the greatest *of these* three just listed. The second interpretation requires that the genitive be one of comparison: the love [of God] is greater *than these*. But if the triad is being treated collectively as a single entity in the comparative "greater," then one must expect that the pronoun be not τούτων but τούτου (not *toutōn* but *toutou*, i.e., the love [of God] is greater *than this* [triad]). That we do not find the singular form virtually rules out this interpretation.

(5) In any case, there is simply no contextual warrant for introducing the love *of God* into this context, as over against (presumably) our love for him and for others.[72]

(6) The greatest strength of the first interpretation—that love alone goes into eternity—lies in the texts affirming that in eternity faith becomes sight and hope is taken over by reality (2 Cor. 5:7; Rom. 8:24–25; 2 Cor. 4:18). If such perspectives are foundational to faith and hope, then faith and hope do not continue, as such, into eternity. But Lacan, Neirynck, Barrett, and others have demonstrated rather forcefully that such texts are misapplied in 1 Corinthians 13:13.[73] Consider hope: it is true that there is a sense in which hope is no longer needed once eternity dawns. But that is not the only sense of hope: in 1 Corinthians 15:19, for instance, Paul writes, "If only for this life we have hope in Christ, we are to be pitied more than all men." Presumably in one sense Paul expects hope to continue beyond this life in the continued enjoyment of that for which we hoped; for there is a sense in which hope is not merely the anticipation of the blessings to come, an anticipation no longer needed once those blessings have arrived, but a firm anchor in Christ himself. Our hope is in God, in Christ; and as such, hope continues forever, doubtless opening up an infinity of new depths of blessings, world without end. Put psychologically, we may ask: Will we stop looking forward in anticipation to what is ahead once we begin to enjoy the new heaven and the new earth? Consider faith: it is true that in one sense faith will be displaced by sight. But there is another sense in which faith is simply thankful trust in God, deep appreciation for him, committed subservience to him. Will there

72. Martin extends his interpretation into chap. 14. There, when Paul tells the Corinthians to follow the way of love, Martin takes the article (τὴν ἀγάπην) to be anaphoric: *the* love to which I have just referred, that *kind* of love, i.e., the love of God. Abstract nouns commonly take the article, so its presence does not instantly suggest anaphoric usage. But more important, Martin's interpretation means that after all the exposition of chap. 13, none of it proves relevant as an example to emulate, except the last two words!

73. Barrett, *The First Epistle to the Corinthians;* and especially F. Neirynck, "De grote drie bij een niewe vertaling van I Cor., XIII, 13," *Ephemerides Theologicae Lovanientis* 39 (1963): 595–615. See also Marc-François Lacan, "Les trois qui demeurent: I Cor. 13:13," *Recherches de Science Religieuse* 46 (1958): 321–43.

be any time in the next fifty billion years (if I may speak of eternity in the categories of time) during which the very basis of my presence in the celestial courts will be something *other* than faith in the grace of God?

It appears, then, that faith, hope, and love, these three, all remain. They are eternal, permanent virtues. That Paul here introduces faith and hope and adds them to love is probably because this triad or some part of it is so common in early Christianity (see Rom. 5:1–5; Gal. 5:5–6; Eph. 4:2–5; Col. 1:4–5; 1 Thess. 1:3; 5:8; Heb. 6:10–12; 10:22–24; 1 Peter 1:3–8, 21–22). But if all three remain eternally, why then is love said to be the greatest of the three?

There is a hint within the chapter itself. After all, this is not the first time faith and hope have been introduced: faith appears in verse 2, and hope in verse 7.[74] Paul in verse 2 can imagine exercising faith without love, but not love without faith; and in verse 7 hope is part of a constellation of virtues that contribute to love, as various colors contribute to white light. In some sense, therefore, love is the all-embracing virtue. One can imagine other ways of setting out the relations that bind faith, hope, and love together, but in Paul's exposition, love is foundational, even of the virtues that characterize God's people in eternity. That is why the greatest of these virtues is love. Moreover, the Scriptures strongly insist that God is love (1 John 4:16); yet it is difficult to imagine how they could have said that God is faith, or that God is hope. That God is love may be John's expression, not Paul's; but the conclusion is the same. Once again, the greatest of these is love.

Two conclusions follow from this exposition. The first is obvious: there does not appear to be biblical warrant, at least from this chapter, for banning contemporary tongues and prophecies on the grounds that Scripture anticipates their early demise. This does not mean, of course, that everything that passes for prophecy or the gift of tongues is genuine. I shall say more about the nature of these gifts in the next chapter.

Second, there is a more startling implication. In the words of one commentator, "Now . . . love and the charismata are set in antithesis to each other, and we have the eschatological argument that the latter will cease. They are accordingly, unlike love, not the appearance of the eternal in time, but the manifesting of the Spirit in a provisional way. Thus these very gifts hold us fast in the 'not yet.' "[75]

Two centuries ago, Jonathan Edwards probed the question as to

74. See Emanuel Miguens, "1 Cor 13:8–13 Reconsidered," *Catholic Biblical Quarterly* 37 (1975): 76–97.

75. Conzelmann, *First Corinthians*.

what makes the church like heaven.[76] His answer: it is love. The church's manifestation in time of the glories that are yet to come is not accomplished in the gift of tongues, nor even in prophecy, giving, teaching. It is accomplished in love. One day all the charismatics who know the Lord and all the noncharismatics who know the Lord will have nothing to fight over; for the so-called charismatic gifts will have forever passed. At that point, both of these groups of believers will look back and thoughtfully contemplate the fact that what connects them with the world they have left behind is not the gift of tongues, nor animosity toward the gift of tongues, but the love they sometimes managed to display toward each other despite the gift of tongues. The greatest evidence that heaven has invaded our sphere, that the Spirit has been poured out upon us, that we are citizens of a kingdom not yet consummated, is Christian love.[77]

76. Jonathan Edwards, *Charity and Its Fruits*, ed. Tyron Edwards (1852; reprint ed., Edinburgh: Banner of Truth Trust, 1969), 323ff.

77. Perhaps it should be said that from a broader, biblical perspective this test is always a necessary but not always a sufficient criterion. For instance, in his first epistle, John lays out three tests: a truth test revolving around christological confession, a moral test revolving around the Christian's principial obedience to Christ, and a love test—and John does not suggest that two out of three constitute a passing grade. Other tests are found elsewhere that serve to check any putative believer's claim to grace; for the New Testament writers are at one in believing that saving grace transforms a person. But although no biblical test is universally sufficient, a particular test *may* be sufficient *in a particular context*. In the context of Corinthian disputes over the χαρίσματα *(charismata)*, Paul's test of love is both necessary and sufficient.

3

Prophecy and Tongues: Pursuing What Is Better (14:1–19)

I want to use the majority of my space in this chapter to address directly a question I have so far avoided: What precisely are such gifts as prophecy, tongues, and the interpretation of tongues? I intend therefore to explore those questions presently before turning to a summary exposition of the text itself.

Reflections on the Nature of Several of the χαρίσματα *(charismata)*

Kinds of Tongues and Interpretation of Tongues (12:10, 29, 30)

What does γλώσσαις λαλεῖν *(glōssais lalein,* to speak in tongues) mean? Discussions of this question are legion. I shall try to simplify the issues by asking and trying to answer the following questions.

Were the tongues in Corinth "ecstatic"? Everything turns on the definition of "ecstatic." One major work offers this definition: "In ecstasy there is a condition of emotional exaltation, in which the one who experiences it is more or less oblivious of the external world, and loses to some extent his self-consciousness and his power of rational thought and self-control."[1] Most noncharismatics who argue that ecstasy characterizes contemporary speaking in tongues mean something more than this (though usually not less), in particular that the languages spoken by tongues-speakers are not real languages but (in the less graceful books) mere gibberish. Strictly speaking, however, there is no necessary connection between ecstasy and the coherence or incoherence of the "tongue" that is spoken. Indeed, there are three quite discrete issues: whether or not ecstasy is involved, whether the utterance is contentful or not, and whether it is a known, human language. These are three distinct questions. Any one of them can stand independently of the others. Most charismatics avoid applying the term *ecstasy* to their tongues-speaking; but this is because they do not take the term to describe the intelligibility or otherwise of their "tongue," but to the psychological state, the degree of dissociation, that they experience. Culpepper writes:

> The main reason charismatics object to tongues being called "ecstatic utterance" is that it seems to suggest one has gone "off his rocker" and lost control of oneself. The first meaning which *Webster's New Collegiate Dictionary* (1975) assigns to ecstasy is that of "a state of being beyond reason and self-control." Glossolalists make the point that Paul assumes that the glossolalist can control his or her speech. This, they say, is exactly what they experience. The point is well taken![2]

Hollenweger helpfully distinguishes between "hot" tongues (those that are spoken in a state of advanced mental dissociation) from "cool" tongues (those uttered where the speaker has perfect control of his or her utterance and remains mentally alert and cognizant of what is going on, even though he or she cannot understand the sounds coming from his or her own mouth).[3] In that sense, hot tongues are ecstatic, cool tongues are not. My perception is that the overwhelming majority of modern tongues-speakers resort to cool tongues; and that is also the self-perception of most tongues-speakers themselves.[4] By and large,

1. G. B. Cutten, *Speaking with Tongues, Historically and Psychologically Considered* (New Haven: Yale University Press, 1927), 157.
2. Robert H. Culpepper, *Evaluating the Charismatic Movement: A Theological and Biblical Appraisal* (Valley Forge: Judson, 1977), 103.
3. Walter J. Hollenweger, *The Pentecostals*, trans. R. A. Wilson (Minneapolis: Augsburg, 1972), 344.
4. This is widely represented in charismatic literature, and is also recognized by competent observers. C. F. D. Moule, *The Holy Spirit* (Grand Rapids: Eerdmans, 1978),

however, "ecstasy" has become such a slippery term that it is probably better left out of the discussion unless it is thoroughly qualified and all sides in the debate know what is meant.[5]

Were the tongues at Corinth "real languages," or something else? To put the matter in technical terms, is the phenomenon of 1 Corinthians an instance of xenoglossia (that is, speaking in unlearned human languages) or glossolalia (that is, speaking in verbal patterns that cannot be identified with any human language)? This is an extraordinarily difficult question to answer convincingly on either side, despite the dogmatic claims made by many proponents on each side. Most contemporary charismatics would be happy with the definition of "tongues" offered by Christensen: "a supernatural manifestation of the Holy Spirit, whereby the believer speaks forth in a language he has never learned, and which he does not understand."[6] This of course simply pushes the question back from the meaning of "tongue" to the meaning of "language." Probably most charismatics are persuaded their utterances are real languages insofar as they believe they actually convey something: they are the tongues of men or of angels. It is a slightly different question whether they believe they are human languages occurring naturally in the world but unlearned by the tongues-speaker. Increasingly, however, some charismatics and a variety of sympathetic observers of the charismatic movement, spurred on by modern linguistic analyses of tapes of tongues utterances (about which I will say more in a few moments), argue that modern tongues and the tongues in Corinth alike are not so-called real languages at all (for instance, Cardinal Suenens,[7] H. Mühlen, who views tongues primarily as a more intense prayer experience in the worship of the inexpressible God,[8] and Green, who suggests that some tongues may be real languages and others not[9]).

One of the strongest defenders of the glossolalist position, over

90, rightly comments: "Those who are familiar with it [i.e., with contemporary tongues-speaking] assure us that it is never 'ecstatic,' if that word is taken to mean out of the subject's control. . . . It is exercised consciously and self-controlledly in such a way that if the gift is available, the use of it can be started or terminated at will."

5. Cyril G. Williams, "Glossolalia as a Religous Phenomenon: 'Tongues' at Corinth and Pentecost," *Journal of Religion and Religions* 5 (1975): 16–32.

6. Larry Christensen, *Speaking in Tongues and Its Significance for the Church* (Minneapolis: Bethany, 1968), 22.

7. Léon-Joseph Suenens, *A New Pentecost?* (New York: Seabury, 1974), 99.

8. Heribert Mühlen, *A Charismatic Theology: Initiation in the Spirit* (London: Burns and Oates; New York: Paulist, 1978), 152–56. See George T. Montague, *Riding the Wind: Learning the Ways of the Spirit* (Ann Arbor: Servant, 1974), 45: "The gift is primarily non-rational prayer ([The one who speaks in a tongue speaks not to men but to God] 1 Cor 14,2). Artless, it uses no phrenetic energy in formulation."

9. Michael Green, *I Believe in the Holy Spirit* (Grand Rapids: Eerdmans, 1975), 162–63.

against xenoglossia, is Williams.[10] He firmly criticizes those word studies of γλῶσσα (*glōssa*, tongue) that insist the term, when it does not
refer to the wagging organ in one's mouth, always means real languages. Not only may the word "indicate the physical organ, known
languages, dialects or sub-dialects, but also the incoherent utterance
of certain forms of spiritual fervency."[11] In any case, he writes, "normal usage is not the only criterion when the subject of investigation
is what appears to be a new phonemenon or at least one that is un-
familiar in a particular context. In such cases a term in common cur-
rency may be given an extension of connotation and sometimes the
new meaning establishes a technical application."[12] Williams is similarly unimpressed with studies that argue the verb *to interpret* normally means "to translate"—and translation presupposes a real
language.[13] Williams is far from saying that tongues are entirely devoid of meaning: he means rather that they may be an expression of
deep feelings and inarticulate thoughts issuing out of the speaker's
deep experience of the Spirit, but not demonstrably conveyed in propositional terms in the sounds themselves. Whereas many commentators would be reasonably happy with this so far as 1 Corinthians is
concerned, they might prefer to see in Acts 2 not glossolalia but xenoglossia. Williams, however, pushes on to consistency, and suggests
that even in Acts 2 we are dealing with glossolalia: after all, even
glossolalia makes *some* sounds that could be identified as real words
in various languages. How else could it be, Williams wonders, that
many of those present accused the believers of being drunk? Would
we accuse someone who was speaking in another human language of
being drunk?[14]

Nevertheless, I remain unpersuaded by Williams's arguments. I shall
discuss Acts 2 in the last chapter, but for the moment I must merely
register my conviction that what Luke describes at Pentecost are real,
known, human languages. More careful word studies have shown that
in none of the texts adduced by Behm[15] or the standard lexica[16] does

10. Cyril G. Williams, *Tongues of the Spirit: A Study of Pentecostal Glossolalia and
Related Phenomena* (Cardiff: University of Wales, 1981), especially 25–45.

11. Ibid., 26, referring to BAG.

12. Ibid., 26.

13. In particular, J. G. Davies, "Pentecost and Glossolalia," *Journal of Theological
Studies* 3 (1952): 228–31. See also R. H. Gundry, " 'Ecstatic Utterance' (N.E.B.)?" *Journal of Theological Studies* 17 (1966): 299–307.

14. Williams, *Tongues of the Spirit*, 31ff.

15. Johannes Behm, "γλῶσσα, ἑτερόγλωσσος," *TDNT*, 1:719–27.

16. In particular, BAGD.

γλῶσσα *(glōssa)* ever denote noncognitive utterance.[17] The utterance may be enigmatic and incomprehensible, but not noncognitive. The ecstatic utterances of the pagan religions prove less suitable a set of parallels than was once thought.[18] Nor is Thiselton entirely convincing when he argues that the verb ἑρμηνεύω *(hermēneuō)* can be used in Philo and Josephus to mean "to put into words" rather than "to translate";[19] for as Turner has pointed out, in 1 Corinthians it is not simply the verb that one must wrestle with, but the use of the verb *in connection with "to speak in (or with) tongues."*[20] MacGorman insists that glossolalia in 1 Corinthians is "Holy Spirit inspired utterance that is unintelligible apart from interpretation, itself an attendant gift. It is a form of ecstatic utterance, a valid charismatic endowment."[21] He goes on to affirm that if the modern reader reads real languages into the picture, then verses such as 14:2, 13, 14, 18, 26 degenerate to sheer nonsense. But in fact, not one of them is nonsense, even if the tongue is a real language, *provided only that the tongues-speaker does not know what he or she is saying*—a point Paul surely presupposes when he exhorts the tongues-speaker to pray for the gift of interpretation, and acknowledges it is possible to pray without the mind (see further discussion, below). Moreover if tongues are principally unintelligible at the intrinsic level until the gift of interpretation is exercised, one wonders in what sense tongues are being "interpreted" at all. Dunn supports the view that the tongues in Corinth were not real human

17. By this I mean utterance without cognitive content, regardless of whether such content is understood by either the speaker or the hearer. See Gundry, " 'Ecstatic Utterance' "; Thomas R. Edgar, *Miraculous Gifts: Are They for Today?* (Neptune, N.J.: Loizeaux, 1983), 110–21.

18. See T. M. Crone, *Early Christian Prophecy. A Study of Its Origin and Function* (Baltimore: St. Mary's University Press, 1973), especially chap. 1, and 220–21; and the excellent treatment by Christopher Forbes, "Glossolalia in Early Christianity" (unpublished paper, Macquarie University, 1985).

19. A. C. Thiselton, "The 'Interpretation' of Tongues: A New Suggestion in the Light of Greek Usage in Philo and Josephus," *Journal of Theological Studies* 30 (1979): 15–36.

20. M. M. B. Turner, "Spiritual Gifts Then and Now," *Vox Evangelica* 15 (1985): 18–19. Moreover, as Forbes has shown ("Glossolalia in Early Christianity," 23–27), Thiselton's argument is flawed at several points. His statistics of the use of διερμηνεύω and διερμήνευσις in Philo ("no less than three-quarters of the uses refer to the articulation of thoughts or feelings in intelligible speech" [Thiselton, "The 'Interpretation' of Tongues," 18]) are substantially reversed if one includes the simple verb ἑρμηνεύω and its cognates: 60 percent now stand against his thesis. That the verb *can* mean "to put into words" or the like, Thiselton has clearly established; that such is the obvious meaning in 1 Cor. 12–14 is less likely. Forbes also demonstrates that Thiselton's arguments from context are not convincing.

21. Jack W. MacGorman, *The Gifts of the Spirit: An Exposition of 1 Corinthians 12–14* (Nashville: Broadman, 1974), 390–91.

languages, partly on the grounds that the subject matter is "mysteries," which he understands to be eschatological secrets known only in heaven, and partly on the grounds that if Paul thought the gift of tongues utilized real foreign languages he could not have *compared* them with real foreign languages in 14:10ff. But "mysteries" in 13:2 are connected with prophecy, not tongues; and the expression *all mysteries*, as we saw in the last chapter, is purposely wildly hyperbolic, since Paul does not think that we can now enjoy more than partial knowledge. In any case, Paul is capable of expressing heavenly mysteries *in Greek:* see 1 Corinthians 15:51–52—so there is no necessary connection between mysteries and noncognitive speech. And in 14:10ff., "Paul could be pointing to the obvious consequences in the secular realm of what the Corinthians fail to see in the spiritual, without which others do not understand; Paul points out how close they come to being ridiculed as 'barbarians' rather than exalted as 'spirituals.' "[22]

Other arguments in favor of taking tongues in 1 Corinthians as noncognitive have been treated elsewhere.[23] Perhaps two more should be mentioned here. Smith says that if the tongues are real but unlearned languages, then each instance is an open miracle—and God is in the awkward position of doing miracles through tongues-speakers while simultaneously instructing his apostle to curb them. Therefore these cannot be real tongues, miraculously bestowed.[24] But if this argument were applied to other spiritual gifts, we would arrive at nonsense. For instance, Paul curbs excesses in prophecy, which presumably is Spirit-prompted. Smith's argument seems to suppose that if the tongues are not real languages, then the Spirit of God may not be so intimately involved. Indeed, if Smith's argument had any real weight, it would be a decisive blow against the notion of a sovereign and providential God; for since all that transpires takes place under the aegis of divine sovereignty (Rom 8:28), why should God forbid anything that does in fact take place? Possible answers to that question lie elsewhere;[25] but certainly Smith's objection does not rule out real languages.

A second objection concerns the use of the verb λαλεῖν *(lalein)*, "to speak" in tongues. Some have suggested that it here retains an older meaning and hints at babbling, utterance empty of cognitive content. Gundry replies with four telling observations: Paul can also use λέγω *(legō)* for speaking in tongues, 14:16—and that verb is regularly used

22. Turner, "Spiritual Gifts Then and Now," 19.

23. Ibid., 19–20; Forbes, "Glossolalia in Early Christianity."

24. Charles R. Smith, *Tongues in Biblical Perspective: A Summary of Biblical Conclusions Concerning Tongues*, 2d ed. (Winona Lake, Ind.: BMH, 1973), especially 26–27.

25. See D. A. Carson, *Divine Sovereignty and Human Responsibility: Biblical Perspectives in Tension* (Atlanta: John Knox, 1981).

for ordinary speech; Paul uses the verb λαλέω *(laleō)* in 14:19 in connection with speaking with the mind, which seems to embrace intelligible speech, so the verb cannot be restricted to unintelligible speech; Paul also uses this verb in 14:29 of prophetic speech, which like tongues is Spirit-prompted but unlike tongues is immediately intelligible; and the same verb is used in 14:34–35 of a woman asking questions, presumably in her normal language.[26]

On balance, then, the evidence favors the view that Paul thought the gift of tongues was a gift of real languages, that is, languages that were cognitive, whether of men or of angels. Moreover, if he knew of the details of Pentecost (a currently unpopular opinion in the scholarly world, but in my view eminently defensible), his understanding of tongues must have been shaped to some extent by that event.[27] Certainly tongues in Acts exercise some different *functions* from those in 1 Corinthians; but there is no substantial evidence that suggests Paul thought the two were *essentially* different.

We have established high probability, I think, that Paul believed the tongues about which he wrote in 1 Corinthians were cognitive.[28] But before any sweeping conclusions can be drawn, another question must be brought to bear.

What bearing does the discipline of linguistics have on the assessment of modern tongues? To my knowledge there is universal agreement among linguists who have taped and analyzed thousands of examples of modern tongues-speaking that the contemporary phenomenon is not any human language.[29] The patterns and structures that all known human language requires are simply not there. Occasionally a recognizable word slips out; but that is statistically likely, given the sheer quantity of verbalization. Jaquette's conclusion is unavoidable: "we are dealing here not with language, but with verbalizations which

26. Gundry, " 'Ecstatic Utterance,' " 304.

27. Some writers, among them Jimmy A. Millikin, "The Nature of the Corinthian Glossolalia," *Mid-America Theological Journal* 8 (1984): 81–107, have argued that tongues in Corinth were a degenerative form of tongues in Acts, a strange mixture of real words and gibberish. But Paul nowhere in 1 Cor. 12–14 treats the gift as if it were itself degenerative. Not the gift, but the weight the Corinthians were placing on it, is the focal point of Paul's attack.

28. Or, more precisely, that the tongues bore cognitive content, whether or not that content was actually *understood* by speaker or hearer. See Abraham Kuyper, *The Work of the Holy Spirit*, trans. Henri de Vries (reprint ed., Grand Rapids: Eerdmans, 1975), 132–38.

29. See especially the much cited works of W. J. Samarin, *Tongues of Men and Angels: The Religious Language of Pentecostalism* (New York: Macmillan, 1972); idem, *Variation and Variables in Religious Glossolalia: Language in Society* (London: Cambridge University Press, 1972).

superficially resemble language in certain of its structural aspects."[30] When studies have been made of tongues uttered in different cultures and linguistic environments, several startling conclusions have presented themselves.[31] The tongues phenomena have been related to the speaker's natural language (e.g., a German or French tongues-speaker will not use one of the two English "th" sounds; and English tongues-speakers will never include the "u" sound of French "cru"). Moreover, the stereotypical utterance of any culture "mirrors that of the person who guided the glossolalist into the behavior. There is little variation of sound patterns within the group arising around a particular guide,"[32] even though other studies show that the tongues patterns of each speaker are usually identifiable from those of others, and a few tongues-speakers use two or more discrete patterns.[33] In any case, modern tongues are lexically uncommunicative and the few instances of reported modern xenoglossia are so poorly attested that no weight can be laid on them.

What follows from this information? For some, the evidence is so powerful that they conclude the only biblical position is that no known contemporary gift of tongues is biblically valid, and ideally the entire practice should be stopped immediately.[34] For others, such as Packer, modern tongues are not like biblical tongues, and therefore contemporary tongues-speakers should not claim that their gift is in line with Pentecost or with Corinth; yet on the other hand the modern phenomenon seems to do more good than harm, it has helped many believers in worship, prayer, and commitment, and therefore should probably be assessed as a good gift from God that nevertheless stands without explicit biblical warrant.[35] I cannot think of a better way of displeasing both sides of the current debate.

Can we get beyond this impasse? I think so, if the arguments of Poythress stand up. How, he asks, may tongues be perceived? There are three possibilities: disconnected sounds, ejaculations, and the like that are not confused with human language; connected sequences of sounds that *appear* to be real languages unknown to the hearer not

30. J. R. Jaquette, "Toward a Typology of Formal Communicative Behaviors: Glossolalia," *Anthropological Linguistics* 9 (1967): 6.

31. See Felicitas D. Goodman, *Speaking in Tongues: A Cross-Cultural Study of Glossolalia* (Chicago: University of Chicago Press, 1972).

32. Ibid., 123.

33. Virginia H. Hine, "Pentecostal Glossolalia: Toward a Functional Interpretation," *Journal for the Scientific Study of Religion* 8 (1969): 212.

34. E.g., John F. MacArthur, Jr., *The Charismatics: A Doctrinal Perspective* (Grand Rapids: Zondervan, 1978), especially 156ff.

35. J. I. Packer, *Keep in Step with the Spirit* (Leicester: Inter-Varsity; Old Tappan, N.J.: Revell, 1984), 207ff.

trained in linguistics, even though they are not; and real language known by one or more of the potential hearers, even if unknown to the speaker.[36] I would add a fourth possibility, which was later treated by Poythress though not at this point classified by him: speech patterns sufficiently complex that they may bear all kinds of cognitive information in some coded array, even though linguistically these patterns are not identifiable as human language.

Our problem so far is that the biblical descriptions of tongues seem to demand the third category, but the contemporary phenomena seem to fit better in the second category; and never the twain shall meet. But the fourth category is also logically possible, even though it is regularly overlooked; and it meets the constraints of both the first-century biblical documents and of some of the contemporary phenomena. I do not see how it can be dismissed.

Consider, then, Poythress's linguistic description of glossolalia:

> *Free vocalization* (glossolalia) occurs when (1) a human being produces a connected sequence of speech sounds, (2) he cannot identify the sound-sequence as belonging to any natural language that he already knows how to speak, (3) he cannot identify and give the meaning of words or morphemes (minimal lexical units), (4) in the case of utterances of more than a few syllables, he typically cannot repeat the same sound-sequence on demand, (5) a naive listener might suppose that it was an unknown language.[37]

The next step is crucial. Poythress reminds us that such free vocalization may still bear content beyond some vague picture of the speaker's emotional state. He offers his own amusing illustration;[38] I shall manufacture another. Suppose the message is:

"Praise the Lord, for his mercy endures forever."

Remove the vowels to achieve:

PRS TH LRD FR HS MRC NDRS FRVR.

This may seem a bit strange; but when we remember that modern

36. Vern S. Poythress, "The Nature of Corinthian Glossolalia: Possible Options," *Westminster Theological Journal* 40 (1977): 131. See also the cautious essay by Francis A. Sullivan, "Speaking in Tongues," *Lumen Vitae* 31 (1976): 145–70.

37. Vern S. Poythress, "Linguistic and Sociological Analyses of Modern Tongues-Speaking: Their Contributions and Limitations," *Westminster Theological Journal* 42 (1979): 369.

38. Ibid., 375.

Hebrew is written without most vowels, we can imagine that with practice this could be read quite smoothly. Now remove the spaces and, beginning with the first letter, rewrite the sequence using every third letter, repeatedly going through the sequence until all the letters are used up. The result is:

PTRRMNSVRHDHRDFRSLFSCRR.

Now add an "a" sound after each consonant, and break up the unit into arbitrary bits:

PATARA RAMA NA SAVARAHA DAHARA DAFARASALA FASA CARARA.

I think that is indistinguishable from transcriptions of certain modern tongues. Certainly it is very similar to some I have heard. But the important point is that it conveys information *provided you know the code.* Anyone who knows the steps I have taken could reverse them in order to retrieve the original message. As Poythress remarks, "thus it is always possible for the charismatic person to claim that T-speech [tongues] is *coded* language, and that only the interpreter of tongues is given the supernatural 'key' for deciphering it. It is impossible not only in practice, but even in *theory,* for a linguist to devise a means of testing this claim."[39]

It appears, then, that tongues may bear cognitive information even though they are not known human languages—just as a computer program is a "language" that conveys a great deal of information, even though it is not a "language" that anyone actually speaks. You have to know the code to be able to understand it. Such a pattern of verbalization could not be legitimately dismissed as gibberish. It is as capable of conveying propositional and cognitive content as any known human language. "Tongue" and "language" still seem eminently reasonable words to describe the phenomenon. This does not mean that all modern tongues phenomena are therefore biblically authentic. It does mean there is a category of linguistic phenomenon that conveys cognitive content, may be interpreted, and seems to meet the constraints of the biblical descriptions, even though it is no known human language. Of course, this will not do for the tongues of Acts 2, where the gift consisted of known human languages; but elsewhere, the alternative is not as simple as "human languages" or "gibberish," as many noncharismatic writers affirm. Indeed, the fact that Paul can speak of different *kinds* of tongues (12:10, 28) may suggest that on

39. Ibid., 375–76.

some occasions human languages were spoken (as in Acts 2), and in other cases not—even though in the latter eventuality the tongues were viewed as bearing cognitive content.

What bearing does the gift of interpretation have on the nature of contemporary tongues? This was addressed in part when the meaning of the verb to interpret was briefly considered, but several other things must be said. The most important is that Paul draws an extremely tight connection between the gift of tongues and the gift of interpretation. If someone wishes to argue that Paul may have used "tongues" or "languages" even though what was spoken was verbalization that bore no cognitive content, Paul's treatment of the gift of interpretation becomes an immediate barrier. After all, the interpretation issues in intelligible speech, cognitive content; and if it is not in fact a rendering of what was spoken in tongues, then the gift of interpretation is not only misnamed but also must be assessed as undifferentiable from the gift of prophecy. The tight connection Paul presupposes between the content of the tongues and the intelligible result of the gift of interpretation demands that we conclude the tongues in Corinth, as Paul understood them, bore cognitive content.

What about the contemporary gift of interpretation? A few years ago a friend of mine attended a charismatic service and rather cheekily recited some of John 1:1–18 in Greek as his contribution to speaking in tongues. Immediately there was an "interpretation" that bore no relation whatsoever to the Johannine prologue. Two people with the gift of interpretation have on occasion been asked to interpret the same recorded tongues message and the resulting different and conflicting interpretations have been justified on the grounds that God gives different interpretations to different people.[40] That is preposterous, if the interpretations are wildly dissimilar, because it would force us to conclude that there is no univocal, cognitive content to the tongues themselves. I know of no major work that has researched hundreds or thousands of examples; but it could be a very revealing study.

More commonly, at least in my experience, triteness triumphs: "Interpretations prove to be as stereotyped, vague, and uninformative as they are spontaneous, fluent, and confident."[41]

This does not prove that there is no valid, modern gift of tongues. But these distortions of interpretation are sufficiently frequent, and the interpretations themselves so commonly pedestrian, that at some

40. See John P. Kildahl, The Psychology of Speaking in Tongues (New York: Harper and Row, 1972), 63; idem, "Psychological Observations," in The Charismatic Movement, ed. Michael P. Hamilton (Grand Rapids: Eerdmans, 1975), 136.
41. Packer, Keep in Step with the Spirit, 212.

point the gift of tongues must, *in some cases,* also be called into question. The evidence is not comprehensive enough to serve as a universally damning indictment; but it is enough to provoke reflective pauses in all thoughtful believers.

In the last chapter, I will reflect further on the bearing of church history and of psychology in assessing the modern tongues movement. At the moment I shall turn to three other gifts.

Apostles (12:28)

There is neither time nor space to treat this subject in a comprehensive fashion; yet something must be said, for quite apart from its intrinsic interest, the subject has a curious relation to the broader questions of spiritual gifts. As long as "apostles" are understood to refer to a select group (the Twelve plus Paul) whose positions or functions cannot be duplicated after their demise, there is a prima facie case for saying *at least one* of the χαρίσματα *(charismata)* passes away at the end of the first generation, a gift tightly tied to the locus of revelation that came with Jesus Messiah and related events. Therefore, there is a precedent for asking if there were other spiritual gifts in Paul's day that cannot be operative in our day. Conversely, once the charismatic movement had rehabilitated all of the other spiritual gifts explicitly mentioned in 1 Corinthians 12–14, it is not surprising that some felt there should be a place for apostles as well. As a result some wings of Pentecostalism do not hesitate to appoint modern apostles.

Certainly Paul does not use the term exclusively in a tightly defined or technical sense. The referent in some passages is disputed: are the apostles in 1 Corinthians 15:7 the Twelve less Judas Iscariot, as I think likely, or a broader group who became, as eyewitnesses of the resurrection, founding missionaries? There are certainly broader uses. Epaphroditus is an "apostle," a messenger, of a congregation (Phil. 2:25); Paul's agents to the churches can also be designated "apostles" (2 Cor. 8:22–23). The force of "apostles" in Romans 16:7 is uncertain on several grounds, but may be roughly equivalent to "missionaries" or the like. Moreover, as has often been remarked, "There could not have been false apostles (2 Cor. xi.13) unless the number of Apostles had been indefinite."[42] Certainly the tendency in some branches of modern scholarship is to downplay the uniqueness and authority of those thirteen (the Twelve plus Paul) traditionally referred to as apostles. All recognize that in time these thirteen came to be looked on as a closed

---

42. Archibald Robertson and Alfred Plummer, *A Critical and Exegetical Commentary on the First Epistle of St. Paul to the Corinthians,* 2d ed. (Edinburgh: T. and T. Clark, 1914).

circle that served in part as the foundation of the church, a position already reflected (it is argued) in the Epistle to the Ephesians and in the Apocalypse (cf. Eph. 2:20; 3:5; Rev. 21:14). Because some date Ephesians rather late, and Revelation later, naturally there are suspicions that such notions formed no part of the understanding of the original apostles about whom such claims are made. Taking a leaf out of this analysis, some branches of the charismatic movement therefore cluster the kinds of apostles in the New Testament in three groups: Jesus Christ himself, a group of one; the Twelve, unrepeatable and irreplaceable; and Paul and all other apostles—an open-ended group that allows modern equivalents.[43] And since it is Paul who is writing 1 Corinthians 12:28, the conclusion is obvious.

This conclusion is nevertheless premature. Dupont has shown that even Acts pictures the missionary and authority status of Paul in the same categories as that of the Twelve;[44] and Jervell, likewise bucking the tide, argues that the perspectives of Acts and of the writings of Paul are indistinguishable so far as the apostolic authority of Paul is concerned.[45] Too much is made of Paul's persistent willingness to reason with his churches, to beg them to reform or to take some action, to function as the servant and example. None of this is incompatible with a strong sense of unique, personal, apostolic authority that may (as threatened in 2 Cor. 10–13) regretfully be applied in its full force if the church does not conform to gentler admonitions.[46] Indeed, this combination of authority and meekness lies at the heart of all levels of Christian leadership; so to pit one against the other, as if the former is called into question by the latter, is to exhibit a very deep misunderstanding.

Of course, the word *apostle* can extend beyond the Twelve plus Paul; but "Lord" can extend beyond Jesus, "elders" and "deacons" can extend beyond ecclesiatical office/functions, and so forth. The primary reason is obvious: nascent Christianity had to use the vocabulary into which it was born, and its own specialized use of certain terms did not immediately displace the larger semantic range of the terms em-

43. See Hywel Jones, "Are There Apostles Today?" *Foundations* 13 (Autumn 1984): 16–25.

44. Jacques Dupont, "La Mission de Paul d'après Actes 26.13–23 et la Mission des Apôtres d'après Luc 24.44–49 et Actes 1.8," *Paul and Paulinism: Studies in Honor of C. K. Barrett*, ed. Morna D. Hooker and Stephen G. Wilson (London: SPCK, 1982), 290–99.

45. Jacob Jervell, *The Unknown Paul: Essays on Luke-Acts and Early Christian History* (Minneapolis: Augsburg, 1984), 77–95.

46. The theme is treated repeatedly in D. A. Carson, *From Triumphalism to Maturity: An Exposition of 2 Corinthians 10–13* (Grand Rapids: Baker, 1984).

ployed. As a result, attempts to establish what apostleship means for
Paul by simply appealing to the full semantic range of the word as it
is found in his writings is deeply flawed at the methodological level.[47]
Only a traditional skepticism will ignore several important strands of
evidence: Jesus himself, according to the synoptic Gospels, appointed
the Twelve, designated them "apostles," and gave them certain distinguishing privileges and responsibilities (Luke 6:13); after the resurrection and ascension, these men felt it necessary on biblical grounds
to make up their number in the wake of the defection of Judas Iscariot
(Acts 1:15–26); Paul saw his own apostleship as on a par with that of
the Twelve, so far as immediacy of call, witness to the resurrection,
grasp of the gospel, and intrinsic authority were concerned. The only
area in which he admitted he was not worthy to be grouped with the
others had to do with the lateness of his conversion and call, and that
from a context in which he was persecuting the church; but even so,
he confessed he had worked harder than all the others (see especially
1 Cor. 9; 1 Cor. 15; Gal. 1–2). There is even a little evidence from Paul's
writings that he recognized the notion of the Twelve sprang from the
Lord Jesus himself[48]—which is in line with the way he viewed his own
ministry.

What use of "apostle," then, do we find in 1 Corinthians 12:28? The
revealing word, I think, is "first": "God has appointed *first of all* apostles." If the summary I have just given is cogent, it is hard to imagine
why Paul would designate "first" in *any* sense those who are apostles
in some derivative fashion—messengers from the churches, perhaps.
It is more likely that he has the narrow scope of "apostles" in mind.
If we ask, "First in what sense?" the answer is uncertain. It could be
"first in the potential for edifying the church"; but that theme does
not assume major proportions until chapter 14. It might be "first in
greatness or importance"; but Paul is about to classify greatness in
terms of love and edification, not personal pomp or importance. It
might be "first in authority in the church"; not only does this theme
seem incidental to the flow of 1 Corinthians 12–13, but I shall argue
shortly that usually the New Testament treats the authority of the
teacher above that of the prophet, even though "prophet" precedes
"teacher" in 1 Corinthians 12:28.[49] It may simply be "first in chronological appointment": in historical order, God first appointed apostles,

47. As, for instance, in David E. Aune, *Prophecy in Early Christianity and the Ancient
World* (Grand Rapids: Eerdmans, 1983), 202–3.

48. See Robert W. Herron, Jr., "The Origin of the New Testament Apostolate,"
Westminster Theological Journal 45 (1983): 101–31.

49. Possibly not even Eph. 2:20 is a genuine exception to this; but see discussion,
infra.

then (New Testament) prophets at Pentecost (about which I shall say more), and then teachers. This seems the most likely interpretation, but in any case, it is clear that the gift of apostleship that Paul mentions in this text is not transferable to persons living in our day. Perhaps that is why it is not apostleship but prophecy that is discussed so centrally in chapter 13. If Paul had wanted to say that tongues cease toward the end of the apostolic age or thereabouts, instead of at the parousia, he had a ready-made precedent in the gift of apostleship, already listed as the *first* appointment in the church. Instead, he links tongues and the gift of knowledge with prophecy, the *second* appointment in the church, and thereby opens the door to the eschatological argument central to that chapter.

Teachers (12:28)

About this gift I shall say very little. The word used (διδάσκαλος, *didaskalos*) does not in the New Testament designate a particular office or role—though by contrast it is intrinsic to the office/role of apostle and of "bishop" or "overseer." "Presumably [teachers] were mature Christians who instructed others in the meaning and moral implications of Christian faith; . . . possibly (as some think) they expounded the Christian meaning of the Old Testament."[50]

Prophecy and Prophets (12:10, 28, 29)

The range of phenomena covered by this word group in the first century is enormous.[51] But just what was included under the rubric of "prophecy" in the New Testament?

The answers to that question are legion. Sometimes they are formulated less in terms of what prophecy *is* than of what prophecy *does.* One commentator, for instance, writes: "Prophesying was the power of seeing and making known the nature and will of God, a gift of insight into the truth and of power in imparting it, and hence a capacity for building up men's characters, quickening their wills, and encouraging their spirits."[52] That is, of course, true; but since it is cast in terms of function, it could be applied equally to gifted preaching—and elsewhere the same commentators make precisely that connection.[53] When Paul says that prophecy is for the "strengthening, encouragement and comfort" (14:3) of the congregation, he does not thereby *define* prophecy, for exposition, prayer, and teaching might serve the same ends. Further, it is not clear (as Turner points out) that

50. C. K. Barrett, *The First Epistle to the Corinthians*, 2d ed. (London: Black, 1971).
51. See Aune, *Prophecy.*
52. Robertson and Plummer, *Corinthians*, 306.
53. Ibid., 301.

14:3 provides a *necessary* criterion of prophecy; for such a view inevitably marginalizes rather arbitrarily such prophecies as those of Agabus (e.g., Acts 21:11).[54]

There is in fact a sustained tradition that identifies New Testament prophecy with what we today call preaching or expounding Scripture.[55] The reasons offered are many. One of the most common is that prophecy in the Old Testament is largely devoted to calls to reform and renewal: it is paraenetic. Therefore paraenetic ministry under the new covenant is also a form of prophecy.[56] Logically this connection cannot be made, unless prophecy and paraenesis are so tightly bound together as never to be found separately or in any other linkage—a manifest absurdity. The argument of Ellis—that the exegesis and application of Old Testament texts in the New Testament are sometimes accompanied by a phrase like "says the Lord" and therefore to be treated as prophecy (thereby serving as a model for *our* exegesis and exposition of Scripture)[57]—has been shown by Aune to be mistaken.[58] Aune points out that the "says the Lord" formula in passages like Romans 12:19, citing Deuteronomy 32:35, does nothing more than identify God as the source of the Old Testament quotation. Moreover, similar application of Scripture in *Barnabas* is labeled as teaching, not prophecy.

On the other hand, Green forges an absolute disjunction between

54. Turner, "Spiritual Gifts Then and Now," 13.

55. E.g., David Hill, *New Testament Prophecy* (Atlanta: John Knox, 1980), 108ff. (though he has some legitimate reservations); E. Earle Ellis, *Prophecy and Hermeneutic* (Grand Rapids: Eerdmans, 1978), 147ff.; Ralph P. Martin, *Spirit and the Congregation: Studies in 1 Corinthians 12–15* (Grand Rapids: Eerdmans, 1984), 14; E. Cothenet, "Les prophètes chrétiens comme exégètes charismatiques de l'Ecriture," in *Prophetic Vocation in the New Testament and Today,* ed. J. Panagopoulos, *Novum Testamentum* Supplements, vol. 45 (Leiden: Brill, 1977) especially 79–81; and many Reformed writers. Some scholars resort to what I can only call slippery language. e.g., Mühlen, *Charismatic Theology,* 149ff.

56. E.g., Packer, *Keep in Step with the Spirit,* 215. He writes that "the essence of the prophetic ministry was forthtelling God's present word to his people, and this regularly meant application of revealed truth rather than augmentation of it. [We may note in passing an odd disjunction here: Packer would be the first to insist that when an Old Testament prophet called the people back to the standards of previous revelation, and his prophetic word was then inscripturated, the result must be labeled some kind of augmentation of revealed truth.] As Old Testament prophets preached the law and recalled Israel to face God's covenant claim on their obedience, with promise of blessing if they complied and cursing if not, so it appears that New Testament prophets preached the gospel and the life of faith for conversion, edification and encouragement. . . . By parity of reasoning, therefore, any verbal enforcement of biblical teaching as it applies to one's present hearers may properly be called prophecy today, for that in truth is what it is."

57. Ellis, *Prophecy and Hermeneutic,* e.g., 186.

58. Aune, *Prophecy,* 343–45.

prophecy and preaching[59] (a point to which I shall return in the last chapter). Schlink makes New Testament prophecy and Old Testament prophecy indistinguishable, insisting moreover that the gift continues today; but she does not recognize the inherent dangers in that position:[60] that is, once again, the finality of canon is threatened, at least theoretically. Prior, alert to the danger, suggests that at least most of the New Testament prophets enjoyed the same authority status as their Old Testament predecessors; but they died out with the apostles, and any subsequent manifestation of the gift must be subordinate to the canon.[61] This position may be theologically safe, but it is difficult to justify exegetically, and it labors under the disadvantage that any subsequent gift of prophecy is rendered *unlike* the gift of prophecy that was exercised in New Testament times. Whereas many writers in noncharismatic traditions attempt to align prophecy and contemporary preaching, others emphasize the essentially *revelatory* nature of tongues and prophecy, concerned to argue that revelatory material of any kind must eventually prove a threat to the stability of Christian truth once and for all delivered to the saints and now preserved in the canon.[62]

This is not the place to analyze each New Testament text that deals with prophecy. Some of the relevant texts lie in the chapter before us, and will be briefly considered in a few minutes, and other studies have laid the necessary groundwork.[63] Aune defines prophecy as "a specific form of divination that consists of intelligible verbal messages believed to originate with God and communicated through inspired human intermediaries."[64] Grudem bases his definition of prophecy in Paul on a detailed study of 1 Corinthians 14:29–30: prophecy is the reception and subsequent transmission of spontaneous, divinely originating reve-

59. Green, *I Believe in the Holy Spirit,* 171–72.

60. Basilea Schlink, *Ruled by the Spirit,* trans. John and Mary Foote and Michael Harper (Minneapolis: Bethany, 1969), 43.

61. David Prior, *The Message of 1 Corinthians: Life in the Local Church* (Leicester and Downers Grove: Inter-Varsity, 1985), 235–36.

62. E.g., MacArthur, *Charismatics;* Richard B. Gaffin, Jr., *Perspectives on Pentecost: New Testament Teaching on Gifts of the Holy Spirit* (Phillipsburg, N.J.: Presbyterian and Reformed, 1979); Leonard J. Coppes, *Whatever Happened to Biblical Tongues?* (Phillipsburg, N.J.: Pilgrim, 1977); and many others.

63. See the bibliography in Turner, "Spiritual Gifts Then and Now"; and especially Aune, *Prophecy,* 247ff. I confess, however, that I am not persuaded of the reliability of Aune's five criteria for identifying prophetic oracles in the New Testament, even with the stipulation that all five do not have to be present in every instance. For instance, the fourth criterion, that the putative oracle must be prefixed by a statement of the inspiration of the speaker, works out rather poorly in the passages Aune adduces; and the fifth, that the saying or speech must not sit easily in the literary context, is an appeal to aporias by another name—a notoriously slippery approach.

64. Ibid., 339.

lation.[65] The verb *to prophesy* denotes this process. Rather similar is the definition of Panagopoulos.[66]

But Grudem's thesis on New Testament prophecy breaks new ground. I am generally sympathetic to it, although I have reservations at two or three critical points. I shall not defend this thesis, as that would be to write a book he has already written, but I shall summarize some of his arguments, indicate my mild dissent now and then, and show how the thesis bears on these chapters.

Grudem seeks to put on a systematic basis what has been suggested by some others, that the prophecy of the New Testament must be distinguished from the prophecy of the Old Testament, especially in its authority status. Some of the reasons include the following.

(1) Adequate definitions of prophecy, like the two previously reported, accept that prophecy presupposes revelation—the prophecy comes from God. But they do not presuppose that each prophecy is in the form of a direct quotation from God, prefaced perhaps by a stern "thus says the Lord": such instances are rare in the New Testament, and somewhat disputed.[67]

(2) For Paul, the legitimate heirs and successors of the Old Testament prophets, so far as their authority status was concerned, were not New Testament prophets, but the apostles—"apostles" defined in a fairly narrow way. Here again Grudem expands on a point advanced by others.[68] Once a prophet was tested and approved in the Old Testament, God's people were morally bound to obey him. To disobey such a prophet was to oppose God. If a prophet speaking in the name of God was shown to be in error, the official sanction was death. But once a prophet is acknowledged as true, there is no trace of repeated checks on the *content* of his oracles. By contrast, New Testament prophets are to have their oracles carefully *weighed* (14:29; so also

65. Wayne A. Grudem, *The Gift of Prophecy in 1 Corinthians* (Washington, D.C.: University Press of America, 1982), 115ff., especially 139–43.

66. J. Panagopoulos, "Die urchristliche Prophetie: Ihr Charakter und ihre Funktion," in *Prophetic Vocation in the New Testament and Today*, ed. J. Panagopoulos, *Novum Testamentum* Supplements, vol. 45 (Leiden: Brill, 1977), 27: "Das prophetische Wort wird *unmittelbar durch Offenbarung* ermittelt oder gegeben und zwar durch Traum, Vision, Audition oder direkte Offenbarung der Herrn, eines Engels oder anderer Vermittlungsorgane; der Prophet empfängt es ohne sien Zutun und verkündet es weiter. . . . Die propheten können aber nicht von sich aus allein solche prophetischen Worte aussprechen, sondern wo und wann Gott selbst will."

67. See Kevin Giles, "Prophecy in the Bible and in the Church Today," *Interchange* 26 (1980): 75–89, who points out that there are very few instances where a New Testament prophet quotes God or the exalted Jesus directly (as in Rev. 2–3)—rather unlike most modern charismatic claims to prophecy, a point to which I shall return in the last chapter.

68. E.g., H. A. Guy, *New Testament Prophecy: Its Origin and Significance* (London: Epworth, 1947).

1 Thess. 5:19–21). The word διακρίνω (*diakrinō*) suggests that the prophecy be *evaluated*, not simply accepted as totally true or totally false.[69] "The presupposition is that any one New Testament prophetic oracle is expected to be *mixed* in quality, and the wheat must be separated from the chaff."[70] Moreover, there is no hint of excommunication as the threatened sanction if the prophet occasionally does not live up to the mark. More importantly, Paul places the authority of Christian prophets *under his own* (14:37–38); and to contravene apostolic authority may eventually bring enormous threat (see 1 Cor. 4.21, 2 Cor. 10.11, 13.1–10, 1 Tim. 1.20).[71] There is even evidence, albeit disputed, that Paul's self-consciousness as an apostle has close similarities to the self-consciousness of the Old Testament prophets.

These exegetical observations undermine the criticism of Gaffin, who against Grudem insists that the evaluation in view is not of the prophecy but of the prophet, or rather of the prophecy in order to pass judgment on the prophet himself—exactly as in the Old Testament:

> The distinguishing or discrimination required functions to determine the source of an alleged prophecy, whether or not it is genuine, whether it is from the Holy Spirit or some other spirit; it does not sift worthwhile elements presumably based on a revelation from those that are not. Perhaps also included is an interpretive function, assessing in some way the significance of the prophecy for the congregation. . . . What also needs to be grasped is that in the case of genuine prophecies, the need for evaluation does not show that they lack the full authority of God's Word. Rather, this evaluation is of a piece with the positive proving, the affirmative testing Paul the apostle commands for his own teaching.[72]

This is rather more assertion than argument, and it flies in the face of too much of the evidence. If Gaffin is right, why is the authority of the prophets at Corinth so emphatically placed under his own (14:37–38, a point to be emphasized in the next chapter)? Why is it the *prophecy* that is to be judged, and this with a tone that suggests normal oper-

---

69. See Grudem, *Gift of Prophecy*, 58–59, 64–66; and 263ff., a reprint of his article, "A Response to Gerhard Dautzenberg," to which reference has already been made. Grudem demonstrates that the verb διακρίνω commonly (though not consistently) bears in Hellenistic Greek the connotation of sifting, separating, evaluating; whereas the simple form κρίνω is used for judgments where there are clear-cut options (guilty or innocent, true or false, right or wrong), and never for evaluative distinction.

70. Turner, "Spiritual Gifts Then and Now," 16.

71. J. Panagopoulos, Ἡ Ἐκκλησία τῶν προφητῶν. Τὸ προφητικὸν Χάρισμα ἐν τῇ Ἐκκλησίᾳ τῶν δύο πρώτων αἰώνων (Athens: Historical Publications, Stefanos Basilopoulos, 1979), insists that New Testament prophets were faithful to the apostolic tradition.

72. Gaffin, *Perspectives on Pentecost*, 70–71.

ating procedure? If Paul wanted to make the point Gaffin detects, why did he not use the verb κρίνω (krinō) instead of the verb διακρίνω (diakrinō, weigh)?

(3) The New Testament does not see prophets as the solution to the problem of apostolic succession. The silence is startling. If the gift of prophecy was regarded as the equivalent in authority to that of Old Testament prophecy, and if it persisted throughout the New Testament era right into the midpatristic period, why, once the apostles had died, were the prophets not presented as the church's bastion against false teaching, its source of light and information in the face of uncertainty? In fact, the latest epistles in the New Testament sound a different note. The emphasis is "Guard the deposit! Keep the faith once delivered to the saints! Return to what was from the beginning!" (2 Tim.; Jude; 1 John respectively). One must either conclude that the prophets died with the apostles—a conclusion so totally at variance with the early Fathers it must be instantly rejected—or that the prophets of the new covenant never enjoyed the authority status of the apostles (in the narrow sense of that term).

(4) Although New Testament prophets apparently spoke on a variety of topics, there is little evidence that they enjoyed the clout in the church that either the apostles demanded in the church or the writing prophets demanded in Israel and Judah. I do not mean that Old Testament prophets were universally revered and uncontested, nor that New Testament apostles were never opposed, maligned, or slighted by Christians. Quite the reverse: it is precisely because of the public status and high claims to authority that there were such polarized reactions. But New Testament prophecy, by contrast with that of the Old, cuts a very low profile. The Thessalonians actually have to be told not to treat prophecies with contempt (1 Thess. 5:20); and in 1 Corinthians 14, Paul has to advance the cause of prophecy above the cause of tongues. There are only two passages in the Pauline correspondence where prophets stand in more exalted company, Ephesians 2:20 and 3:5. The former is crucial: the church, we are told, is built on the foundation of the apostles *and prophets*. In an extended treatment, Grudem argues that the construction means "the apostles who are prophets";[73] certainly the New Testament writers sometimes view the

---

73. Grudem, *Gift of Prophecy*, 82–105. One crucial point is the construction τῶν ἀποστόλων καὶ προφητῶν (the second noun anarthrous), which groups the two nouns together in some way. Such grouping *can* of course preserve distinction between the two members (e.g., Acts 23:7); but, argues Grudem, it *can* also identify them (e.g., Col. 1:2). Which it is must be determined from the context, and Grudem offers an admirable list of contextual factors to support his view. His list of more than twenty examples where a single article governs two substantives that have the same referent

apostles as prophets (see 1 Cor. 13:9; 14:6; and possibly Rev. 1:3, if the traditional authorship is correct). There are difficulties with his view that he himself acknowledges; but his lengthy discussion demonstrates, at the least, how complex is the detailed exegesis of that verse, and how cautious our deductions should be under *any* interpretation of it. If we conclude, against Grudem, that the "prophets" in question here enjoy a role with the apostles in providing the revelatory foundation for Christianity (although that is not quite what is said), we must hasten to admit that this is an anomalous use of "prophets" in the New Testament. It is as illegitimate for Gaffin[74] to use this verse as the controlling factor in his understanding of the New Testament gift of prophecy as it would be to conclude from Titus 1:12 ("Even one of their own prophets has said, 'Cretans are always liars, evil brutes, lazy gluttons' ") that New Testament prophets were pagan poets from Crete.

(5) There are instances of prophecies in Acts that are viewed as genuinely from God yet having something less than the authority status of an Old Testament prophecy. Perhaps most startling is Acts 21:4 where certain disciples "by means of the Spirit"—almost certainly a signal of prophecy, see 11:28—tell Paul not to go up to Jerusalem. Paul goes anyway, persuaded that he is being prompted by the Spirit to visit the city. Perhaps, as Grudem suggests,[75] these prophets had received some revelation about the apostle's impending sufferings, and *interpreted* them to mean Paul should not go. Whatever the case, the prophecy, so far as Paul was concerned, needed evaluating, and, in the form he received it from them, rejecting. The prophecy of Agabus in Acts 21:10–11 stipulates that the Jews at Jerusalem would bind the man who owns Paul's girdle and hand him over to the Gentiles. Strictly speaking, however, in the event itself, Paul was not bound by the Jews but by the Romans; and the Jews did not hand Paul over to the Romans, but sought to kill him with mob violence, prompting a rescue

---

includes few instances of two *plural nouns* in this array: for instance, in Col. 1:2, just cited, we read τοῖς ἐν Κολοσσαῖς ἁγίοις καὶ πιστοῖς ἀδελφοῖς, but strictly speaking the former is a substantivized adjective. In the expression τοὺς δὲ ποιμένας καὶ διδασκάλους (Eph. 4:11), it is not entirely certain that the referent is the same for both nouns. But there are certainly convincing examples where plural participles are involved; and similarly for singular nouns. Of course, Grudem does not argue that this construction *demands* that the two substantives have a single referent; but it certainly allows for it, much more so, it might be added, in the Pauline corpus than elsewhere in the New Testament. For an exhaustive list of the occurrences of this construction in the New Testament, see D. A. Carson, Paul A. Miller and James L. Boyer, *A Syntactical Concordance to the Greek New Testament* (Chicago: University of Chicago Press, forthcoming).

74. Gaffin, *Perspectives on Pentecost*, 93–95.

75. Grudem, *Gift of Prophecy*, 79–82.

by the Romans. I can think of no reported Old Testament prophet whose prophecies are so wrong on the details. The rebuttal of Gaffin, in my judgment, does not pay close enough attention to the text.[76]

(6) The constraints placed on prophecy in this chapter—see verses 29, 30, 36—make it clear that the gift of prophecy stands considerably tamed. Moreover, it is precisely because prophecy operates at this lower level of authority that Paul can encourage women to pray and prophesy in public under the constraints of 1 Corinthians 11 (whatever they mean), while forbidding them to exercise an authoritative teaching role over men (1 Tim. 2:11ff.) or to evaluate the content of the prophecies (1 Cor. 14:33b–36). The latter point of course is immensely controverted; but I shall say more about it in the next chapter.

My hesitations about this thesis are two, neither of which does irreparable damage to it, but only refines it.

First, the thesis oversimplifies the contrast between Old Testament prophets and New Testament prophets. The Old Testament, for instance, records the existence of "schools" of the prophets; and it is far from clear that everyone in a particular "school" enjoyed the status of Amos or Isaiah. There is no single, stereotypical Old Testament prophecy and a different stereotypical New Testament prophecy. Indeed, it has been compellingly suggested that Numbers 12:6–8 and 11:29 give evidence within the Old Testament of two kinds of prophecy—one "charismatic and enigmatic" and the other "Mosaic."[77] The suggestion may nevertheless provide indirect support for Grudem since the "charismatic and enigmatic" kind is picked up by Joel's prophecy, which is said by Peter to be fulfilled on the day of Pentecost (Acts 2:16ff.). Grudem's general point stands, but as we shall see in the last chapter, it needs some qualification.

Second, Grudem describes the two levels of authority as, respectively, an authority of general content and an authority that extends to the very words of the prophet. This goes beyond the evidence, and is open to several objections.[78] Exegetically, the distinction does not seem securely based in Paul. It appears rather as an attempt to find a consistent explanation for distinctions in authority that *are* there; but another explanation may be possible. Moreover, Grudem's distinction masks a difficult point in the prophetic psychology. When Old

---

76. Gaffin, *Perspectives on Pentecost*, 65–67.

77. Peter Jones, "Y a-t-il deux types de prophéties dans le NT?" *Revue Réformée* 31 (1980): 303–17. Similarly, Joseph Brosch, *Charismen und Ämter in der Urkirche* (Bonn: Peter Hanstein, 1951), 80–81, makes a distinction between the major Old Testament prophets and the "schools of the prophets" in Samuel's time, and suggests that New Testament prophecy is closer to the latter.

78. See Turner, "Spiritual Gifts Then and Now," 16.

Testament prophets were declaring the word of the Lord, they were not always presenting what they believed to be verbatim quotes. We may agree that the inscripturated form of those prophecies was so superintended by God that the *result* was God's truth right down to the words (that was Jesus' view of the Old Testament [Matt. 5:17]), but it is not obvious that when, for instance, Paul was explaining his itinerary to the Corinthians in his second canonical letter to them he was *psychologically* aware of a revelatory process operating that extended to the words he was dictating. The question arises therefore whether there is any difference between the psychological self-awareness of the Old Testament prophet and the New Testament prophet. What evidence is there that it was a different gift, so far as the prophets' self-perceptions were concerned? Grudem's distinction may be salvaged if the difference in authority level lies only in the prophecy qua result, and not in prophecy qua revelatory experience: but (wrongly, he assures me), he has not always been understood that way. In any case, in the prophecy of Agabus, the errors turn not on quibbles over words but on aspects of the content. Turner remarks:

> This is where Grudem's distinction breaks down (and he is not unaware of the problems): semantically it is not the surface structure of the wording, but the semantic structure of the propositions of a communication that is primarily significant. And this suggests, what seems reasonable on other grounds too, namely, that there was no *sharp* distinction between apostolic prophecy and prophets' prophesyings—rather, a spectrum of authority of charisma extending from apostolic speech and prophecy (backed by apostolic commission) at one extreme, to vague and barely profitable attempts at oracular speech such as brought "prophecy" as a whole into question at Thessalonika (1 Thess. 5:19f.) at the other. A prophet's speech might fall anywhere on the spectrum, so the task of evaluation fell on the congregation.[79]

That Grudem has rightly delineated some distinguishing limitations of New Testament prophecy is in my judgment beyond cavil. It will not do to question his entire synthesis because we have questions about some of his formulations. In the last chapter I shall offer tentative suggestions about how to resolve some of these tensions—in particular how we can speak of prophecy as revelatory yet avoid jeopardizing the canon, and how we can best distinguish between the authority of apostolic prophesying and the authority of (other) New Testament prophets' prophesyings. At the same time I shall briefly

79. Ibid.

assess modern charismatic claims to prophecy. For the moment, however, I must return to 1 Corinthians 14.

The Superiority of Prophecy over Tongues (14:1–19)[80]

That Paul should restrict the focus of discussion from the χαρίσματα *(charismata)* in general to two of them, prophecy and tongues, strongly suggests that there was some dispute or uncertainty about these two in the Corinthian church. It is even possible that the Corinthians lumped both gifts under the rubric *prophecy*, and it is Paul that is making the distinction.[81] After all, on the day of Pentecost when the believers spoke in tongues, Peter insisted that this tongues-speaking was evidence that the last day promised by Joel had dawned, the day on which sons and daughters would *prophesy* (Acts 2:17, citing Joel). The range of the "prophet" word group was certainly broad enough to encompass tongues-speaking. In this view, it seems likely that in the eyes of some Corinthians the tongues form of prophecy was greatly to be preferred over the intelligible form of prophecy, presumably because it was more spectacular. Paul in this chapter draws a distinction between the two, and reverses the order of rank on the basis of which one best edifies the church.

Whether Paul was the first to make the distinction between prophecy and tongues or not, if the background at Corinth is anything like what I am suggesting, there is an important deduction to be made. Although some of Paul's arguments in this chapter are of the generalizing sort, applicable to all the spiritual gifts, Paul's chief concern is the relative weight given to prophecy and tongues. This means that Paul may *not* be saying that tongues is the least of the gifts on some absolute scale, but only that it is less important than prophecy on the scale of reference adopted; equally, it means that Paul may *not* be saying that *prophecy* is the *greatest* of the gifts on some absolute scale, but only that it is more important than tongues on the same scale of reference. The relative value of prophecy over against, say, apostleship, teaching or giving is not what is primarily in view. This observation is not jeopardized by 12:31a, which encourages the Corinthians to desire the greater gifts. That exhortation assumes that the spiritual gifts can be ranked, of course, but instead of providing such ranking,

80. For the discussion on the relation of 14:1 to chaps. 12 and 13, and defense of the view that 14:1 begins with imperatives, see the second chapter.

81. See Thomas W. Gillespie, "A Pattern of Prophetic Speech in First Corinthians," *Journal of Biblical Literature* 97 (1978): 83–84; R. A. Harrisville, "Speaking in Tongues: A Lexicographical Study," *Catholic Biblical Quarterly* 38 (1976): 35–48.

Paul hastens to transcend the spiritual gifts entirely with his chapter on love. Taking up the argument in 14:1, he does not attempt to rank all the gifts he has listed in chapter 12. Rather, assuming that spiritually minded believers will want the greater gifts, and having encouraged them along such lines, he proceeds to distinguish which is the greater of two—the two that apparently stand at the heart of Corinthian debate. And here, as Mills puts it, "Paul's main objection is not to the practice of glossolalia so much as to the *estimate* of the practice."[82]

Potential of a χάρισμα (charisma) for Building the Church (14:1–5)

That thought, of course, is simply a corollary of the love expounded in the previous chapter. The importance of love does not mean it should be pursued *at the expense* of spiritual gifts:[83] they too are to be eagerly desired. We have already noticed (in the second chapter) that there is no clash between this encouragement and Paul's insistence that the spiritual gifts are sovereignly distributed.[84] Here the apostle immediately becomes more specific. Eagerly desire spiritual gifts, he says, *especially* the gift of prophecy. The expression underlying the New International Version's "especially" means "rather" or "but rather."[85] It does not affirm that the best spiritual gift is prophecy; it simply specifies that the Corinthians are to seek this one in particular. The reasons for that specificity can only be learned from the context; such reasons, as I have already pointed out, are cast in the form of a sustained contrast between prophecy and tongues.

The person who speaks in a tongue does not in the first instance speak to men but to God. No one understands him (14:2). Some non charismatics seek to reduce the scope of that "no one" to "no one who does not know the (human) language that is being spoken."[86] That is barely possible; but since the preceding line draws a contrast between speech directed to people and speech directed to God, it seems more natural to understand the "no one" in a broader, principial fashion. The content of this tongues-speech is "mysteries." The word may be

82. Watson E. Mills, *A Theological/Exegetical Approach to Glossolalia* (Lanham, Md.: University Press of America, 1985), 99.
83. The second chapter deals with Martin's reconstruction of this verse, including a perceived quotation from the Corinthian letter.
84. See further Robert Banks and Geoffrey Moon, "Speaking in Tongues: A Survey of the New Testament Evidence," *Churchman* 80 (1966): 288.
85. μᾶλλον δέ. See BAGD s.v. 3.d.
86. E.g., Robert L. Thomas, *Understanding Spiritual Gifts: The Christian's Special Gifts in the Light of 1 Corinthians 12–14* (Chicago: Moody, 1978), 205–6.

used here in a nontechnical sense to suggest that "the speaker and God are sharing hidden truths which others are not permitted to share."[87] By contrast, the one who prophesies strengthens, encourages, and comforts others. This does not mean that prophecy is the only gift that has those virtues: teaching and tongues that are interpreted do as well. In other words, these *functions* of prophecy are not *definitional*.[88] The context specifies that the issue is *intelligibility:* among spiritual gifts of speech (others such as giving or administration are not in view), only those that are intelligible result in the immediate edification of the church. True, the tongues-speaker may be edifying himself (14:4);[89] but that is too small a horizon for those who have meditated on 1 Corinthians 13. This does not mean Paul is prepared to abolish tongues. On the contrary, he would love all of them to speak in tongues (which of course implies that some of them did not). This cannot mean that Paul's conception of the ideal in the church, as a considered theological stance, is that every Christian speak in tongues— any more than his desire in 7:7 that all be celibate as he is means his considered theological stance is that the ideal church must be utterly celibate. After all, Paul has just finished insisting, in chapter 12, that not all *do* speak in tongues. The text before us simply means that Paul knows the gift of tongues is from God and is therefore a good gift, and he wants his beloved converts to enjoy as many good things as possible. One of those is tongues. "But rather," he says—the same expression as in 14:1—"I would like you to prophesy." Once again, the "but rather" does not *itself* establish a comparison in intrinsic worth. The expression refers to what Paul prefers, but does not itself give the reason why. The reason is provided in the context and the point is now driven home (14:5): in any comparison of prophecy and tongues, *in the church* the edification of the church is of paramount concern. On the other hand, it appears as if tongues can have the same *functional* significance as prophecy if there is an interpreter present. Of

---

87. Barrett, *The First Epistle to the Corinthians.*

88. Grudem, *Gift of Prophecy,* 181–84.

89. Some commentators find the notion of self-edification so difficult that they interpret this *in malem partem:* Paul is actually rebuking the tongues-speaker for edifying himself (e.g., Thomas, *Understanding Spiritual Gifts,* 207–8). But this scarcely fits the context, when Paul goes on to encourage tongues-speaking (v. 5), which here must be tongues-speaking *without* interpretation, and therefore in private and for self-edification, since once tongues are followed by interpretation there is no difference between this pair of gifts and prophecy, so far as the functional scale Paul is using is concerned. Moreover, contra Thomas, 1 Cor. 10:23–24 is no parallel. Paul is not there prohibiting the Christian "from misusing his Christian liberty by seeking his own profit or edification" (p. 208), but in the context of chaps. 8–10 doing so at someone else's expense. See further my comments on 12:7 in the first chapter.

course, against Hummel[90] and others, this does not mean there is *no* difference between tongues-plus-interpretation and prophecy. Verses 18–25 are still to come!

Edification Depends on Intelligibility of Tongues (14:6–12)

Paul has introduced the question of intelligibility; now he stresses and enlarges upon it. The string of gift words in 14:6 (revelation/knowledge/prophecy/word of instruction) should probably be rendered like this: "How shall I benefit you unless I report to you a revelation or some knowledge, or unless I prophesy to you or teach you?"—that is, the first two words probably refer to content, and the latter two to the form of content Paul's speech would take.[91] The point is clear: edification demands intelligible content, and tongues, by themselves, cannot provide it. That Paul has to labor the point with examples from musical instruments and military bugle calls suggests how deeply committed to advancing the superiority of tongues the Corinthians (or at least some of them) must have been. Distinct notes from an instrument in coherent array constitute music and engender pleasure; distinct notes from a military horn elicit obedience; understanding another's language makes communication possible. "So it is with you," Paul writes—and the application of these illustrations is obvious. "Since you are eager to have spiritual gifts[92] [here an assumption, with perhaps just a hint from the context that their desire was nevertheless unfortunately warped], try to excel in gifts that build up the church." Thus Paul's stress on intelligibility continues on from its introduction in the first five verses.

Stipulations for Tongues-Speakers (14:13–19)

Whether the opening "for this reason" (διό, *dio*) refers to 14:1–12 or just to verse 12,[93] the rendering of the rest of the verse is probably as in the New International Version: the tongues-speaker, in consequence of the importance of edifying the church and the concomitant need for intelligible utterance in the church, should pray for another

90. Charles E. Hummel, *Fire in the Fireplace: Contemporary Charismatic Renewal* (Downers Grove: Inter-Varsity, 1978), 151.

91. See Grudem, *Gift of Prophecy*, 138–39. He also points out that this pairing might be seen to generate an abab structure: revelation is communicated by prophecy, knowledge is communicated by teaching. But this may be too schematized.

92. On the unexpected πνευμάτων, instead of the expected πνευματικῶν, see K. S. Hemphill, "The Pauline Concept of Charisma: A Situational and Developmental Approach" (Ph.D. diss., Cambridge University, 1976).

93. Compare Charles Hodge, *I and II Corinthians* (Edinburgh: Banner of Truth Trust, 1974), and Thomas, *Understanding Spiritual Gifts*, 210.

gift—the gift of interpretation.[94] Verse 14 does not introduce a new subject, a switch from speaking in tongues to praying in tongues, for 14:2 has already established that speaking in tongues is primarily directed to God. In other words, speaking in tongues *is a form of prayer.* Paul acknowledges that such prayer is valid prayer—his spirit praying—but his mind remains "unfruitful." This may mean that such prayer leaves him without mental, intellectual, or thought benefit; but it may mean that under such circumstances, since his mind is not engaged in the exercise, it does not produce fruit in the hearers—the presupposition being that the edification of the hearers requires intelligibility of utterance, and intelligibility of utterance requires that the mind of the speaker be engaged. In light of the sustained emphasis in this chapter on the edification of the hearers, this latter interpretation is marginally more likely.

If that is the correct way to understand verse 14, then verse 15 probably means something like this: What then shall I do? Well, having prayed for the gift of interpretation, I will pray with my spirit (that is, I will continue to speak in tongues), but I will also pray with my mind (that is, the prayer will be repeated, this time with the mind engaged—presumably the interpretation of the prayer with the spirit). The same is true for singing with the spirit (apparently this is a more melodious or metrical form of tongues-speaking/praying). There is no evidence that this justifies entire congregational participation, as in many contemporary charismatic churches. For a start, that would violate Paul's principle that not all have the same gift; and moreover, since this too is a form of tongues-speaking, interpretation should be required. Still less is there justification for linking this with the hymn singing of Ephesians and Colossians:[95] that the latter was "in the Spirit" is not a sufficient criterion.

That Paul has been talking about what he expects the tongues-speaker to do in the church is now confirmed by verse 16. Again Paul allows that the tongues-speaker whose utterances are not interpreted may be praising God with his spirit; but the non-tongues-speaker in the congregation does not know what the tongues-speaker is saying,

---

94. There is another way to understand this verse. The man who speaks in a tongue should go ahead and pray (in a tongue), in order that an interpreter, presumably some person other than the tongues-speaker, may interpret. In that case, the ἵνα clause does not constitute the prayer's content but its purpose. See Thomas, *Understanding Spiritual Gifts,* 210–11. But that presupposes that speaking in a tongue is different from praying in a tongue—a postulate refuted infra. Moreover, with no interpreter in the context, it is much more natural that the subject of the verb *interpret* is the tongues-speaker himself.

95. So Martin, *The Spirit and the Congregation,* 70–71.

and cannot join in with the corporate "Amen." The word I have rendered "non-tongues-speaker"[96] simply means the outsider, the layman, with the nature of the guild from which he is excluded determined by the context. This person must be a Christian, or there would be no expected "Amen" from his or her lips; hence the conclusion that this is a non-tongues-speaker. Again the principles of the passage are summarized: "You may be giving thanks well enough, but the other man is not edified" (14:17).

Reverting again to the first person, Paul thanks God that he speaks in tongues more than all of his readers. Like a wise pastor, he thus identifies himself with those he seeks to correct.[97] But more movingly yet, like other passages in Paul's epistles (such as the astonishing list of his sufferings in 2 Cor. 11), this one suddenly provides a remarkable insight into Paul the Christian—an insight of which we would have been ignorant had not the circumstances of a particular church, in the providence of God, elicited these words from him. "But in the church," he continues, "I would rather speak five intelligible words to instruct others than ten thousand words in a tongue" (v. 19).

There is no stronger defense of the private use of tongues, and attempts to avoid this conclusion turn out on inspection to be remarkably flimsy.[98] If Paul speaks in tongues more than all the Corinthians, yet in the church prefers to speak five intelligible words rather than ten thousand words in a tongue (which is a way of saying that under virtually no circumstance will he ever speak in tongues in church, without quite ruling out the possibility), then where does he speak them? It will not do to suppose Paul is counseling private, quiet use of tongues *during the assembly* when another is ministering. To adapt Paul's argument, where then would be the tongues-speaker's "Amen," if he or she was not paying attention? We have already seen that Paul envisages praying with the spirit as a form of valid prayer and praise; what he will not permit is unintelligibility in the church. The only possible conclusion is that Paul exercised his remarkable tongues gift *in private.*

This is a point of considerable significance, from a pastoral point of view; but I shall take up such matters in the final chapter.

Throughout history there have been pendulum swings of various sorts. The church, unfortunately, is not exempt. At times there are enormous pressures to intellectualize and formulate the gospel; at

96. ἰδιώτης.

97. See Henry Chadwick, " 'All Things to All Men' (I Cor. ix.22)," *New Testament Studies* 1 (1955): 268–69.

98. See Edgar, *Miraculous Gifts*, 171ff.; well rebutted by Turner, "Spiritual Gifts Then and Now," 22–23.

others, enormous pressures to "feel" one's religious faith and develop passion for God—profound, emotional outbursts of contrition, praise, adoration. At most times in history, of course, groups espousing each of these polarities co-exist, one perhaps on the decline, the other on the ascendancy; and most groups embrace some mixture of the two, without much thought as to their proportion. Only rarely have Christians, such as the early English Puritans, self-consciously committed themselves to wholistic integration of the two. Noncharismatic evangelicals *tend* to the former stereotype; charismatics *tend* toward the latter. Both have their dangers.

One lesson, however, comes through these first verses of 1 Corinthians 14 with startling force. Whatever the place for profound, personal experience and corporate emotional experience, the assembled church is a place for intelligibility. Our God is a thinking, speaking God; and if we will know him, we must learn to think his thoughts after him. I am not surreptitiously invalidating what Paul has refused to invalidate. I am merely trying to reflect his conviction that edification in the church depends utterly on intelligibility, understanding, coherence. Both charismatic and noncharismatic churches need to be reminded of that truth again and again.

4

Order and Authority: Restraining Spiritual Gifts (14:20–40)

There is a sense in which the contrast between the gifts of prophecy and tongues, developed by Paul in the first nineteen verses of this chapter, continues in the second half of the chapter. Certainly tongues and prophecy are set over against each other in verses 20–25. Although verse 26 lists several of the χαρίσματα *(charismata)*, its primary function is to set the stage for renewed discussion of tongues (vv. 27–28) and prophecy (vv. 29–33). Even verses 33b–36, on what I judge to be the most likely interpretation, are not unrelated to the gift of prophecy. The closing verses include a warning (vv. 37–38) and a final pithy contrast between prophecy and tongues (vv. 39–40).

Nevertheless several noteworthy characteristics set this part of the chapter off from what precedes. Paul's tone becomes a shade more strident, heralded in the first instance by the words *brothers, stop thinking like children* (14:20). The contrast between prophecy and tongues in verses 20–25, though still related to the themes of intelligibility and edification, introduces unbelievers as a new factor. Here Paul cites antecedent Scripture as precedent for the very purpose of tongues. Verses 26–40 assume that the values of intelligibility and edification have been adopted, and seek to implement those values with simple, practical rules, rules shaped by an overarching conviction that public worship must mirror the orderliness and peace of the God whom we worship.

We shall examine each of the sections in turn.

The Relation of Tongues and Prophecies to Unbelievers (14:20–25)

The word *brothers* (14:20) helps to soften the sharpness of the rebuke that follows it. The Corinthians thought of themselves as mature; Paul for his part has already had occasion in this epistle to tell them he considers them so infantile they have not even attained the place where they can consume solid foods (3:2). In the context of chapter 14, this can only mean that Paul sees the errors he is correcting as indices of spiritual immaturity. The very gift that some exercise as a token, in their view, of special enduement of the Spirit, has become so overblown in their minds and thereby so distortive of proper spiritual proportion that Paul can accuse them of remarkable childishness. "Overconcentration on glossolalia is a mark of immaturity. There is indeed a right way for Christians to be childlike—in their freedom from guile . . .; but in their intelligence they ought to be mature."[1] At least some Corinthians wanted to measure their maturity by the intensity of their spiritual experiences, without consideration of other constraints, such as love's demands that brothers and sisters in Christ be edified; and thus they became "mature" or advanced, wittingly or unwittingly, in evil, and immature in their thinking. Paul wants to reverse this trend.

The relation between verse 20 and verses 21–25 is uncertain. Probably Paul is casting about for another way to show the Corinthians that the high estimation in which they hold tongues is misplaced, and decides to tackle the relation of tongues to unbelievers, hitherto not considered. These verses are extraordinarily difficult, primarily because tongues are said to be a sign for unbelievers in verse 22, while

1. F. F. Bruce, *1 and 2 Corinthians*, New Century Bible (London: Marshall, Morgan and Scott, 1971).

in verses 23–25 unbelievers respond *negatively* to tongues and *positively* to prophecy, at first glance contradicting the judgment of verse 22. Of the many explanations that have been advanced, the following deserve mention.

First, Edgar, eager to show that "tongues" are always real, human, known languages, argues that tongues are a sign for unbelievers in that, as on the day of Pentecost, they serve as an evangelistic tool.[2] This means, of course, that the connection Paul makes with the "strange tongues" of the quotation from Isaiah (v. 21) is a little obscure. Edgar dogmatically affirms that his view is the only one that makes sense of the passage; and it stands in line, he says, with Acts 2, where real languages are used, and for evangelistic purpose. But as we shall see in my last chapter, it is not entirely clear that the tongues of Acts 2 were used evangelistically, except in the derivative sense that they attracted many people together who heard the first Christians praising God in the diverse languages of the hearers. The evangelistic message of Acts 2 is found in Peter's sermon, delivered in *one* language (presumably Aramaic), and cast as an explanation of the tongues. Edgar's interpretation of 1 Corinthians 14:22 not only requires him to adopt incredible interpretations of much of the rest of the chapter, but, astonishingly, he does not comment on verse 23. Yet that is precisely where the nub of the debate lies. Sadly, Edgar's work is angry, and will therefore not receive the attention that parts of it deserve (for instance, his examination of the meaning of γλῶσσαι).

A variation on this view is that of Thomas,[3] who with more sophistication argues that tongues were used evangelistically to communicate with the unbeliever and frankly admits that Paul is divorcing his use of Isaiah 28:11–12 from its own context. The explanation that he offers for verses 23–25 is that these verses "point out the inappropriateness of tongues in an assembly composed primarily of believers. The gift had a perfectly valid purpose in a group where unbelievers predominated (v. 22), but prophecy is much more useful among Christians. . . . This view provides the only adequate way of reconciling verse 22 with verses 23–25."[4] But I am afraid it is not adequate; for verses 23–25 do not give as the reason for the inappropriateness of tongues the predomination of believers over unbelievers, but that *the unbeliever himself* will conclude that the tongues-speaker is raving.

2. Thomas R. Edgar, *Miraculous Gifts: Are They for Today?* (Neptune, N.J.: Loizeaux, 1983), 146ff. For trenchant rebuttal, see M. M. B. Turner, "Spiritual Gifts Then and Now," *Vox Evangelica* 15 (1985): 20.
3. Robert L. Thomas, *Understanding Spiritual Gifts: The Christian's Special Gifts in the Light of 1 Corinthians 12–14* (Chicago: Moody, 1978), 224–25.
4. Ibid., 225.

One would have thought, under Thomas's reconstruction, that the only person who appreciated what was going on was the unbeliever; but that is precisely what Paul does *not* say.

Second, some writers of dispensational persuasion say that Paul's point quoting the passage from Isaiah is to affirm that tongues are a sign exclusively for *Jewish* people—"from which it follows," writes Hodges, "that the average heathen visitor to the Christian assembly (far more likely to be a Gentile than a hostile Jew) would be exposed to a phenomenon never intended for him in the first place."[5] The exegetical naïveté is somewhat staggering, and turns in part on how the New Testament writers use the Old Testament. Such fundamental issues aside, however, it is remarkable that in verses 23–25 Paul does not distinguish the unbeliever's response to tongues and to prophecy along the lines of his race and what is appropriate to it, but along the lines that the unbeliever deduces from the one activity, tongues, that the speaker is raving; and from the other, prophecy, from which he gains understanding, that he is a sinner and in need of the grace of God.

Third, a far more sophisticated variation on a racial distinction, or perhaps better, a covenantal distinction, is that of Robertson.[6] He rightly draws attention to the fact that behind Isaiah 28:11 stands the covenantal curse of Deuteronomy 28:49–50: if the people of God turn from him, they are told, "The LORD will bring a nation against you from far away, from the ends of the earth, like an eagle swooping down, a nation whose language you will not understand, a fierce-looking nation without respect for the old or pity for the young." Robertson then notes that Isaiah 28:11, picking up this theme in connection with the Assyrian invasion of Israel as divine punishment, is followed by the messianic promise of Isaiah 28:16: God will lay a stone in Zion, a tested and precious cornerstone, and "the one who trusts will never be dismayed"—cited by Paul in Romans 9:31–33. Even the tongues at Pentecost are in line with this: even though all present on that day were presumably Jewish or committed proselytes, nevertheless tongues at Pentecost "represent the taking of the kingdom away from Israel and the giving of the kingdom to men of all nations. . . . No longer will God confine himself to one people, speaking a single language."[7] Thus, "Tongues serve as a sign to indicate that God's redemptive program has shifted from a Jewish-centered activity to an activity involving all

5. Zane C. Hodges, "The Purpose of Tongues," *Bibliotheca Sacra* 120 (1963): 231.
6. O. Palmer Robertson, "Tongues: Sign of Covenantal Curse and Blessing," *Westminster Theological Journal* 38 (1975): 49–53.
7. Ibid., 47–48.

nations of the world."[8] As for the apparent awkwardness between verse 22 and verses 23–25, Robertson observes that in verse 22 only tongues, strictly speaking, are said to be *a sign* for anyone, in this case unbelievers; prophecy is merely *for* believers. Paul, Robertson admits, has had to transfer "unbelievers" from a Jewish context to a Gentile context; but the point is that tongues constitute a sign and prophecy does not: " 'Tongues' serve as an indicator; 'prophecy' serves as a communicator. 'Tongues' call attention to the mighty acts of God; 'prophecy' calls to repentance and faith in response to the mighty Acts of God."[9] Since this crucial change in God's covenantal purposes is now ancient history, there is now no longer any purpose to tongues, "which are attached vitally—but irretrievably—to a particular juncture in the history of redemption."[10]

This last sentence, of course, is again remarkably reductionistic; for even if Robertson's interpretation of 14:21–25 were right, that would not prove he has exhausted *all* that the Bible has to say about the purpose of tongues. It is certainly difficult to think how the use of tongues in private devotion (discussed in the last chapter) can be integrated into Robertson's synthesis. A more devastating weakness with this interpretation, however, is that the unbeliever in 1 Corinthians 14 is a Gentile. Robertson cannot legitimately retreat to the observation that Old Testament categories of unbelief, primarily Jewish, are habitually transferred to the Gentile unbelief of Paul's world; for his argument turns on seeing signs as a *covenantal* curse on *Jews*. Moreover, it is far more likely that Paul in verse 22 is saying that tongues are a sign for unbelievers, and prophecy *is a sign for* believers (not simply "prophecy is *for* believers," as Robertson's interpretation demands), even though the extra words are left out. The omission is not unexpected in Greek. The matter is well discussed by Turner.[11] Moreover, the dichotomy that makes tongues an indicator and prophecy a communicator is not very felicitous anyway; for Paul has gone to considerable trouble in verses 1–19, especially verse 5, to say that tongues themselves may be "a communicator" provided there is an interpretation.

Fourth, Johanson resolves the tension between verse 22 and verses 23–25 by postulating that verse 22 is in fact a rhetorical question, Paul's summing up of his opponents' views in order to oppose them

8. Ibid., 48.
9. Ibid., 52.
10. Ibid.
11. Turner, "Spiritual Gifts Then and Now," ad loc.

in verses 23–25.[12] This is part of the trend I mentioned in the second chapter—the trend to discover quotations of the opponents' positions wherever there is an exegetical difficulty. This one does not meet the three criteria I set out in that chapter. The Johanson thesis labors under the further disadvantage that the connectors are inappropriate. For instance, at the beginning of verse 23, instead of a strong adversative we find ὥστε (*hōste*, so then), which can be salvaged for the theory only by postulating an ellipsis.

Fifth, another proposal argues that tongues must be understood as a *positive* sign here.[13] Ruef suggests that it was the sign by which Gentile Christians were accepted by Christian Jews, in the same way that the tongues-speaking of Cornelius and those with him apparently opened the way to their acceptance as Christians by the believers in Jerusalem (Acts 10–11). But once these Gentiles have actually been accepted as believers, Ruef argues, the proper sign for them, as for other believers, is prophecy. Continuing the practice of tongues at that point will only confuse the outsider, the unbeliever who is watching.

There seems little to commend this view. For reasons we shall see in the next chapter, the episode with Cornelius is best understood as a critical salvation-historical turning point, not a paradigm of the way Jews commonly tested the validity of the conversion of Gentiles. In epistles with demonstrated focus on Jew/Christian/Gentile relationships (e.g., Galatians), the test of tongues Ruef advances is nowhere in view. Moreover, the flow of the argument through 1 Corinthians 12–14 spawns no suspicion that Jew/Gentile conflict lurks behind the abuse of tongues. To put the same issue more positively, these chapters consistently pit prophecy against tongues in the area of intelligible communication. That context is lost by this interpretation. Ruef's proposal also means that Paul has abused Isaiah 28:11, for God was not speaking a *positive* sign through the Assyrians. This is of some importance, for verse 22 opens with the logical "so then."

Recently a more believable variation on this proposal has been advanced by Thiessen.[14] He removes the Jew/Gentile conflict from the discussion and suggests that the Corinthian church was trying to make tongues a criterion for membership. Paul replies, in effect, that this is inappropriate because tongues are a sign *not* for believers but for unbelievers, just as in Isaiah 28 the strange tongues come to those who do *not* hear, who do *not* belong to the *Gemeinde* (the believing com-

---

12. B. C. Johanson, "Tongues, a Sign for Unbelievers? A Structural and Exegetical Study of 1 Corinthians XIV.20–25," *New Testament Studies* 25 (1978–79): 180–203.

13. John Ruef, *Paul's First Letter to Corinth* (London: SCM, 1977).

14. Gerd Thiessen, *Psychologische Aspecte paulinischer Theologie* (Göttingen: Vandenhoeck and Ruprecht, 1983), 82–88.

munity). Prophecy is the appropriate sign of the believer. This preserves a positive sense to "sign" in both cases. But a central weakness to the interpretation remains: the text focuses attention not on confirmation of the *church's* assessment of the individual, but of the *individual's* reaction before the two phenomena, tongues and prophecy.

Sixth, Roberts suggests that tongues would have been a sign of some kind of spiritual activity, and thus positive, without it being clear just what the source of that tongues phenomenon was.[15] Tongues are therefore a positive sign, but not communicative. If an unbeliever enters the church and hears everyone speaking tongues, he will say, "You are possessed"—not a reproach, merely a statement of fact, possibly mingled with mild admiration. But that is not enough to make the unbelieving onlooker a Christian. That requires content, and the resulting moral reformation. That is why prophecy is superior to tongues. The point of the quotation from Isaiah is simply that tongues are an ineffective means of communicating God's will.

This is surely an abuse of Isaiah 28:11. The measure of the effectiveness of the strange tongues, in the context of Isaiah, is not in their ability to communicate but in their signal of divine judgment—which was remarkably effective. Moreover, the contrast in verse 22 is not between a gift that serves as a mildly positive but incommunicative sign to unbelievers, and another gift that serves as a positive and communicative sign, *also to unbelievers*, but between a sign to unbelievers and a sign *to believers*.

Seventh, there is a growing number of scholars who adopt one form or another of the interpretation that I shall briefly defend here.[16] Not all of them agree on the details, but the general shape of the proposal is capturing majority approval.

In the context of Isaiah 28:9–13, the "strange tongues" of foreigners (i.e., the Assyrian troops) represent God's visitation in judgment on his people. They had refused to listen to him and repent when he spoke clearly; now he will visit them through invading hordes by whom he will "speak" in a language (Assyrian) whose content they will not

15. P. Roberts, "A Sign—Christian or Pagan?" *Expository Times* 90 (1978): 199–203.

16. Among many others, cf. J. P. M. Sweet, "A Sign for Unbelievers: Paul's Attitude Toward Glossolalia," *New Testament Studies* 13 (1966–67): 240–57; Bruce, *1 and 2 Corinthians*; Frederick Dale Bruner, *A Theology of the Holy Spirit: The Pentecostal Experience and the New Testament* (Grand Rapids: Eerdmans, 1970), 299–300; Jack W. MacGorman, *The Gifts of the Spirit: An Exposition of 1 Corinthians 12–14* (Nashville: Broadman, 1974), 96–105; Turner, "Spiritual Gifts Then and Now," 20–21; Krister Stendahl, *Paul Among Jews and Gentiles* (London: SCM, 1977), 115–16; Wayne A. Grudem, *The Gift of Prophecy in 1 Corinthians* (Washington, D.C.: University Press of America, 1982), 185–202; B. Dominy, "Paul and Spiritual Gifts: Reflections on 1 Corinthians 12–14," *Southwestern Journal of Theology* 26 (1983): 64–65.

understand, even though in it they will "hear" a message of judgment. The "strange tongues" therefore do not convey content to the unbelieving Israelites, but they do serve as a sign—a *negative* sign, a sign of judgment. This is the example to which Paul appeals. In the Law it is written (and by "Law" here he means what we would call the Old Testament Scriptures) that at a crucial juncture in the history of the covenant community, God "spoke" to his people through "strange tongues." But when he did so, he was speaking a message of judgment. It appears, then, that when God speaks through strange tongues and the lips of foreigners to unbelievers, at least here it is a sign of his judgment upon them.[17]

It may have been that some believers in Corinth were justifying their undiscriminating overemphasis on tongues by extolling their virtue as a witness to unbelievers, as a *sign* to them of God's powerful presence in the life of the church. Paul replies, in effect: Yes, you are partly right. Tongues are a sign for unbelievers. But if you examine how the Scriptures describe the relationship between unbelievers and "strange" (i.e., foreign and unknown)[18] tongues, you discover that they constitute a *negative* sign. They are a sign of God's commitment to bring judgment. But when in the same verse (v. 22), Paul says that prophecy is a sign for believers, does he not mean this in a *positive* sense?

Indeed, the most frequent criticism of this interpretation—in fact, the only one that is regularly raised against it—is that it uses "sign"

17. On the text form of Paul's quotation, see F. S. Malan, "The Use of the Old Testament in 1 Corinthians," *Neotestamentica* 14 (1981): 134–70. On the exegetical questions surrounding the interpretation of the Masoretic Text, see Grudem, *Gift of Prophecy*, 185ff.

18. Many noncharismatics deduce from Paul's appeal to Isa. 28:11 that the tongues of 1 Cor. 12–14 have to be real, human, foreign languages unknown to the speaker. Paul appeals to Isa. 28, however, not to establish the nature of the tongues in Corinth, but what they might signify to unbelievers. It meets the needs of Paul's appeal if the tongues at Corinth conveyed propositional information, not mere feeling. (On this point, see my third chapter.) To push the analogy much beyond that point leaves no stopping place: e.g., we might want to argue that in the two cases the tongues-speakers were saying the same things, or that since the tongues-speakers in Isaiah's day were foreign pagan troops, therefore the tongues-speakers in Corinth were pagan. *Reductio ad absurdum.* It is not quite enough to say, with Gundry, "At Corinth interpretation was necessary because the audiences were local [i.e., most would have known some combination of only Greek, Latin and perhaps Aramaic]. On the Day of Pentecost interpretation was necessary because the audience was cosmopolitan." (From R. H. Gundry, " 'Ecstatic Utterance' [N. E. B.]?" *Journal of Theological Studies* 17 [1966]: 303.) For this view of tongues makes sense out of the situation in Acts 2; but it leaves one wondering in 1 Cor. 12–14 why foreign languages should be granted at all, if no one was there to understand them.

in a *negative* sense with respect to the gift of tongues, and in a *positive* sense with respect to the gift of prophecy. But two things must be said in defense of this interpretation. First, it is possible that verse 22 is commenting on the situation in *Isaiah's* day. The unbelievers faced judgment, and were addressed by God in the unintelligible language of foreigners; but there remained a godly remnant who benefited, not from tongues, but from prophecy—Isaiah's prophecy (see Isa. 8:16).[19] In other words, the distinction as to whether a certain phenomenon served as a positive sign or a negative sign extends back into the context of Isaiah. Second, the word σημεῖον (*sēmeion*, sign), especially in the Septuagint, often simply means "an indication of God's atti-tude." Whether those indications are positive or negative is a subor-dinate issue. Grudem provides long lists of examples in which signs are entirely positive (e.g., the rainbow [Gen. 9:12, 13, 14]; the blood on the doorpost [Exod. 12:13]; the mark on the forehead [Ezek. 9:4, 6]), entirely negative (the bronze censers of Korah, Dathan, and Abiram [Num. 16:38]; the defeat of Pharaoh Hophra [Jer. 44:29]). In the former series, the "signs" show God's approval and blessing; in the latter, his disapproval and impending judgment. Indeed, many signs are simul-taneously negative and positive: negative to the rebellious and unbe-lieving, and positive to the Lord's faithful people (e.g., the signs and wonders at the time of the exodus were negative to Pharaoh and to the Egyptians [Exod. 10:1–2; 11:9–10; Deut. 6:22; Neh. 9:10]; but they were positive to Israel [Deut. 4:34–35; 6:22; 7:19]). Even in the New Testament, a "sign" can indicate God's approval and blessing (e.g., Acts 2:22, 43; 4:30; John 2:11) or God's disapproval and threat of im-pending judgment (Luke 11:30; 21:11, 25; Acts 2:19).[20] In other words, it is more intrinsic to the word *sign* (σημεῖον, *sēmeion*) that something about God be "sign-ified" than that the "sign al" be positive or nega-tive. Paul may therefore not have cared if the "sign" of tongues is negative and the "sign" of prophecy is positive, even within the same verse; for in *both* instances the commonality was for him more decisive.

If this approach to the sign value of tongues is taken in verse 22, then there is no longer any difficulty in understanding verse 23. When outsiders or unbelievers come into a Christian assembly where every-one is speaking in tongues, it will not be surprising if they simply conclude that the believers are possessed (which is probably what the word μαίνεσθε [*mainesthe*] means). The two words I have rendered "outsider" and "unbeliever" probably refer to the same kinds of peo-

19. See Ralph P. Martin, *The Spirit and the Congregation: Studies in 1 Corinthians 12–15* (Grand Rapids: Eerdmans, 1984), 72–73.
20. Grudem, *Gift of Prophecy*, 195–96.

ple: non-Christians. Because the first word is used in 14:16 to refer to the Christian without the gift of tongues, some have preferred to think it here refers to some sort of "halfway" Christian, a catechumen perhaps.[21] But that imposes too narrow a referent on the term, and fails to recognize its intrinsic genius: it simply means "outsider"; but what this person stands outside of can be determined only by context. Because the flow of the argument in these verses contrasts believers with unbelievers, newcomers with the established Christian community, it seems best to see in "outsiders and unbelievers" a double description of the non-Christian visitor to the congregation.

It appears, then, that these tongues do *not* have exactly the same *function* as those in Acts 2; but I shall return to this point in the last chapter.

If an unbeliever enters the congregation when everyone is prophesying, instead of speaking in tongues, then communication takes place. It may even be communication designed by the Spirit to expose the secrets of his own heart and thereby to convict him of sin, bringing him to repentance and worship (14:24–25).[22] Schlatter rightly observes that this picture fosters the assumption that Paul was concerned, in evangelism, to begin by producing a consciousness of guilt.[23] Certainly his goal was not so much to generate the maximum possible number of tongues-speakers as to bring sinners to their knees in repentance and worship. Moral renewal, like love, is one of the essential factors that distinguishes genuine Christianity from all its rivals.

Of course, this interpretation of the passage means that although prophecy serves as a sign to believers, it also has more positive effect on unbelievers than does the gift of tongues. This does not mean Paul is reversing ground; for the prophesying of verse 24 is not evangelistic preaching. The unbeliever comes in and *overhears* what is going on in the *assembly*, and by that means is brought to recognition of need, and to repentance and worship. The point is that even so far as outreach

21. So N. M. Pritchard, "Profession of Faith and Admission to Communion in the Light of 1 Corinthians 11 and Other Passages," *Scottish Journal of Theology* 33 (1980): 64–65.

22. It is unlikely that the content that brought about such a sense of guilt was what Käsemann calls "sentences of holy law" (e.g., texts structured like 1 Cor. 3:17; 14:38; 16:22a); see Ernst Käsemann, *New Testament Questions of Today*, trans. W. J. Montague (London: SCM, 1969), 66–81; for as Martin, *The Spirit and the Congregation*, 68, points out, in 14:28 the prophecy is directed toward believers, and the unbelievers simply overhear.

23. Adolf Schlatter, *Paulus—Der Bote Jesu: Eine Deutung seiner Briefe an die Korinther*, 3d ed. (Stuttgart: Calwer, 1962), 382. Conzelmann says Schlatter's remark is a pietistic, legalist shift in the text's meaning, and misguided; but as he does not say why, I cannot evaluate his reasons.

is concerned, tongues must take a back seat to prophecy. The question of intelligibility has returned, but now with reference to unbelievers.

Those of us who have spent any time on the borders between the ranks of the charismatic movement and the noncharismatics can easily sympathize with Paul's warnings. I have known more than one Christian group in a university setting, for instance, where the leadership was taken over by aggressive charismatics. These leaders succeeded not only in splitting the group, but also in driving away some students who had become interested in Christian things but who were now alienated by the perplexing phenomenon of tongues.[24]

One other issue emerges from these verses. When Paul says that the unbeliever comes into the assembly while *everyone* is speaking in tongues (v. 23) or while *everyone* is prophesying (v. 24), how far can the universality of such descriptions be pressed? That leads us to the next section.

Order in Public Worship (14:26–36)

The preliminary question this section raises, then, is this: Who may prophesy? At one level, the answer is obvious: only those who are so gifted. In Paul's view, that is only *part* of the church, since his rhetorical question *are all prophets?* in 12:29 demands a resounding no! Within that framework, 14:24 may not mean that everyone in the congregation either was or could be prophesying when the unbeliever walked in, still less that they were all doing so simultaneously. It may simply mean that when the unbeliever entered, all that he heard from everyone who participated, one by one, was prophesying (or, in v. 23, speaking in tongues) But verse 31 is more difficult: "You can all prophesy in turn so that everyone may be instructed and encouraged." Is it fair to restrict the scope of this verse? If not, how can it be reconciled with Paul's repeatedly expressed commitment to the principle that the various spiritual gifts are *distributed* to the church, with no gift universally poured out?

There are, I think, only three possible answers. It is possible that verse 31 is not as comprehensive as it first sounds. It may be that "you . . . all" does not refer to every person in the church without exception, but to every person in the church without distinction—men, women, slaves, nobles, and so forth, provided he or she has the gift. Or it may be that Paul simply presupposes that "you . . . all" refers to those who

---

24. It is no telling rebuttal to point out that some are also converted through the agency of the group responsible for the split: God has always been quick to use even the wrath of man to praise him.

are recognized as prophets; that is, all of you prophets may prophesy, one by one. But it is probably marginally more natural to read the Greek in the widest possible sense. In that case, many have suggested that we need to distinguish between those who prophesy now and then, and those whose gift is so developed, or so deployed, or whose prophecies when evaluated receive such high assessments, that they achieve the semistatus of "prophets."[25] The debates are intricate, the results uncertain and unsatisfying; but they may have some bearing on the attempt, in the final chapter, to synthesize the material gathered so far on the nature of prophecy.

The introductory question of verse 26 anticipates what Paul thinks can be learned from the discussion so far. His position, in a word, is that *whatever* the χάρισμα *(charisma)*, all that is done when the believers "come together" (i.e., meet as the gathered church) must be done for the edification of the church. Of the nature of each gift here mentioned we cannot be certain. Does the person who brings a "hymn," for example, simply introduce a known composition for all to sing? Does it mean a fresh contribution each time, as many have suggested? The brief answer is that we possess too little information to warrant firm conclusions. It is clear that the Corinthian service was not boring! I shall draw out one or two implications for our own corporate worship at the end of this chapter. At the moment, we need to hear Paul descending to the extremely practical as he attempts to curtail the enthusiasm of those in Corinth who speak in tongues and prophesy.

Tongues (14:27, 28)

In brief, Paul imposes three specific limitations on tongues-speakers in the church. First, there must be an interpreter present (though how that interpreter is identified in advance is not specified);[26] second, only

25. See Henry Barclay Swete, *The Holy Spirit in the New Testament* (1920; reprint ed., Grand Rapids: Baker, 1976), 377; E. Earle Ellis, "The Role of the Christian Prophet in Acts," in *Apostolic History and the Gospel: Studies in Honor of F. F. Bruce*, ed. W. Ward Gasque and Ralph P. Martin (Exeter: Paternoster, 1970), 62; Turner, "Spiritual Gifts Then and Now," 14–16; Grudem, *Gift of Prophecy*, 235ff.; J. Reiling, "Prophecy, the Spirit and the Church," *Prophetic Vocation in the New Testament and Today*, ed. J. Panagopoulos, *Novum Testamentum* Supplements, vol. 45 (Leiden: Brill, 1977), 67; Francis A. Sullivan, "Speaking in Tongues," *Lumen Vitae* 31 (1976): 21–46.

26. Archibald Robertson and Alfred Plummer, *A Critical and Exegetical Commentary on the First Epistle of St. Paul to the Corinthians*, 2d ed. (Edinburgh: T. and T. Clark, 1914). They interpret εἰς in 14:27 to mean "one": let there be *one* interpreter, regardless of whether there are two or three tongues-speakers. They suggest this is not only the more natural way to take the word, but that if only *one* interpreter were used for all utterances in tongues, there would be extra insurance against several speaking at once. But once the principle of only one speaking at a time is laid down, the extra

one tongues-speaker may speak at a time; and third, only two or at the most three may speak. Whether this last restriction stems from a concern that the meetings do not become unwieldy, or from a concern that tongues-speakers must not assume a more prominent place than prophecy, which also has its set limits (14:29), is uncertain.

It is clear that tongues-speakers are understood to have control over themselves. If the allotted two or three have had their say, Paul expects the others to keep quiet, which confirms that the gift is not of the sort where the individual loses all self-control. It also hints at a remarkable and dynamic tension between the Spirit who is producing the gift and the individual who is its vehicle. Paul does not argue that after two or three have spoken, the Spirit will not grant the gift to anyone else; and therefore the fourth and subsequent tongues-speakers at any meeting must be fraudulent, or inspired by some spirit other than the Holy Spirit. Precisely the same dynamic tension operates in the gift of prophecy (vv. 29–30). The compulsion of the Spirit is not of the order where the prophet loses ability to hold his or her peace; and if a revelation comes to the fourth party, after three prophets have had their say, that does not provide warrant to the prophet to break the firm guidelines Paul is imposing on the church.

One cannot help but see some decided differences between this sort of prophesying, and that, say, of Jeremiah.

Prophecy (14:29–33a)

Some of the main points in these verses have already been dealt with in these chapters: the limitation on the numbers of prophets who speak at one meeting; the fact that the prophets retain control of their spirits throughout the prophesying, hinting at a dynamic tension between the promptings of the Holy Spirit and the constraints of the order imposed by the spiritually gifted apostle; the presupposition that the informational base of prophecy is not study but revelation (v. 30); the fact that the evaluation of prophetic messages is couched

restriction perceived by Robertson and Plummer seems unnecessarily restrictive, not least since εἷς not infrequently serves as an indefinite pronoun in New Testament Greek, i.e., "someone" (NIV). There is a second ambiguity: the Greek of the first clause of v. 28 could be rendered either "But if no interpreter is present" (Hans Lietzmann and Werner Georg Kümmel, *An die Korinther I. II*, Handbuch zum Neuen Testament, vol. 9 [Tübingen: J. C. B. Mohr, 1969]) or "But if he is not an interpreter" (Johannes Weiss, *Der erste Korintherbrief*, 10th ed. [Göttingen: Vandenhoeck und Ruprecht, 1897]). The former rendering is perhaps marginally more natural, but raises the question of how to know in advance if an interpreter is present; the second rendering is in line with the interpretation of v. 13 I provided in the third chapter. I see no way of deciding which rendering is best.

in language that presupposes the message may contain a mixture of the valuable and the worthless.[27]

One other question must be posed: Who are the "others" who "should weigh carefully what is said" (v. 29)? On the face of it, this word could embrace either the prophets[28] or some larger group, even the entire Corinthian assembly. Almost certainly the responsibility to weigh what the prophets say rests with the entire congregation, or, more precisely, with the congregation as a whole. Certainly that is true elsewhere in the New Testament (e.g., 1 Thess. 5:21; see also 1 John 4:1–6). One commentator rightly remarks that if Paul had wanted to say "the rest (of the prophets)," the Greek more plausibly should have been οἱ λοιποί *(hoi loipoi)* rather than οἱ ἄλλοι *(hoi alloi)*.[29] Grudem raises a psychological point:

> If we understand οἱ ἄλλοι to be restricted to a special group of prophets, we have much difficulty picturing what the rest of the congregation would do during the prophecy and judging. Would they sit during the prophecy waiting for the prophecy to end and be judged before knowing whether to believe any part of it? . . . Especially hard to believe is the idea that teachers, administrators and other church leaders without special gifts of prophecy would sit passively awaiting the verdict of an elite group.[30]

Moreover, there is no evidence that this careful weighing of the content of Christian prophecy should be confused with the gift of discerning spirits (12:10).

It seems best, then, to see in "the others" the church as a whole. This does not necessarily mean that everyone in the congregation should participate equally in the evaluating process, or that there may not be some further restriction as to participation (indeed, I think Paul imposes such a restriction in verses 33b–36, discussed further on), but

27. See the discussion in the third chapter, interacting primarily with Grudem. David E. Aune, *Prophecy in Early Christianity and the Ancient Mediterranean World* (Grand Rapids: Eerdmans, 1983); 217–22, has some valuable material; but his discussion is marred by several exegetical false steps, and a failure to distinguish between the Old Testament's evaluation of the *prophet* and this Pauline concern to evaluate the *prophecy.*

28. So, among many others, H. Greeven, "Propheten, Lehrer, Vorsteher bei Paulus: Zur Frage der 'Ämter' in Urchristentum," *Zeitschrift für die neutestamentliche Wissenschaft* 44 (1952–53): 6; K. Maly, *Mündige Gemeinde* (Stuttgart: Katholisches Bibelwerk, 1967), 218.

29. Frédéric Godet, *Commentaire sur la première épitre aux Corinthiens*, 2d ed., 2 vols. (Neuchâtel: L'Imprimerie Nouvelle L.-A. Monnier, 1965).

30. Grudem, *Gift of Prophecy*, 60–62.

only that the responsibility for evaluation is not permitted to rest with the prophets, but is extended to the broader community.

There is an important corollary to this testing. If this was the common practice in churches regulated by Paul, it follows that a prophet who treated his or her prophecy as so immediate and direct and untarnished a product of divine inspiration that it should be questioned by no true believer, would not only be stepping outside the Pauline restrictions but would, presumably, ultimately fall under the suspicions of the church.

One of the more troubling aspects of some parts of the modern charismatic movement is the frequency with which prophecies are given as direct quotations from the Lord (even though that pattern is extraordinarily rare in the New Testament). This aberration (and from the biblical point of view, that is what it is) is then compounded by far too little attention to the importance of Paul's exhortation to weigh carefully what is said, or, in 1 Thessalonians 5, to test everything (in the context of prophecies) and to hold on to what is good. The inevitable result is that some charismatic leaders *and their followers* treat the prophecies of their leaders as if they possess the unqualified authority of God himself, and such authority on American religious television programming is then easily transmuted into a fund-raising device. God has given the leader a prophecy that commands him to build something and to tell the people to send in so much money; no community of believers carefully checks out this claim, *nor does the leader submit himself or herself to the evaluation of a spiritually minded community.* The resulting exploitation is manipulative, arrogant, sometimes dishonest, corrosive of the leader's humility and destructive of the followers' spiritual maturity. Paul's restrictions, thought fully applied by some of these contemporary charismatic leaders, would immediately reduce these shameful abuses.

The divine reality behind these restrictions is given in verse 33a: our God is a God not of disorder but of peace. This truth does not of course sanction mere traditionalism in worship, or sanctify stuffiness; but it does warn us sharply about the dangers of the opposite end of the spectrum. That is not wise and biblically informed Christian worship that pursues freedom at the expense of order, or unrestrained spontaneity at the expense of reverence.

Restrictions on Women (14:33b–36)

This highly disputed passage begins its daunting array of challenges with a text-critical problem and uncertainty as to whether verse 33b belongs to the preceding verses or to the passage before us.

The interpretation of verses 33b–36 is extremely difficult. For a start, even the nature of the link between verse 33b and verse 34 issues in a conclusion based on balanced probabilities. Do we read, "For God is not a God of disorder but of peace, as in all the congregations of the saints"; or "As in all the congregations of the saints, women should remain silent in the churches"? The latter is stylistically inelegant, in that in Greek the words rendered "congregations" and "churches" by the New International Version are the same word: that is, "As in all the churches of the saints, women should remain silent in the churches." On the other hand, what some see as stylistic inelegance, others see as powerful emphasis. Moreover, if verse 33b is linked with what precedes, it is difficult to see what the line of thought is. The sentence "For God is not a God of disorder but of peace, as in all the congregations of the saints" is either trite (Of course God will be the same God everywhere!) or meaningless (Exactly what is being compared? God and the congregations of the saints? God's peaceful order with what is in all the congregations of the saints?). On the whole, it seems best to take verse 33b with what follows. But even if someone prefers the other option, little is changed in the interpretation of verses 34–36, since the phrase *in the churches* (in the plural) is found in verse 34.

The nub of the difficulty is that in 1 Corinthians 11:2–16, Paul is quite prepared for women to pray and prophesy, albeit with certain restrictions; but here, a first reading of the text makes the silence he enjoins absolute. The solutions that have been advanced are, like devils in certain instances of demon possession, legion. I can do no more than list a few, and mention one or two of my hesitations about them, before turning to the interpretation I find most contextually and exegetically secure.

Some continue to see the demand for silence as an absolute rule. This is done in one of two ways. First, several seek to escape the tension between 11:2–16 and 14:33b–36 by arguing that only the latter passage has reference to the public assembly: the former deals only with the home or with small group gatherings.[31] In that case, there is noth-

---

31. So Philipp Bachmann, *Der erste Brief des Paulus an die Korinther*, 4th ed. (Leipzig: A. Deichertsche Verlagsbuchhandlung, 1936); Hermann Olshausen, *A Commentary on Paul's First and Second Epistles to the Corinthians* (Minneapolis: Klock and Klock, 1984); John W. Robbins, *Scripture Twisting in the Seminaries. Part I: Feminism* (Jefferson, Md.: The Trinity Foundation, 1985). Also to be noted is the argument of Noel Weeks, "On Silence and Head Covering," *Westminster Theological Journal* 35 (1972): 21–27, who holds that in 11:5 the "uncovering" is symbolic of the act of praying. Correspondingly its dative form (ἀκατακαλύπτῳ) has instrumental force: i.e., Every woman praying or prophesying, *by means of the uncovering of the head*, dishonors her head. In this way the passage turns out to be an absolute prohibition, so far as public assembly is concerned. (It is worth pointing out in passing that Weeks, along with most commentators, assumes 11:2–16 deals with public meetings of the church—

ing in 1 Corinthians to prevent the interpreter from taking the prohibition of chapter 14 absolutely, so far as the church assembly is
concerned. This interpretation does not seem very likely, for (1) Paul
thinks of prophecy primarily as revelation from God delivered through
believers *in the context of the church* where the prophecy may be evaluated (14:23–29). (2) Distinctions between "smaller house groups" and
"church" many have not have been all that intelligible to the first
Christians, who commonly met in private homes. When the "church"
in a city was large enough (as at Jerusalem, Antioch, Ephesus, and
possibly Corinth) to overflow the largest private accommodation, it
must have been difficult, once opposition was established, to find a
public venue large enough to accommodate *all* the believers of that
city; that is, the house groups in such instances *constituted* the assembly of the church. (3) The language of 11:16 ("If anyone wants to be
contentious about this, we have no other practice—nor do the churches
of God"), seems to suggest a *church* concern, not merely the concern
of private or small-group piety. The "we"/"church of God" parallel
means either Paul has never allowed the practice, and the churches
have followed his lead; or Paul and the church in Ephesus (from which
he is writing) constitute the "we" that have not followed the practice,
and again the other churches have adopted the same stance. Either
way, when Paul adopts the same tone elsewhere (see especially 14:33b,
36), he is talking about conduct *in an assembly.* (4) The immediately
succeeding verses (11:17–34) are certainly devoted to an ordinance
designed for the assembly. (5) If someone points out that 11:2–16, unlike 14:33b–36, does not include the phrase *in the church*, it must also
be observed that 11:2–16 does not *restrict* the venue to the private
home or small group. (6) Whether the restriction in 11:2–16 requires
some kind of hat or a distinctive coiffure, it becomes faintly ridiculous
in proportion to the degree of privateness envisaged. If the restriction
pertains to every venue *except* the church assembly, does this mean
the Christian wife must postpone her private prayer until she has
hurried to her chambers and donned her headpiece? The restriction
is coherent only in a public setting. (7) Above all, the universality of
the promise of Joel, cited at Pentecost, that the Holy Spirit would be

unlike the view we have just examined.) But this interpretation invokes a strained
syntactical argument. If the "uncovering" is symbolic of praying and prophesying,
then one cannot reasonably take such "uncovering" as an instrumental dative modifying praying or prophesying. Stripped of the symbolism, the verse would then read,
in effect, "Every woman praying or prophesying, by means of praying or prophesying,
dishonors her head." And as in the previous interpretation, the approach of Weeks
does not adequately reckon with the fulfilled Joel prophecy recorded in Acts 2, to the
effect that both young men *and women* will prophesy.

poured out on men and women such that both would prophesy as constituent members of the community of the new covenant, seems somehow less than transparent if the women may display their inheritance only outside the context of the gathered messianic community.

The second way in which some understand the prohibition in 14:33b–36 as an absolute rule, thereby requiring creative measures in the exegesis of 11:2–16, is by taking the permission granted in the latter passage to be mere concession: women may indeed pray and prophesy (under the restriction of the head covering, whatever that is), but this is conceded with extreme reluctance to those who cannot manage to submit to the rule of chapter 14.[32] But the praying and prophesying exercised by women in chapter 11 is not cast as a concession. Moreover, the church enjoyed the heritage of Pentecost and the fulfillment of the prophecy of Joel, as we have seen, which promised that both men *and women* would have the Spirit poured out on them and they would prophesy (Acts 2:18).

Some are willing to leave a contradiction, and say no more.[33] Apart from any doctrine of Scripture, it is hard to believe that Paul could contradict himself as boldly as some think he has within the space of a few pages. A variation on this approach interprets verses 34–36, or some part of them, as a gloss of no relevance in establishing Pauline theology.[34] Many of these writers exercise a similar source-critical skill with all the other passages in the Pauline corpus that seem to restrict women in any way. The authentic Paul is the Paul of passages like 1 Corinthians 11:2–16 and Galatians 3:27ff. I confess I am always surprised by the amount of energy and ingenuity expended to rescue Paul from himself and conform him to our image. In any case, from a purely text-critical point of view, the evidence that these verses are original, and in their original location (and not, as in some manuscripts, with verses 34–35 placed after 14:40), is substantial.[35]

---

32. Thomas, *Understanding Spiritual Gifts*, 230–31.

33. E.g., John Koenig, *Charismata: God's Gifts for God's People* (Philadelphia: Westminster, 1978), 174; MacGorman, *The Gifts of the Spirit*, 113, who says Paul has already set a precedent for self-contradiction in 1 Cor. 8:4–6 versus 10:21!

34. E.g., F. X. Cleary, "Women in the New Testament: St. Paul and the Early Pauline Tradition," *Biblical Theology Bulletin* 10 (1980): 78–82; D. J. Doughty, "Women and Liberation in the Churches of Paul and the Pauline Tradition," *Drew Gateway* 50 (1979): 1–21; W. O. Walker, "The 'Theology of Women's Place' and the 'Paulinist' Tradition," *Semeia* 28 (1983): 101–12; G. W. Trompf, "On Attitudes Toward Women in Paul and Paulinist Literature: 1 Corinthians 11:3–16 and Its Context," *Catholic Biblical Quarterly* 42 (1980): 196–215; Hans Conzelmann, *First Corinthians: A Critical and Historical Commentary on the Bible*, ed. George W. MacRae, trans. James W. Leitch, Hermeneia series (Philadelphia: Fortress, 1974).

35. See Bruce M. Metzger, *A Textual Commentary on the Greek New Testament* (Lon-

Equally unlikely is the view of Kähler, to the effect that the subordination Paul has in mind is not of women to men, but of women to the order of worship he is establishing.[36] But we must ponder why women are singled out. Do not men also have to submit to the ecclesiastical structures Paul is setting forth? Moreover the verb for "submit" or "subordinate" normally involves subordination of a person or persons to a person or persons, not to an order, procedure, or institution.

To her credit, Fiorenza suggests that the reasoning behind many such judgments is based on theological bias, so she is prepared to let Paul be Paul.[37] However, she thinks the restriction is placed on wives only. After all, 1 Corinthians 7 displays Paul's "ascetic preference for the unmarried state";[38] and thus it is "apparent that Paul, here is 'taking over bourgeois moral concepts which denote not absolute but conventional values.' "[39] Fiorenza finds Paul's attitude surprising since we know of missionary couples. Paul derives his stance from "the Jewish Hellenistic propaganda tradition" that "places the demand for subordination of wives in the context of the Law."[40] Verse 36 betrays the fact that Paul expects strong response from the church against these restrictions; for indeed, Paul himself recognizes that his argument "sounds preposterous" and "goes against the accepted practice of the missionary churches in the Hellenistic urban centers. He therefore claims for his regulations the authority of the Lord (v. 37)."[41]

Here we have Paul not only strapped into a bourgeois mentality, but also guilty of the worst sort of religious jingoism: knowing what he says is preposterous and preparing for the backlash by appealing to the Lord's authority! I confess I cannot help entertaining the suspicion that Fiorenza's exegesis tells us more of her than it does of Paul.

Another cluster of interpretations argues that the problems behind Paul's demand for silence are local, probably doctrinal, and/or cul-

don: United Bible Society, 1971), 565; G. Zuntz, *The Text of the Epistles: A Disquisition upon the Corpus Paulinum* (London: British Academy, 1953), 17; and especially E. Earle Ellis, "The Silenced Wives of Corinth (1 Cor. 14:34–35)," in *New Testament Textual Criticism: Its Significance for Exegesis: Studies in Honor of Bruce M. Metzger*, ed. Eldon J. Epp and Gordon D. Fee (Oxford: Clarendon, 1981), 213–20, though I disagree with his interpretation of the passage.

36. E. Kähler, *Die Frau in den paulinischer Briefen* (Zürich: Gotthelf-Verlag, 1960), 61; see also Karl Barth, *Church Dogmatics* (Edinburgh: T. and T. Clark, 1966), 3/4:172.

37. Elisabeth Schlüsser Fiorenza, "Women in the Pre-Pauline and Pauline Churches," *Union Seminary Quarterly Review* 33 (1978): 153–66.

38. Ibid., 161.

39. Ibid., 161, citing K. Niederwimmer, *Askese und Mysterium* (Göttingen: Vandenhoeck und Ruprecht, 1975), 115.

40. Fiorenza, "Women in the Pre-Pauline and Pauline Churches," 161.

41. Ibid., 161.

tural.[42] These positions are defended with varying degrees of sophistication. The argument that some of the women were too noisy cannot be taken very seriously;[43] for we must ask why Paul then bans *all* women from talking. And were there *no* noisy men? Nor is it plausible that the women are silenced because they were uneducated; for again, we must ask why Paul does not silence uneducated *people*, not just women. And since Paul's rule operates in *all* the churches (vv. 33b–34), it would be necessary to hold that *all* first-century Christian women were uneducated—which is palpable nonsense.[44]

The more sophisticated approach argues that women were exploiting their emancipation, refusing the ruling of verse 29, and falling into various heresies. The "Law" to which Paul appeals in verse 34 is his own prior ruling, alluded to again in verse 37. Moreover, verse 36 makes it clear that the crucial issue at stake was the word of God: "The Corinthians were claiming to have originated the divine message, with their women giving the lead."[45] The doctrinal error may have been related to 15:12—a claim to have already been raised; and this claim "may well have carried with it—on the part of women—a tacit denial of their married state on the ground that as 'risen ones' they no longer owed marital allegiance."[46]

But none of this is convincing, and some of it is misleading. There is *no* evidence that Paul ever uses the word *law* to refer to his own ruling. There is, as we shall see, a much more natural interpretation of that word. Surely the thrust of verse 36 is the charge that the Corinthians were trying to stand apart from the other churches (see 14:33b). In other words, verse 36 does not *define* the problem but *describes* the attitude that supports it. And what evidence is there here that the women "gave the lead"? The attempt to link this situation with a similar one in 1 Timothy arouses all the same kinds of objections about the exegesis of 1 Timothy. There is a more foundational objection: These approaches are unbearably sexist. They presuppose that there was a major heresy in which one of the following was true:

42. E.g., Richard Boldrey and Joyce Boldrey, *Chauvinist or Feminist? Paul's View of Women* (Grand Rapids: Baker, 1976); J. Keir Howard, "Neither Male nor Female: An Examination of the Status of Women in the New Testament," *Evangelical Quarterly* 55 (1983): 31–42; Martin, *The Spirit and the Congregation*, 86ff.; William F. Orr and James Arthur Walther, *1 Corinthians*, Anchor Bible, vol. 32 (Garden City, N.Y.: Doubleday, 1976).

43. Howard, as in the last note.

44. See especially Stephen B. Clark, *Man and Woman in Christ: An Examination of the Roles of Men and Women in Light of Scriptures and the Social Sciences* (Ann Arbor: Servant, 1980), 185–86.

45. Martin, *The Spirit and the Congregation*, 87.

46. Ibid., 88.

only women were duped, yet Paul brutally silences *all* the women, regardless of whether they were heretics or not; both some men and some women were duped, but Paul silences only the latter, thus proving to be a chauvinist; or Paul was entirely right in his ruling, because *all* the women and *only* women were duped—which perhaps I may be excused for finding hard to believe. Has that ever happened in the history of the church? The truth of the matter is that this passage raises no question of heresy, but if it did, some explanation would have to be given for the fact that Paul's response silences women, not heretics.

Yet another cluster of interpretations attempts to resolve the difficulty by ascribing verses 34–35, or some parts of them, to the position of the Corinthians, perhaps even a quote from their letter.[47] There are many variations to this cluster, but the central purpose of these approaches is to assign the parts that do not seem to cohere with Paul's thought, as enunciated elsewhere, to the Corinthian position Paul is setting out to refute. If the Law (v. 34) means the Old Testament, one must find some place where women are told to be silent; and (we are told) there is not one. Therefore "law" must refer to something else. One common view is that it represents Torah, which in the first instance means "teaching," but was commonly used to cover both Scripture and associated Jewish traditions. So the law, here, refers to Jewish tradition that the Corinthians have unwisely adopted. Verses 34–35 summarize that position. Paul's horrified response is given in verse 36; that the word *only* (μόνους, *monous*) is masculine may suggest that Paul is saying, in effect, "Did the word of God originate with *you men only?*" Moreover, it has been argued that the first word of verse 36, ἤ (*ē*), must not be taken here as a comparative particle ("or"), but as a disjunctive particle, expressing shock and overturning what immediately precedes ("*What!* Did the word of God originate with you men only?").[48]

47. E.g., Walter C. Kaiser, Jr., "Paul, Women, and the Church," *Worldwide Challenge* 3 (1976): 9–12 (which I have discussed in D. A. Carson, *Exegetical Fallacies* [Grand Rapids: Baker, 1984], 38–40); Neil M. Flanagan, "Did Paul Put Down Women in 1 Cor. 14:34–36?" *Biblical Theology Bulletin* 11 (1981): 10–12; Gilbert Bilezekian, *Beyond Sex Roles: A Guide for the Study of Female Roles in the Bible* (Grand Rapids: Baker, 1985), 144–53; Gottfried Fitzer, *"Das Weib schweige in der Gemeinde": Über den unpaulinischen Charakter der Mulier-taceat-Verse in 1. Korinther 14*, Theologische Existenze Heute 10 (Munich: Chr. Kaiser, 1963); J. Murphy-O'Connor, "Interpolations in 1 Corinthians," *Catholic Biblical Quarterly* 48 (1986): 90–92.

48. Chris Ukachukwu Manus, "The Subordination of Women in the Church. 1 Co 14:33b–36 Reconsidered," *Revue Africaine de Théologie* 108 (1984): 183–95; D. W. Odell-Scott, "Let the Women Speak in Church: An Egalitarian Interpretation of 1 Cor 14:33b–36," *Biblical Theology Bulletin* 13 (1983): 90–93.

Again, however, the arguments are not as convincing as they first seem. That the word for "only" is masculine is irrelevant: people considered generically are regularly referred to in the masculine gender in Greek.[49] It is more natural to read verse 36 as addressed to the church, not just to the men in the church. If verses 34–35 constitute a quotation, this "quotation" breaks every one of the formal criteria for the *certain* quotations that I set out in the second chapter. Moreover, although Paul uses the word *law* in several ways, he *never* uses it to refer to Jewish tradition; and the precise expression, "the law says," occurs only twice elsewhere in Paul (Rom. 3:19; 1 Cor. 9:8), both with reference to the Old Testament law. Although it is true that the first word in verse 36 is probably a disjunctive particle, nevertheless the proffered explanation does not follow. Odell-Scott and Manus understand verses 33b–35 as the proposition against which the disjunctive "what!" responds. But more likely verse 36 is responding to that attitude in the church that thinks it can act independently from the rest of the Christian churches (vv. 33b–34).

There is in addition a variety of interpretations that cut more or less independent swathes. For instance, Ellis sees the restriction applied to wives only, in the light of the distinctions in roles he holds Paul expects to be maintained in the Christian home.[50] Perhaps these women were questioning their husbands' prophecies, provoking some very embarrassing situations. But in much of the ancient world, marriage for women meant an *improvement* in freedom and social stature. Even if these verses deal primarily with the *married* woman, I suspect both Paul and his readers would assume the a fortiori argument: if married women are enjoined to be silent, then how much more the single ones? Besides, does Ellis really think that Christian women enjoyed full freedom and perfect egalitarianism in function in the church as long as they were single, and then from the day of their marriage onward became silent for fear of offending the husbands to whom they were to submit? These considerations effectively dismiss those interpretations that admit Paul insists on certain role distinctions between

49. It is astonishing to be told that the masculine plural μόνους *(monous)* "requires some such paraphrase as 'you fellows only' " (so Charles H. Talbert, "Paul's Understanding of the Holy Spirit: The Evidence of 1 Corinthians 12–14," in *Perspectives on the New Testament: Studies in Honor of Frank Stagg*, ed. Charles H. Talbert [Macon, Ga.: Mercer University Press, 1985], 106).

50. Ellis, "Silenced Wives." For yet another interpretation, see Robert J. Karris, "Women in the Pauline Assembly: To prophesy [1 Cor 11,5] but not to speak [14,34]?" in *Women Priests: A Catholic Commentary on the Vatican Declaration*, ed. Leonard Swidler and Arlene Swidler (New York: Paulist, 1977), 205–8.

the sexes, but that limits such distinctions to the home, denying they have any bearing on the church.

All of these interpretations share another decisive weakness. They do not adequately explain why these words should be found here in this context, dealing with prophecy and tongues. After all, Paul has not yet abandoned the subject (as is clear from vv. 39–40). If we accept the text as it stands, we must ask why Paul seems to interrupt the flow of his thought to add this little unrelated section into his chapter.

Another interpretation has been set out by various writers and meets the objections put to it. The view has been ably defended elsewhere;[51] I can merely sketch it in here. Paul has been requiring that the church in Corinth carefully weigh the prophecies presented to it. Women, of course, may participate in such prophesyings: that was established in chapter 11. Paul's point here, however, is that they may *not* participate in the oral weighing of such prophecies. That is not permitted in the churches. In that connection, they are not allowed to speak—"as the Law says." Apparently in sympathy with the view that makes this appeal to "law" a feature of the *Corinthian* position, Evans suggests that to take this as *Paul's* appeal to law sounds "strangely unlike" him.[52] That is a strange assessment, since Paul in this chapter has already appealed once to "the law" (see 14:21), by which he means the Old Testament Scriptures. By this clause, Paul is probably not refer-ring to Genesis 3:16, as many suggest,[53] but to the creation order in Genesis 2:20b–24,[54] for it is to that Scripture that Paul explicitly turns on two other occasions when he discusses female roles (1 Cor. 11:8, 9; 1 Tim. 2:13). The passage from Genesis 2 does not enjoin silence, but it suggests that because man was made first and woman was made for man, a pattern has been laid down regarding the roles the two play. Paul understands from this creation order that woman is to be subject to man—or at least that wife is to be subject to husband. In the context of the Corinthian weighing of prophecies, such submission could not be preserved if the wives participated: the first husband who uttered a prophecy would precipitate the problem. More broadly, a strong case can be made that Paul refused to permit any woman to

51. M. E. Thrall, *I and II Corinthians* (Cambridge: Cambridge University Press, 1965); James B. Hurley, *Man and Woman in Biblical Perspective* (Grand Rapids: Zondervan, 1981), 185–94; Grudem, *Gift of Prophecy*, 245–55; see W. J. Dumbrell, "The Role of Women—A Reconsideration of the Biblical Evidence," *Interchange* 21 (1977): 14–22.

52. Mary J. Evans, *Woman in the Bible* (Downers Grove: Inter-Varsity, 1983), 95.

53. E.g., R. Banks, "Paul and Women's Liberation," *Interchange* 18 (1976): 100; and then he points out that this is not so much a command as a statement of the consequences of the first couple's sin.

54. See Hurley, *Man and Woman in Biblical Perspective*, 192.

enjoy a church-recognized teaching authority over men (1 Tim. 2:11ff.);[55] and the careful weighing of prophecies falls under that magisterial function. This does not mean that women should not learn: let them ask their husbands about various aspects of these prophecies, once they return home. Why should the Corinthians buck not only the practice of all the churches (v. 33b) but also the Scriptures themselves (v. 36)? Are they so enamored with the revelations that they have received that they dare to pit them against the authentic deposit found in Scripture and in the apostolic tradition? And if they feel they are merely interpreting that tradition under the promptings of the Spirit, are they not troubled to see that all the churches have translated the same texts, and the same gospel, into quite different ecclesiastical practices? Are you the only people the word of God has reached (see v. 36b)?[56]

Several final observations on this interpretation may prove helpful. First, the major objection is that it seems inconsistent for Paul to permit women to prophesy, and then to forbid them from weighing prophecies. But the objection carries little weight *provided* the view of prophecy I am outlining is understood to be the one with which Paul operated. It constitutes a problem *only* if prophecy has the same authority status that the great writing prophets of the Old Testament enjoyed (whether or not such authority was immediately recognized). In certain respects, then, it is proper for Paul to elevate teaching above prophecy, especially if the teaching is considered part of the nonnegotiable apostolic deposit that serves in part as one of the touchstones enabling the congregation to weigh the prophecies granted to the church, and especially if the prophecies themselves, unlike the apostolic deposit, are subject to ecclesiastical appraisal. This does not mean, of course, that the utterances of any particular teacher need not be verified: I am not saying that prophecy must be evaluated, but teaching need not be. The New Testament includes too many passages that encourage the church to take responsibility for evaluating teachers and teaching. It *does* mean that prophecy cannot escape such evaluation; and it presupposes that there is a deposit of apostolic teaching, a given content, that is nonnegotiable and can serve as the criterion both of further teaching and of prophecy. Second, this interpretation

---

55. Ibid.; Clark, *Man and Woman in Christ;* Douglas J. Moo, "1 Timothy 2:11–15: Meaning and Significance," *Trinity Journal* 1 (1980): 62–83; idem, "The Interpretation of 1 Timothy 2:11–15: A Rejoinder," *Trinity Journal* 2 (1981): 198–222.

56. Verse 36 must not be understood to be addressed to women only: the masculine μόνους *(monous)* eliminates such a view. The entire Corinthian *church* is being held responsible for the deviations Paul disapproves, as is suggested already by the contrast between Corinthian *church* practice and that of other *churches* (v. 33b—assuming this clause is to be read with vv. 34–36).

fits the flow of chapter 14. Although the focus in the second part of the chapter is still on tongues and prophecy, it is more closely related to the order the church must maintain in the enjoyment of those grace-gifts. Verses 33b–36 fall happily under that description. The immediately preceding verses deal with the evaluation of prophets; these verses (vv. 33b–36) further refine that discussion. The general topic of 1 Corinthians 12–14 has not been abandoned, as the closing verses of chapter 14 demonstrate. There is no other interpretation of these disputed verses that so neatly fits the flow of the argument. Third, this is not all the Bible has to say about relationships between men and women in Christ. I have said nothing, for instance, about the command for men to love their wives even as Christ loved the church—an exquisitely high standard characterized by unqualified self-giving. Nor have I listed the many things Paul expects Christian women to do. Yet, fourth, if this interpretation is correct, and there are some role distinctions between men and women to be observed, it is essential to recognize that this teaching is for our good, not for our enslavement.

Warning (14:37–38)

Part of the answer to the questions in the preceding verse (36) must be something like: No, we admit that the word of God first came to us through you; *you* first preached it to us.[57] Verse 37 then follows naturally with a focus on apostolic authority, but this is so elevated that it stands a quantum leap above that of the prophets at Corinth. Indeed, Paul can actually make the acceptance of the authority of what he writes a necessary criterion of the validity of all claims to spiritual giftedness, including prophecy.

Several observations on the text will help to clarify the thrust of Paul's claim.

First, the words rendered "what I am writing to you" are a translation of a *plural* expression, "*the matters* about which I am writing to you" or the like. This strongly suggests that Paul has in mind not the single injunction dealing with the silence of women, but everything he has said in this epistle[58]—and principally, beyond. But even if one were to decide that the relative pronoun has exclusive reference to

57. See James B. Hurley, "Did Paul Require Veils or the Silence of Women? A Consideration of I Cor. 11:2–16 and I Cor. 14:33b–36," *Westminster Theological Journal* 35 (1972–73): 218.
58. See Aune, *Prophecy*, 257–58, who suggests the reference is to what Paul has said in chap. 14; Robertson and Plummer, *Corinthians*, who think the entire epistle is in view, but with no binding implications for the contemporary church, since Paul has only the Corinthian church in mind.

chapters 12–14, it is hard to imagine that Paul himself understood chapters 1–11 to be *less* authoritative.

Second, the textual variant—whether we should render it "is of the Lord" or "is the Lord's command"—has little bearing on the authority claim Paul is making. The latter is marginally more likely; but that means the use of "command" (ἐντολή, *entolē*) is a little different from that in 1 Corinthians 7, where "the Lord's command" refers to what Jesus taught in the days of his flesh. Paul is not making that claim here: he simply means that what he has been writing is backed by the authority of the risen Christ himself. This shows that "the Lord's command" was not a stereotyped expression, but could vary in force according to context.

Third, the word *Lord* is placed in an emphatic position. Paul is therefore associating submission to what he writes with submission to the Lord. Not to submit to what the apostle writes is thus to deny the lordship of Jesus, which is the Christian's central confession as stipulated at the beginning of these three chapters (12:3). It is hard to resist seeing an *inclusio* (a figure of speech in which everything in these three chapters, sandwiched between two strong references to the lordship of Jesus, must be read in the light of that lordship). As we shall see in a moment, there are other hints that Paul is harking back to 12:1–3 and drawing his argument to a close.[59]

Fourth, that Paul's authority should be placed so decisively above that of the prophets has obvious bearing on our understanding of prophecy in Corinth. Paul clearly believes that prophecy is revelatory (see v. 30); equally clearly, he does not conclude on this ground that the authority of the prophets is therefore absolute. Rather, he holds that, principally, the prophetic word "must at every point agree with the apostolic deposit or it is to be rejected."[60] I shall try to wrestle a little more with the notion of "revelation" in the next chapter, but clearly this principle must go some way to stilling the alarms of contemporary noncharismatics who detect in any revelatory gift of prophecy a threat to the apostolic deposit, and thus to Scripture itself. The presupposition seems to be that if a prophecy is in any sense revelatory, it must be true, and thus authoritative—and therefore what is there to prevent a contemporary "prophet" from, say, annulling var-

---

59. In addition, this section also becomes tightly tied to chap. 13, if we follow Nils Johansson, "I Cor. xiii and I Cor. xiv," *New Testament Studies* 10 (1963–64): 383–92, who, admittedly too strongly, argues that Paul so understands Christ as the very manifestation of ἀγάπη *(agapē)* in chap. 13 that "the Lord's command" becomes equivalent to "love's command."

60. George Mallone, *Those Controversial Gifts* (Downers Grove: Inter-Varsity, 1983), 39.

ious components of the new covenant in much the same way that the New Testament writers claim to fulfill and therefore transcend certain aspects of the old covenant? But the remarkable fact is that Paul takes the prophecy *of his own day* to be in some sense revelatory (14:30) and yet to have less authority than his own written word. One cannot fail to perceive that those interpretations of New Testament prophecy that insist it enjoys the same authority status as Old Testament canonical prophecy see in the phenomenon a great deal more than the apostle himself allows. Conversely, of course, this verse presupposes not only considerable authority vested in the apostle Paul, but his self-conscious awareness of it. Some of the protestations over the obscurity of this verse are located, I think, in the failure to recognize this fact.[61]

Fifth, the use of πνευματικός *(pneumatikos)* is striking: literally, "If anybody thinks he is a prophet or *a spiritual*"—that is, a spiritual person, a pneumatic. The three chapters began with consideration of what spirituality consists in (see discussion of 12:1–3 in my first chapter). Now that Paul has concluded his arguments, he can say not only that the prophet will recognize the authority of his remarks, but also that the spiritual person, the person with the Holy Spirit, will do so. Here, then, is a foundational test of the Spirit's presence, of "spirituality" if you like: submission to the apostolic writings, not simply because they are the writings of an apostle, but because they are the *Lord's* command, and therefore tied irrevocably to the believer's confession, "Jesus is Lord!" (12:1–3).

Sixth, this apostolic authority grounds the open threat of verse 38. The initial clause does not mean "if he is ignorant of this," despite the verbal similarity to 12:1,[62] for after three chapters of exposition, Paul may reasonably expect his readers are not *ignorant* of what he has to say. What he fears, rather, is that some may *ignore* what he has to say. If anyone succumbs to that temptation, Paul warns, "he himself will be ignored [sc., by God]." That, surely, is the severity of the threat—not, with some variant readings that try to soften the thrust, "let him not be recognized [i.e., by the congregation]," or still less "he himself will be ignored [sc., by the congregation]."[63] The latter two are inadequate as a threat in the light of the immense claims Paul has made,

---

61. E.g., Conzelmann, whose failure to grasp this point is startling: "It is not clear how Paul grounds his assertion that his exposition is a command of the Lord himself: with the help of the intermediate idea that everything that is generally valid in the church is a command of the Lord? Yet this idea is better suited to the interpolation than to Paul, and is suggested by it. Is Paul himself speaking as a prophet, with the same authority as accrues to the judicial statement in v. 38?"

62. I.e., εἰ δέ τις ἀγνοεῖ, ἀγνοεῖται (v. 38) calls to mind οὐ θέλω ὑμᾶς ἀγνοεῖν (12:1).

63. C. K. Barrett, *The First Epistle to the Corinthians*, 2d ed. (London: Black, 1971).

as Hemphill rightly points out.[64] The Corinthians may pursue their own self-interested definitions of what is spiritual, and run the risk of being ignored *by God;* or they may recognize afresh that their confession of Jesus as Lord is not only the significant criterion of the Spirit's presence (12:1–3) but something that can be tested by enthusiastic obedience to that Lord's commands, mediated through the apostle.

Summary (14:39–40)

Paul wraps up.[65] So far as the competing claims of prophecy and the gift of tongues are concerned, prophecy is heartily encouraged, and tongues are not to be forbidden.

Some time ago, a pastor in England discussed some of these matters with a well-known charismatic clergyman. The charismatic, doubtless thinking of Paul's words, "Do not forbid speaking in tongues," asked my friend what he would do if someone began to speak in tongues at one of the meetings of the church he served. The pastor replied, "I'd allow the tongues-speaker to finish, and if there were an interpretation immediately forthcoming, and no proselytizing in the ensuing weeks, I'd have no objection."

Then he paused, and asked in return, "But what would you do if there were *no* public tongues-speaking in your church for six months or so?"

"Ah," replied the charismatic, "I'd be devastated."

"There is the difference between us," the pastor replied; "for you think tongues-speaking is indispensable. I see it as dispensable, but not forbidden." And that, surely, is Paul's distinction.

Of course, more can be said from a pastoral point of view; and I shall offer a few practical suggestions in the final chapter. It is clear that Paul wants the public meetings of the church to be conducted

64. K. S. Hemphill, "The Pauline Concept of Charisma: A Situational and Developmental Approach" (Ph.D. diss., Cambridge University, 1976), 159. See also Lietzmann and Kümmel, *An die Korinther I. II;* J. Moffatt, *The First Epistle of Paul to the Corinthians* (London: Hodder and Stoughton, 1934); Thomas Charles Edwards, *A Commentary on the First Epistle to the Corinthians*, 4th ed. (London: Hodder and Stoughton, 1903), and F. W. Grosheide, *Commentary on the First Epistle to the Corinthians* (Grand Rapids: Eerdmans, 1953). This threat of course fits the description of what Ernst Käsemann, *New Testament Questions*, 66–81, calls "sentences of holy law"; but the category is somewhat problematic. See Robert M. Grant, " 'Holy Law' in Paul and Ignatius," in *The Living Text: Studies in Honor of Ernest W. Saunders*, ed. Dennis E. Groh and Paul K. Jewett (Lanham, Md.: University Press of America, 1985), 65–71.

65. Martin's view (*The Spirit and the Congregation*, 75–76), that once again we have a quotation from the Corinthians' letter to Paul, is adequately discussed in the second chapter.

"in a fitting and orderly way" (v. 40); and for him that means not less than the observance of the rules he has enunciated in the second half of chapter 14. "For God is not a God of disorder but of peace" (14:33a).

Concluding Reflections

Before leaving chapter 14, I must say more about first-century practices when the church gathered together. In part, these reflections are tangential to this discussion, but because chapter 14 preserves a glimpse of what went on, or what Paul expected to go on, in at least one first-century church, and because these verses have fueled debate over patterns of corporate worship, a few remarks may not be entirely out of order.

Let Schweizer set the stage: "It is completely foreign to the New Testament," he writes, "to split the Christian community into one speaker and a silent body of listeners."[66] The same point has been made by many more popular writers:[67] chapter 14 reflects a church service where there is dynamic interplay, sharing, give and take—*not* detailed liturgy climaxed by lengthy exposition delivered by one properly recognized authority.

There are immense complexities to this subject that cannot be probed here (such as the role and number of elders in the early church, the ways in which the pastoral Epistles should be related to 1 Corinthians, and much more). If I may be forgiven for offering suggestions without taking time to substantiate their worth, three might be put forward. (1) These verses (especially 1 Cor. 14:26ff.) do not describe *all* that should take place in every meeting of the church. Nothing is mentioned, for instance, of corporate prayer or reading of Scripture, both of which are mentioned elsewhere (1 Cor. 14:16; 1 Tim 4:13 respectively). Moreover, if the "word of instruction" (14:26) is (as seems likely) equivalent to the "word of knowledge" or "word of wisdom" identified in chapter 12, then there is nothing here that describes regular teaching ministry—even though regular teaching of the apostolic tradition is one of the distinguishing characteristics of elders. This focus on the apostolic tradition can be traced back to the earliest days of the church (see Acts 2:42). When was it communicated or explicated if not when the church met together? Moreover, if 1 Corinthians 14:26ff. is taken

---

66. Eduard Schweizer, "Worship in the New Testament," *The Reformed and Presbyterian World* 24 (1957): 205; reprinted in *Neotestamentica: German and English Essays 1951–63* (Zürich: Zwingli, 1963), 295.

67. E.g., Jon Zens, "Building up the Body—One Man or One Another?" *Baptist Reformation Review* 10/2 (1981): 10–29; Robert Banks, *Paul's Idea of Community* (Grand Rapids: Eerdmans, 1980).

as an exhaustive list of the activities carried out in Corinthian public meetings, when did the Corinthians gather for the Lord's Supper (see 11:17ff.)? We are forced to recognize that verses 26ff. do not purport to tell us everything that went on in the Corinthian assembly, but, as seems obvious on the face of it, only what restrictions Paul lays out for the Corinthians so far as the participatory χαρίσματα *(charismata)* are concerned.[68] (2) Those who do not think that the account of Paul's appointment of elders on the return swing of the first missionary journey (Acts 13–14) is anachronistic recognize that there were elders operating in the Pauline churches virtually from their inception; and we must ask what these elders were doing. We must similarly ask when and where in the church's life those who were recognized teachers (as in 12:28) discharged their gifts. The approach of Schweizer, at first attractive, suddenly seems a trifle reductionistic. (3) I suspect that there is biblical warrant for thinking, on somewhat more remote grounds, that there were aspects of corporate worship characterized by a great deal of spontaneity, Spirit-led sharing, mutual edification, and the like, and other aspects characterized by solemnity, formal reading, and explication of the Scriptures already given, enunciation of apostolic truth, and corporate prayers and singing. So far as our practices today are concerned, this means we should give more thought to developing in our own contexts *both* trends found in the biblical evidence. Even if we cannot satisfy both emphases in every service, the least we must do is develop structures in which both emphases are worked out in proper proportion in the total life of the church.

Beyond these comments I must not venture.[69] It is enough to remark that Paul's chief aim in these verses is not to lay out an exhaustive list of necessary ingredients in corporate worship, but to insist that the unleashed power of the Holy Spirit characteristic of this new age must be exercised in a framework of order, intelligibility, appropriateness, seemliness, dignity, peace. For that is the nature of the God whom we worship.

68. It is a rather startling selectivity in some noncharismatic groups that appeals to 14:26ff. to justify their ad hoc worship patterns while staunchly refusing to be touched in any way by charismatic (in the modern sense) phenomena.

69. For an extended discussion of the congregational worship reflected in these verses, see James D. G. Dunn, "The Responsible Congregation (1 Co 14,26–40)," in *Charisma und Agape (1 Ko 12–14)*, P. Benoit et al., eds. (Rome: St. Paul vor den Mauern, 1983), 201–69, which includes reports of extensive oral interaction with several New Testament scholars.

5

Unleashed Power and the Constraints of Discipline: Toward a Theology of Spiritual Gifts

In many ways this chapter has been the most difficult to prepare. I am no longer constrained by a single, sustained text, but must pick and choose what seems most important to the topic; and I must articulate conclusions without adequate space to justify them. My only excuse is that this sort of preliminary synthesis seems preferable to leaving large numbers of loose strands dangling.

I hasten to add that the subtitle of this final chapter, "Toward a

Theology of Spiritual Gifts," is unforgivably presumptuous. The truth of the matter is that what you read will be long on the "toward" and short on the "theology." What I propose to offer you are reflections on a variety of topics related to 1 Corinthians 12–14, in a final bid to bring integration to the four preceding chapters and to link the results to broader streams of biblical thought and contemporary experience.

Reflections on Tongues, Miracles, and the Baptism in the Spirit in Acts

I shall begin with some remarks on each of the four crucial passages in Acts, and then offer some observations of a more general kind.

Acts 2

It must be insisted that in Luke's description of the utterances on the day of Pentecost we are dealing with xenoglossia—real, human languages never learned by the speakers. Williams's summary of what went on cannot easily be squared with the text: he claims "that sounds uttered by the speakers seemed to some Jewish hearers as identifiable words in languages dimly recalled. It is even possible that interspersed among inarticulate utterances would be actual identifiable words. This occurs sometimes in modern glossolalia."[1] This will not do. We saw in the third chapter that the word for "tongue" (γλῶσσα, *glōssa*) cannot easily be reduced in meaning to free verbalization bearing no cognitive content; and Luke attests that the hearers on the day of Pentecost asked in amazement how they could hear distinctive utterances (lit.) in their own "dialects" (τῇ ᾿ιδί α διαλέκτῳ, *tē idia dialektō*, 2:8). What they heard was *not* an occasional word accidentally intruded into a stream of lexical gibberish, a mere statistical inevitability, but "the wonders of God" (2:11). These wonders were enunciated in the languages of recognized linguistic groups (Parthians, Medes, Elamites). It goes beyond the text to argue that this was a miracle of hearing rather than one of speech,[2] for Luke's purpose is to associate the descent of the Spirit with the Spirit's activity *among the believers*, not to postulate a miracle of the Spirit *among those who were still unbelievers*.[3]

---

1. Cyril G. Williams, *Tongues of the Spirit: A Study of Pentecostal Glossolalia and Related Phenomena* (Cardiff: University of Wales, 1981), 36.

2. See M. M. B. Turner, "Spiritual Gifts Then and Now," *Vox Evangelica* 15 (1985): 17; J. Kremer, *Pfingstbericht und Pfingstgeschehen: Eine exegetische Untersuchung zu Apg.2.1–13* (Stuttgart: KBW, 1973): 120–26.

3. I cannot here discuss the position of those who argue that regardless of what Luke means, he is so removed from the historical reality that his report cannot seriously be taken as a reliable record of what took place. For the most recent reflection on this stance, see Christopher Forbes, "Glossolalia in Early Christianity" (unpublished paper, Macquarie University, 1985), 6–8.

What, then, of the charge of drunkenness (2:13)? Does this not suggest that many people heard only gibberish, and not real languages at all? Is this not an implicit support of glossolalia, not xenoglossia?[4] Such a conclusion would be premature. After all, if three thousand people repented and were baptized after Peter's sermon (2:41), presumably the crowd before which the believers were speaking in tongues was many times larger. No one could hear *every* tongue; presumably no single person was so incredibly well-educated as to have been able to identify every tongue, even if each tongue had been heard in turn.[5] Some may not have heard their own tongue, but someone else's, and dismissed the entire episode without putting in the energy to walk around and see if there was a tongue that *was* recognizable. It has also been suggested, with some plausibility, that the charge of drunkenness may have emerged from the resident Aramaic-speaking Jews who did not recognize *any* of the languages being spoken and who thus found *nothing* intelligible in the utterances.[6] Turner wisely comments, "Of course one should not try artificially to harmonize Luke's details—but nor should one unnecessarily make a fool of him when one can plausibly explain how he may have viewed the scene."[7]

Judging from the flow of the Book of Acts, one cannot seriously doubt that this experience of the Spirit on the day of Pentecost is presented by Luke as the fulfillment of the prophecy by John the Baptist: after him would come the one who would baptize in the Holy Spirit (Matt. 3:11; Mark 1:8; Luke 3:16; John 1:33). That promise is taken up by the resurrected Christ in Acts 1:5, where it serves as the basis for his injunction to remain in Jerusalem until the gift of the Spirit is given. Acts 2 must be read in that light. There are two entailments. First, it is gratuitous for Shallis to argue that what Luke describes in Acts 2 is not the baptism in the Spirit (since that language is not specifically used in Acts 2) but the filling of the Spirit.[8] Shallis compounds an argument from silence with overspecification of the semantic range of "baptism in the Spirit" and "filling with the Spirit," and with a failure to grasp the flow of Luke's argument. Second, and

4. See Charles R. Smith, *Tongues in Biblical Perspective*, 2d ed. (Winona Lake, Ind.: BMH, 1973), 25–40.

5. See I. Howard Marshall, *Acts* (Leicester: Inter-Varsity, 1980), 70–71.

6. E.g., R. H. Gundry, " 'Ecstatic Utterance' (N.E.B.)?" *Journal of Theological Studies* 17 (1966): 304; Thomas R. Edgar, *Miraculous Gifts: Are They for Today?* (Neptune, N.J.: Loizeaux, 1983), 126; Klaus Haacker, "Das Pfingstwunder als exegetisches Problem," in *Verborum Veritas: Festschrift für G. Stälin*, ed. Otto Böcher and Klaus Haacker (Wuppertal: Brockhaus, 1970), 125–31.

7. Turner, "Spiritual Gifts Then and Now," 17.

8. Ralph Shallis, *Le miracle de l'Esprit* (Fontenay-sous-Bois, France: Editions Telos, 1977), 250–51.

more important, the coming of the Spirit at Pentecost is thus tightly tied to a redemptive-historical appointment. What further bearing it may have on individual Christian experience we shall shortly try to explore. There is, however, no basis in the command to wait for the gift of the Father (in Acts 1:4) to justify contemporary, postconversion tarrying experiences in anticipation of a personal Pentecost. It is striking that of the two dozen or more conversions mentioned in Acts after this point, there is no further exhortation to wait for the gift of the Spirit. In short, Pentecost in Luke's perspective is first of all a climactic salvation-historical event.

Luke's salvation-historical focus is also attested by his handling of the prophecy from Joel (Acts 2:16–21). Joel had predicted that "in the last days" certain things would take place in connection with the eschatological pouring out of the Spirit on all people (see Acts 2:17); and, says Peter, referring to the manifestations of the Spirit occurring all around him, "this is what was spoken by the prophet Joel" (2:16). There may or may not then be further implications about how believers continue to show the Spirit throughout these last days: that could be deduced only from a further examination of how Luke and other New Testament writers treat this theme. Certainly Luke's emphasis in Acts 2 is not on paradigms for personal experience but on the fulfillment of prophecy. The salvation-historical argument that seeks to explain Pentecost in terms of what the prophets said, and therefore in terms of identifying Jesus as the promised Messiah (2:22ff.), receives the major part of the stress.[9] Indeed, Evans has drawn attention to numerous parallels between Joel and Acts 2 (compare Joel 1:2, 3, 5 and Acts 2:14b, 15a, 22a, 37a, 39a, 40c), suggesting that Luke grasped a very tight connection between their Pentecost experience and the "prophetic narrative" of the prophet.[10]

It is most striking, as Guy points out,[11] that Peter understands the *tongues* phenomena to be the fulfillment of what Joel says regarding *prophecy:*

        " 'Your sons and daughters will prophesy,

---

9. See J. I. Packer, *Keep in Step with the Spirit* (Leicester: Inter-Varsity; Old Tappan, N.J.: Revell, 1984), 205ff.; and more generally, Robert Banks and Geoffrey Moon, "Speaking in Tongues: A Survey of the New Testament Evidence," *Churchman* 80 (1966): 278–94.

10. Craig A. Evans, "The Prophetic Setting of the Pentecost Sermon," *Zeitschrift für die neutestamentliche Wissenschaft* 74 (1983): 148–50.

11. H. A. Guy, *New Testament Prophecy: Its Origin and Significance* (London: Epworth, 1947), 91. See also Forbes, "Glossolalia in Early Christianity," 9–11; David E. Aune, *Prophecy in Early Christianity and the Ancient Mediterranean World* (Grand Rapids: Eerdmans, 1983), 199.

your young men will see visions,
your old men will dream dreams.
Even on my servants, both men and women,
I will pour out my Spirit in those days,
and they will prophesy.' " [2:17b–18]

In other words, prophecy is an expression that embraces tongues; or, put more generally, prophecy, tongues, revelatory dreams, and visions are all lumped together in a single category as the expected attestation that the Spirit has been poured out. So far as the New Testament evidence is concerned, the only one to make a sharp distinction between prophecy and tongues is Paul; and for him, the crucial factor in that distinction is not the source of the gift or the nature of the gift, but the intelligibility and corresponding public usefulness of the gift. That factor could not have been introduced in Acts 2, precisely because these tongues were understood; that is, they were intelligible without some further gift of interpretation.

What this does is again attest the broad semantic range of "prophecy," a point I shall develop further. Moreover, if this judgment is right, it suggests that Luke was not particularly interested in identifying tongues, *as opposed to prophecy*, as the crucial, identifying sign of the baptism in the Holy Spirit. It may even be that Luke understood several manifestations of the Holy Spirit to be appropriate fulfillments of Joel, each attesting in its own way that the blessed Holy Spirit, the Spirit of prophecy, had been poured out.

There is no evidence that the three thousand converts (2:41) who accepted Peter's message and were baptized actually spoke in tongues. The "all of them" (2:4) who did were either the apostles (1:26) or, more likely, all the first believers who were gathered together in one place (2:1) when the Spirit descended.

Of these, it appears that all spoke in tongues, for 2:4 reads (in the NIV), "All of them [i.e., those believers gathered at the one place—presumably the 120 or so?] were filled with the Holy Spirit and began to speak in other tongues as the Spirit enabled them." On this basis, even the more cautious charismatics tend to infer too much. For example, one popular writer, referring to this verse, comments: "I believe, although there is no specific teaching on this, that it would be considered the norm in the New Testament experience for the candidate for Baptism of the Holy Spirit to speak another language when this blessing came upon him."[12]

The reasons this inference does not stand up are several. First, as

12. Pat Robertson, *My Prayer for You* (Old Tappan, N.J.: Revell, 1977), 32.

a friend has pointed out to me,[13] it is just possible that verse 4 is not saying quite so much. We may compare 2:44ff.: there we are told that "all the believers were together and had everything in common. Selling their possessions and goods . . ."—which might lead the unwary to think that *every* believer sold *everything*, even though by verse 44 we are told that they met in *their* homes, and in Acts 5 Peter assumes that each believer has the right to give or not give as much or as little as he or she wished. This presumably means that not everyone sold everything after all, even if those who retained their homes (for instance) were very generous with them. In other words, the "all" in 2:44 may not be exhaustive *and distributed to the second verb*. Similarly in 2:4: it is possible that the "all" who were filled with the Holy Spirit did not *all* begin to speak in tongues: rather, they—all of them comprehensively, but not necessarily individually—began to speak in tongues, as the Holy Spirit enabled them. Nevertheless in my judgment it is considerably more likely that all who were filled with the Spirit also spoke in tongues on that first Christian Pentecost: note the distributive "each" in the preceding verse. I mention this first point simply to warn against milking texts for what *may* not be there.

Second, even if this text affirms that all who were filled with the Spirit spoke in tongues (as I think it does), it does not follow that this is the normative New Testament stance. We have already seen that Paul flatly denies that all speak in tongues (1 Cor. 12; see discussion in the first chapter).

Third, if this verse is made normative for all Christian experience, even though it stands without close parallel in the New Testament, it seems extraordinarily arbitrary *not* to see verses 2–3 as *equally* normative: there ought to be the sound of a mighty, rushing wind, and separated tongues of fire resting on each Spirit-filled person.

Fourth, and of greater importance, this individualistic interpretation fails to wrestle with the centrality of Luke's focus on salvation history. Put another way, we must ask if *Luke* saw in the experience of these verses a paradigm for attesting what it means to be filled with the Spirit. That must be argued from his treatment of this and related themes, not merely presupposed.

Although these tongues were real, human languages and communicated cognitive messages, it is by no means clear that such messages were essentially evangelistic. We are told the crowds heard the tongues-speakers declaring "the wonders of God" (2:11; τὰ μεγαλεῖα τοῦ θεοῦ, *ta megaleia tou theou*). The verbal form of the same expression occurs in 10:46 (καὶ μεγαλυνόντων τὸν θεόν, *kai megalynontōn ton theon*) and 19:17 (καὶ ἐμεγαλύνετο τὸ ὄνομα τοῦ κυρίου Ἰησοῦ, *kai emegalyneto*

13. Rev. Ken Hall, in private correspondence, dated 21 June 1985.

to onoma tou kuriou Iēsou), where praise is in view, not evangelism per se. Similarly in chapter 2 the people hear praise, and in their own languages, but this generates questions (sympathetic and otherwise), not conversions. It is Peter's *preaching*, presumably in Aramaic, that brings about the thousands of conversions;[14] the tongues themselves, I suppose, constitute what modern jargon would call preevangelism.

This is in line with one feature of tongues in 1 Corinthians 12–14, and out of step with another characteristic of tongues in those chapters. It is in line with the fact that tongues in 1 Corinthians 14 are understood to be first and foremost *address to God* (1 Cor. 14:2), a gift used in prayer (14:14). The crowds hear the believers on the day of Pentecost praising God: the church needs to learn afresh the compelling power of uninhibited praise, even as a kind of indirect witness to unbelievers who are looking on. But tongues in Acts 2 are *un*like those in 1 Corinthians 12–14 in that unbelievers understand them, even without any display of the gift of interpretation. But this is the only place in the New Testament where they serve that function. What is clear, I think, is that noncharismatics who attempt to make the evangelistic use of tongues their normative and exclusive purpose are doubly wrong: tongues are not primarily evangelistic even in Acts 2, and in any case this is the only passage where uninterpreted tongues are even understood by unbelievers.

If only the initial circle of believers actually spoke in tongues on that first Christian Pentecost, then there is no direct evidence that establishes the connection between water baptism and Spirit baptism. Acts 2:41, on any interpretation of it,[15] is simply irrelevant, as it has to do with the three thousand, not with the original group. The reception of the Holy Spirit promised by Peter (2:38) and presumably received by the three thousand was not, so far as we are told, attested by tongues. *Presumably* the initial group had already undergone baptism; but there is no explicit evidence. One might reasonably conclude that Luke is not particularly concerned to establish a proper order among baptism, faith, and baptism in the Holy Spirit.

Acts 8

This passage is remarkable in that the Samaritans are said to believe the gospel of the kingdom that Philip preaches, and then they are

14. See H. Horton, *The Gifts of the Spirit* (Springfield, Mo.: Gospel Publishing, 1975), 152; Michael Green, *I Believe in the Holy Spirit* (Grand Rapids: Eerdmans, 1975), 164–65.

15. Exercising considerable restraint, I shall refrain from commenting here on the exact nature and significance of Christian baptism; for my sole purpose in this and related discussions farther on is to demonstrate that Luke does not attempt to lay out a programmatic order among baptism, faith, and baptism in the Holy Spirit.

baptized (8:12); yet they do not receive the Holy Spirit until Peter and John travel to Samaria and lay their hands on them (8:17). The text does not explicitly say that this reception of the Spirit was attested by tongues, but it seems likely, since Simon must have witnessed some kind of powerful phenomenon to prompt him to offer money to the apostles. The crucial question, in the context of the contemporary debate between charismatics and noncharismatics, is whether the Samaritans were Christians once they had believed Philip's message and been baptized. If so, a prima facie case can be made for the reception of the Spirit as a second stage experience, at least potentially paradigmatic.

Some noncharismatics, including Dunn and Hoekema, strongly urge that the Samaritans were *not* converted until the Holy Spirit came upon them.[16] Indeed, they say, that is precisely Luke's point: no one is genuinely saved *until* the Holy Spirit is received. But it has been ably pointed out, in some detail, that the language of belief and baptism, applicable to the Samaritans *before* the Holy Spirit descends on them, is regular Lukan terminology for becoming a Christian. There is not space to offer a detailed report of the debate;[17] but in my judgment the attempt to make Luke say the Samaritans were not believers until they received the Holy Spirit is not true to Luke's purposes.

There is nevertheless considerable difficulty with the typology that treats Acts 8 as normative for individualizing Christian experience: first faith and baptism, and subsequently a special enduement of the Holy Spirit. The problem in part is that the debate has been cast in simple antitheses: either the charismatic insistence that the Samaritans were converted immediately upon hearing is correct, or the noncharismatic insistence that the Samaritans were not converted until after they had received the Spirit is correct. But we are not limited to those alternatives. It is far from clear, judging from the diversity of his approaches (see Acts 2:38ff.; 8:12ff.; 10:44–48) that Luke is particularly interested in the question of normative order of faith, water rite, experience of the Holy Spirit, and the like.

16. James D. G. Dunn, *Baptism in the Holy Spirit*, Studies in Biblical Theology 15 (London: SCM, 1970), 55–68; Anthony A. Hoekema, *Holy Spirit Baptism* (Grand Rapids: Eerdmans, 1972), 36–37.

17. See especially M. M. B. Turner, "Luke and the Spirit: Studies in the Significance of Receiving the Spirit in Luke-Acts" (Ph.D. diss., Cambridge University, 1980), 161ff. See also the discussion by David Ewert, *The Holy Spirit in the New Testament* (Scottdale, Penn.: Herald, 1983); Green, *I Believe in the Holy Spirit;* Howard M. Ervin, *Conversion-Initiation and the Baptism of the Holy Spirit: A Critique of James D. G. Dunn, "Baptism in the Holy Spirit"* (Peabody, Mass.: Hendrickson, 1984), 25–28; Harold D. Hunter, *Spirit-Baptism: A Pentecostal Alternative* (Lanham, Md.: University Press of America, 1983), 83–84.

Suppose then we back off and list the places where Luke either explicitly mentions tongues in connection with the Spirit or at least (as here) hints at them. We find four passages: the initial experience of the Spirit at Pentecost, where the Spirit was poured out on Jews (Acts 2); this chapter, where the Spirit comes upon Samaritans, roughly half-breeds racially and operating with only the Pentateuch from the Jewish canon (Acts 8); the episode with Cornelius, certainly used by Luke, as we shall see, to mark the recognition of *Gentiles* as full Christians by the Jewish believers in Jerusalem (Acts 10–11); and the disciples of John the Baptist in Ephesus, who as we shall see fall into a kind of salvation-historical warp (Acts 19). In each case Luke is introducing a new group, until as the gospel expands throughout the empire there are no new groups left. And in each case the manifestation of the Spirit's presence in tongues is part of a *corporate* experience. Never in Acts is this the experience of an individual convert, even though Luke has many opportunities for reducing the scale from the group to the individual (e.g., Lydia [Acts 16:11–15]; the Philippian jailer [16:16–40]; and about twenty others).

It appears, then, that in Acts 8 the gift of the Holy Spirit is withheld to draw the connection between the Samaritans and the Jerusalem church through the apostles, Peter and John. Judging from what we know of relations between Jews and Samaritans, if this connecting link had not been forged, the Samaritans may well have wished to preserve an autonomy that would have divided the church from its inception, and which became principially impossible once their reception of the Holy Spirit was so publicly dependent on the Jerusalem apostles. For their part, the Christian Jews may well have been less than eager to accept the Samaritans as full Christian brothers and sisters unless such a link had been forged. Certainly that is an essential motif in the conversion of Gentiles in Acts 10–11.

Indeed, there is a deeper theme that Luke has been developing. I do not have space to enlarge upon it, but I may summarize it this way. Throughout the Book of Acts, Luke carefully records the early church's rising struggle to understand the precise relationship it has to the law of Moses. As the church increasingly grasped the atoning significance of Jesus' death and the eschatological significance of Jesus' resurrection, it could no longer view the law and its institutions in exactly the same way. Stephen casts doubt on the finality of the temple; Peter learns not only that the food laws no longer apply but also that whatever God declares clean is to be treated as clean, irrespective of antecedent law. Part of this debate develops into the question of how Gentiles are to be related to the Messiah. Those who want to uphold the finality of the Mosaic legislation as a covenant insist that Gentiles must first become Jewish proselytes, pledging themselves by circumcision to obey Moses—and only then are they eligible to accept Jesus, the Jewish Messiah. The alternative view prevails at the Jerusalem Council (Acts 15); and one of the decisive arguments turns on Peter's experiences with Cornelius and his kin (Acts 15:8; see Acts 10–11, about which I will say more in a moment). Now all of this constitutes a major theme in Acts; and it is relatively easy to integrate the four dramatic displays of the Spirit's outpouring with that and related salvation-historical themes. It is not easy to relate them to anything else.

In this light, Hunter's suggestion that the bestowal of the Spirit in Acts 8 cannot have anything to do with Jerusalem authentication since no similar authentication appears to be necessary for the Ethiopian eunuch (8:26–39) misses the point.[18] Not only is the eunuch an *individual,* and therefore not a threat to early *corporate* division, but, more important, since he had gone up to Jerusalem to worship (8:27) he was most likely a proselyte. Within the constraints imposed by the law on eunuchs, he worshiped as a Jew. He therefore cannot serve as an adequate counterexample to the interpretation of Acts being sketched out here.

Some have suggested that Peter's handling of Simon, including the frightening "May your money perish with you," proves that conversion did not take place when he, along with the other Samaritans, believed and were baptized. But the argument, if valid, proves too much, for Peter's stern words are uttered not only after the Samaritans have come to faith, but even after the Spirit has fallen. The difficult questions that Simon raises for us lie not in the realm of the existence or otherwise of a postconversion enduement of the Holy Spirit, but in the realm of the nature of apostasy. That subject would take us too far afield to warrant even brief exploration here.

Acts 10–11

It is worth noting that in this instance the Spirit falls on Cornelius and his family and friends while Peter is still preaching his sermon; and this enduement of the Spirit, attested by tongues, is then followed by water baptism, the rite intimately associated with conversion. But Luke makes nothing of this particular sequence. By itself, it is no more normative than the sequences in Acts 2 and Acts 8. Yet clearly the entire episode is extremely important to Luke, for not only does he tell it to us with painstaking detail in chapter 10, but the salient points are all repeated in chapter 11. This profligacy in the use of space can

18. Hunter, *Spirit-Baptism,* 71ff.

only mean that Luke understands the points he is making to be crucial to the development of his chosen themes—so crucial he does not want anyone to miss them.

When we press a little closer, we observe that the tongues uttered in this instance do not communicate anything to unbelievers; at this point there are no unbelievers present. On this score the situation is like that in Acts 8 (on the assumption tongues were spoken in Samaria), but unlike the situation in Acts 2. The Jewish believers with Peter are astonished that the Holy Spirit is poured out even on the Gentiles (10.45), apparently thinking up to this point that Gentiles would surely have to become Jewish proselytes before they could become eligible for this gift. The reason why they know that the Spirit has fallen on the Gentiles is given in verse 46: "they heard them speaking in tongues and praising God." From this it is not entirely certain whether the praise constituted the *content* of the tongues-speaking, or was parallel to it; but the former is marginally more likely. The Jewish believers draw the appropriate conclusion: there is nothing to prevent Cornelius and the rest from being baptized as Christians; for (they argued), "They have received the Holy Spirit just as we have" (10:47). It is going beyond the text to conclude, with Millon, that the Jewish believers actually understood the content of the tongues.[19] That would presuppose either some unmentioned use of the gift of interpretation or some unmentioned knowledge of languages unknown to the tongues-speakers. It is more likely that they heard the tongues and recognized them to be of a piece with their own Pentecost experience; and therefore they drew the appropriate conclusions.

More telling yet is the flow of the narrative in chapter 11. Once back in Jerusalem, Peter finds himself challenged by the Jerusalem church, still steeped in the presupposition that to be a believer in Jesus Messiah it is necessary first to be a Jew (or, equivalently, a Jewish proselyte). Peter recounts the entire episode, climaxing with the words, "As I began to speak, the Holy Spirit came on them as he had come on us at the beginning. Then I remembered what the Lord had said, 'John baptized with water, but you will be baptized with the Holy Spirit.' So if God gave them the same gift as he gave us, who believed in the Lord Jesus Christ, who was I to think that I could oppose God!" (11:15–17). The explicit references to Acts 2 are obvious, but as in chapter 10, it is unnecessary to conclude that Peter actually understood the tongues that were spoken, or that they were exactly the same

19. G. Millon, *Les grâces de service. La manifestation de l'Esprit pour l'utilité: charismes, diaconies et opérations selon 1 Corinthiens 12:4–7* (Mulhouse: Centre de Culture Chrétienne, 1976), 78.

languages, or that the noise of rushing wind was heard, or that tongues of fire appeared on each believer. All that is necessary is that Peter heard the tongues and, associating this with Pentecost, concluded that the same blessed Holy Spirit who had been poured out on Jewish believers had also been poured out by God on Gentiles—by God who, as the triple vision of the sheet made clear, can make all things clean. The conclusion, embraced both by Peter and by the Jerusalem church, was that these Gentile believers were fellow believers: repentance unto life had been granted even to those who had not come under the Mosaic covenant.

In short, tongues in Acts 10–11 serve *not* to communicate God's wonderful works to unbelievers, but primarily to attest to the Jerusalem church (and thus to Jewish believers) that Gentiles may be admitted to the messianic community without first coming under pledged commitment to the law of Moses.

Acts 19[20]

This rather strange account has in the past sometimes been used to justify a postconversion experience of the Spirit, on the basis of the King James Version's rendering of verse 2: "Have you received the Holy Spirit since you believed?" Today, almost all sides accept the rendering of the New International Version: "Did you receive the Holy Spirit when you believed?"[21] Contemporary debate focuses much more on the meaning of "disciples" in verse 1, whether or not there is a delay between the water baptism of verse 5 and the descent of the Spirit in verse 6, and the like.

But usually too little attention is placed on the unique anomaly the group represents. In Luke's narrative the event follows the somewhat parallel situation of Apollos: he "was a learned man, with a thorough knowledge of the Scriptures. He had been instructed in the way of the Lord, and he spoke with great fervor and taught about Jesus accurately, though he knew only the baptism of John" (18:24–25).

It is very difficult to know exactly where Apollos, and for that matter the Ephesians of Acts 19, stood. But I would be prepared to defend a reconstruction along the following lines. They had apparently become followers of John the Baptist, had received his baptism (whether

20. For discussion of the way in which Apollos (Acts 18) is to be related to this narrative of "disciples" in Ephesus (Acts 19), see C. K. Barrett, "Apollos and the Twelve Disciples of Ephesus," *The New Testament Age: Studies in Honor of Bo Reicke*, ed. William C. Weinrich, 2 vols. (Macon, Ga.: Mercer University Press, 1984), 1:29–39.

21. εἰ πνεῦμα ἅγιον ἐλάβετε πιστεύσαντες. Apparently the Western text also tried to smooth out the difficulties surrounding the Ephesians' response to Paul's question by exchanging ἔστιν for λαμβάνουσίν τινες.

personally or conceivably from one of John's converts), and had followed the Baptist's ministry long enough to know that he had pointed beyond himself to Jesus, the one whose sandals he was not worthy to loosen. Apollos at least (and probably the Ephesians) had also learned enough about Jesus to be described as one who "taught about Jesus accurately" (18:25). This probably suggests knowledge not only of Jesus' public ministry and teaching, but also of his death and resurrection. But apparently they knew nothing of Pentecost and what it signified of eschatological transformation. This ignorance could have developed because they (or the people who taught them) left Jerusalem (like tens of thousands of other diaspora Jews) shortly after the Passover feast— that is, they learned of Jesus' death and resurrection, but not of the coming of the Spirit. This placed them in exactly the same situation as the believers in Acts 1, except that Pentecost had already taken place. To put it another way, these "disciples"[22] in Acts 19 are living one dispensation earlier than the actual state of play in the unfolding sweep of redemptive history.

We may imagine, then, that when Paul found these Ephesian disciples, he sensed something was lacking and began to probe them with questions. At the risk of overdramatization, we might imagine an exchange like this:

"Are you believers?"

"Yes."

"Do you believe in Jesus?"

"Oh, yes!"

"What do you believe about Jesus?"

"Well, among other things, that he was announced by John the Baptist, that he was the Messiah who went around doing good and preaching the kingdom of God, and that he was crucified and rose again on the third day."

"And you have come to believe in him?"

"Oh, yes!"

"Did you receive the Holy Spirit when you believed?"

(Pause) "No, we have not even heard there is a Holy Spirit" (which *may* simply mean "that there is a Holy Spirit to be received," not *necessarily* that they had not even heard the words *Holy Spirit* before).

"But you were baptized as believers?"

"Of course!"

"Then what baptism did you receive?"

"John's baptism, of course."

---

22. Only here in Acts is the plural noun *disciples* anarthrous.

The penny drops: Paul understands what has happened, and the rest of the narrative follows easily enough.

It is important to recognize that if this is anything like what happened, there are two entailments: Paul presupposes by this line of questioning that reception of the Spirit at conversion is normal and expected; the distinctive abnormality of the Ephesians' experience could not be repeated today, since it is inconceivable that someone could be found who was a baptized follower of the Baptist, an enthusiastic supporter of the Baptist's witness to Jesus, apparently also a believer in Jesus' death and resurrection, but ignorant of Pentecost.

In the context of Acts 19, then, unlike the situation in Acts 2, tongues do not communicate the praise of God to unbelievers; and unlike in Acts 8 and Acts 10–11, they have nothing to do with accrediting new groups to the Jerusalem Jewish Christians. Rather, they serve as the attestation to the Ephesian believers themselves of the gift of the Spirit that transfers them as a group from the old era to the one in which they should be living.

The words "they spoke in tongues and prophesied" (19:6) *may* refer to two separate phenomena; but, like "speaking in tongues and praising God" in 10:46, the two verbs *may* be referring to the same reality. I am uncertain.

Miscellaneous Reflections on Acts

The essentially salvation-historical structure of the Book of Acts is too often overlooked. Therefore, as Fee laments, the exegesis of Acts in most charismatic circles is hermeneutically uncontrolled.[23] The way Luke tells the story, Acts provides not a paradigm for individual Christian experience, but the account of the gospel's outward movement, geographically, racially, and above all theologically. The "tarrying" or "waiting" for the Spirit is tied to Pentecost; in the subsequent accounts of tongues-speaking, the gift of the Spirit comes through apostles to entire groups who are not waiting for him. Meanwhile Luke repeatedly records instances where individuals are said to be filled with or full of the Holy Spirit, with no reference to speaking in tongues (e.g., Acts 4:8, 31; 6:3, 5; 7:55; 9:17; 11:24; 13:9, 52). If being Spirit-filled without speaking in tongues was God's path for some of them, it is hard to see why tongues-speaking should be made the criterion for proper obedience to God today.[24]

---

23. Gordon D. Fee, "Hermeneutics and Historical Precedent—a Major Problem in Pentecostal Hermeneutics," *Perspectives on the New Pentecostalism*, ed. Russell P. Spittler (Grand Rapids: Baker, 1976), 118–32.

24. Millon, *Les grâces*, 82, rightly points out that when Paul writes his epistles he certainly does not distinguish between Christians baptized in the Holy Spirit and otherwise. See further Packer, *Keep in Step with the Spirit*, 205–6.

Not much more appealing is the thesis of Stronstad.[25] He adopts a charismatic exegesis of numerous passages in Acts, and argues that his interpretations are most natural *provided* one does not read Paul into Luke. Paul, he admits, allows no second-blessing theology; but Luke does. If redaction criticism has taught us anything, it is to let individual authors speak on their own terms without premature harmonization or systematization.

The problem with Stronstad's thesis is twofold. First, I disagree with his exegesis of Luke-Acts at numerous critical junctures, so I do not find the particular antithesis between Luke and Paul that shapes his entire thesis. But second, the antithesis itself is not well conceived. If Luke and Paul develop complementary theologies, that is one thing (e.g., if Paul stresses only one conversion, but does not rule out some kind of postconversion spiritual enduement, while Luke stresses the latter); but if Luke and Paul develop contradictory theologies, that is another (e.g., if Paul will not permit any form of second-blessing theology, while Luke insists upon it). The polarity may please that part of the modern mood that finds in the New Testament a diverse and even mutually contradictory array of theologies, with the canon providing the *range* of allowable options, but the price is high. One can no longer speak of canonical theology in any wholistic sense. Worse, mutually contradictory theologies cannot both be true, and one cannot even speak of the canon establishing the allowable range of theologies, since one or more must be false. Stronstad's thesis generates more problems than it solves.

Nothing I have said should be taken to mean that for Luke tongues-speaking, because it has primarily salvation-historical *functions*, is necessarily forever past. Charismatics have erred in trying to read an individualizing paradigm into material not concerned to provide one. But noncharismatics have often been content to delineate the function of tongues where they appear in Acts, without adequate reflection on the fact that for Luke the Spirit does not simply inaugurate the new age and then disappear; rather, he *characterizes* the new age.

Under the old covenant, God dealt with his people in what we might call a tribal fashion. Despite remnant themes, the Scriptures picture God working with his people as a tribal grouping whose knowledge of God and whose relations with God were peculiarly dependent on specially endowed leaders. The Spirit of God was poured out, not on each believer, but distinctively on prophet, priest, king, and a few designated special leaders such as Bezalel. When these leaders stooped to

25. Roger Stronstad, *The Charismatic Theology of Luke* (Peabody, Mass.: Hendrickson, 1984).

sin (e.g., David's affair with Bathsheba and consequent murder of Uriah) the people were plunged into the distress of divine judgment.

But Jeremiah foresaw a time when this essentially tribal structure would change.

> "In those days people will no longer say,
>
> 'The fathers have eaten sour grapes,
> and the children's teeth are set on edge.'

Instead, everyone will die for his own sin; whoever eats sour grapes—his own teeth will be set on edge."

> "The time is coming," declares the LORD,
>   "when I will make a new covenant
> with the house of Israel
>   and with the house of Judah.
> It will not be like the covenant I made with their forefathers. . . .
> This is the covenant I will make with the house of Israel
>   after that time," declares the LORD.
> "I will put my law in their minds
>   and write it on their hearts.
> I will be their God,
>   and they will be my people.
> No longer will a man teach his neighbor,
>   or a man his brother, saying, 'Know the LORD,'
> because they will all know me,
>   from the least of them to the greatest,"
>
> declares the LORD.
> "For I will forgive their wickedness
>   and will remember their sins no more." [Jer. 31:29–34]

In short, Jeremiah understood that the new covenant would bring some dramatic changes. The tribal nature of the people of God would end, and the new covenant would bring with it a new emphasis on the distribution of the knowledge of God down to the level of each member of the covenant community. Knowledge of God would no longer be mediated through specially endowed leaders, for *all* of God's covenant people would know him, from the least to the greatest. Jeremiah is not concerned to say there would be no teachers under the new covenant, but to remove from leaders that distinctive mediatorial role that made the knowledge of God among the people at large a secondary knowledge, a mediated knowledge. Under the new covenant, the people of God would find not only that their sins were forgiven but that they too would know God in a more immediate way.

The same kind of hope is set forth by Ezekiel, who quotes the sovereign Lord in these terms:

> "I will sprinkle clean water on you, and you will be clean; I will cleanse you from all your impurities and from all your idols. I will give you a new heart and put a new spirit in you; I will remove from you your heart of stone and give you a heart of flesh. And *I will put my Spirit in you and move you to follow my decrees and be careful to keep my laws.*" [Ezek. 36:25–27, italics added; see 11:19–20]

Elsewhere, we read:

> "I will pour water on the thirsty land,
>   and streams on the dry ground;
> I will pour out my Spirit on your offspring,
>   and my blessing on your descendants.
> They will spring up like grass in a meadow,
>   like poplar trees by flowing streams.
> One will say, 'I belong to the LORD';
>   another will call himself by the name of Jacob;
> still another will write on his hand, 'The LORD's,'
>   and will take the name of Israel." [Isa. 44:3–5]

The same theme pervades many Old Testament texts that anticipate what we might generically label the messianic age. Moses himself recognizes that the *desideratum* was a universal distribution of the Spirit; for when Joshua complains to him that Eldad and Medad are prophesying in the camp and indignantly demands that they be stopped, the aged leader responds, "Are you jealous for my sake? I wish that all the LORD's people were prophets and that the LORD would put his Spirit on them!" (Num. 11:27–29).

It is of this that Joel prophesies (Joel 2:28–32 in English versions); and according to Peter, it is this that is fulfilled on the day of Pentecost (Acts 2). But that means Joel's concern is not simply with a picky point—more people will prophesy some day—but with a massive, eschatological worldview. What was anticipated was an entirely new age, a new relationship between God and his people, a new covenant; and experientially this turns on the gift of the Spirit. Put more generically, what the prophets foresaw was what some have labeled "the prophetic Spirit."[26] *All* who live under this new covenant enjoy the gift of this prophetic Spirit; and this is no mere creedal datum, but a lived, transforming, charismatic (in the broad, New Testament sense

26. See especially Turner, "Luke and the Spirit."

of that word identified in my first chapter), vital experience. It is in that sense that all who live under the new covenant are prophets: they enjoy this enduement of the Spirit, with various rich and humbling manifestations distributed among them.[27]

It is the dawning of the new age that was signaled by Pentecost, and that is why Peter's quotation of Joel's prophecy is so significant. According to all four Gospels, John the Baptist predicted that Jesus Messiah would usher in that age: *he* would baptize his people in the Holy Spirit. Jesus, especially in the Gospel of John, explicitly connects his death, resurrection, and exaltation with the coming of the Spirit. His return to the Father via the cross and the empty tomb is the necessary condition for the Spirit's coming (e.g., John 7:39; 16:7). Indeed, the Holy Spirit, that "other Counselor," is in certain respects Jesus' replacement during this period between the "already" and the "not yet" so characteristic of New Testament eschatology; he is the means by which the Father and the Son continue to manifest themselves to believers (e.g., John 14:23).[28] The same theme is picked up

27. This analysis is profoundly tied up with another question recently brought to the forefront of debate by Aune *(Prophecy)*. Much contemporary scholarship holds that first-century Judaism believed the age of prophecy had passed with the last of the writing prophets. If God continued to speak it was only indirectly, via the בַּת-קוֹל. Prophecy would not be resumed until the messianic age, or just prior to it. Aune disputes this. Contrary to repeated statements, Josephus twice speaks of prophecy in reference to his contemporary situation; and prophecy, studied historically instead of theologically, continues right through the disputed period (see David E. Aune, "The Use of προφήτης in Josephus," *Journal of Biblical Literature* 101 [1982]: 419–21). Despite his protestations, however, Aune's appeal to *historical* (as opposed to *theological*) categories offers no escape; for he himself is repeatedly forced by the evidence to draw out the many *distinctions* between Old Testament canonical prophecy and prophecy in the later period (see Aune, *Prophecy*, especially 106ff., 139, 153, 195). The failure to integrate these distinctions into Aune's broader thesis also has some bearing on his treatment of the relative degrees of authority in Old Testament prophecy, Josephus, New Testament prophets, apostles, and so forth; for the "prophets" of the late Second Temple period saw themselves in a different light from that of their canonical forebears, and gave utterances that were formally and materially different from them. The truth of the matter is that in the first century "prophecy" is a rubric so vast in semantic range that it can include phenomena with no significant relation to canonical prophecy. This semantic range, as we have seen, is attested in the New Testament: e.g., one of the Cretan "prophets" said, "Cretans are always liars, evil brutes, lazy gluttons" (Titus 1:12), which certainly does not place Epimenides on a par with Isaiah, so far as the writer of the Pastorals is concerned. Similarly, the principial distribution of what I have called "the prophetic Spirit," characteristic of Christian experience after Pentecost, does not require that each Christian prophet have precisely the same authority status as the prophet Isaiah, or even that the nature of the prophecy delivered be substantially similar. The spread of the categories is too large, and the range of qualifying circumstances too complex, to sanction such brutal reductionism.

28. See further M. M. B. Turner, "The Concept of Receiving the Spirit in John's Gospel," *Vox Evangelica* 10 (1977): 26–28.

by Peter on the day of Pentecost: "Exalted to the right hand of God, [Jesus] has received from the Father the promised Holy Spirit and has poured out what you now see and hear" (Acts 2:33). It has been shown in some detail that for Luke the coming of the Spirit is not associated merely with the *dawning* of the new age but with its *presence*, not merely with Pentecost but with the entire period from Pentecost to the return of Jesus the Messiah.[29]

Certainly the Spirit's purposes are Christocentric. Some gifts, notably tongues, *function* in Acts in ways particularly related to the *inception* of the messianic age. But it does not follow that Luke expects them to cease once the period of inception has passed and the new age is under way, for the manifestations of the Spirit are tied *to the Spirit, to the new age*, fulfilling Old Testament prophecy, and not *merely* to their inception. On the one hand, granted Luke's interest in the salvation-historical inception or inauguration of the messianic age, we shall abuse his text if we force it into a Procrustean bed to make it tell us that a *particular* manifestation of the Spirit attests the Spirit's presence or filling or baptism in every believer this side of Pentecost: Luke simply does not set out such guidelines. Yet on the other hand, there is no exegetical warrant for thinking certain classes of the Spirit's manifestations cease once the crucial points of redemptive history have passed. Throughout this age, the Christian personally *knows* the Lord by the Spirit; the believer senses him, enjoys his presence, communes with him. The Spirit in a Christocentric fashion manifests himself in and to the believer; the believer in turn shows the Spirit. The wide range of χαρίσματα *(charismata)* that show the Spirit is much broader, as Paul insists, than the few over which so much fuss has erupted today, but they certainly *include* these few. The only χάρισμα

29. See especially Turner, "Luke and the Spirit"; idem, "Spiritual Gifts Then and Now," especially 41ff. For a similar reading of the Old Testament evidence, see W. J. Dumbrell, *Covenant and Creation: An Old Testament Covenantal Theology* (Exeter: Paternoster, 1984). Conservatives from both the Reformed and the charismatic camps have frequently argued that there is no difference between the *experience* of Old Testament and New Testament believers, but only between their respective understandings of God's salvific purposes. To put it another way, Old Testament and New Testament believers are equally regenerate (a decidedly New Testament term). So, for instance, John Rea, "The Personal Relationship of Old Testament Believers to the Holy Spirit," in *Essays on Apostolic Themes: Studies in Honor of Howard M. Ervin,* ed. Paul Elbert (Peabody, Mass.: Hendrickson, 1985), 92–103. But the evidence adduced inevitably pertains to special leaders, such as David or one of the prophets or priests. It ignores not only the Old Testament passages, already cited, that anticipate a *new* and more widely distributed experience of the Spirit, but also the pulsating New Testament stance, especially strong in Paul, that sees the Holy Spirit in the life of the Christian and the church as the decisive evidence that the *new* age has dawned and the messianic reign has begun. The structure of New Testament eschatology is jeopardized by the failure to discern such distinctions.

(charisma) bound up with obsolescence is apostleship in the tightly defined sense. The reason for the obsolescence of this χάρισμα *(charisma)* lies not in its connection with the Spirit but in its connection with the resurrected and exalted Christ, who now no more appears to human beings as the personal, resurrected Lord. Until his return, he manifests himself to us only by his Spirit; and therefore the peculiar commission and authority of the first apostles, which turned on personal contact with the resurrected Jesus, cannot be duplicated today.

It is the failure to recognize this essentially eschatological structure that mars Warfield's insistence that miracles ceased.[30] The heart of his argument is that miracles of various kinds served primarily as attestation first of Jesus and then of the apostles. Since Jesus and the apostles have passed from the scene, and the deposit of truth they conveyed is bound up in the canon, the need for attestation has also passed. All claims to miracles, including tongues, healings, prophecies, and the like must therefore be deemed spurious.

But this argument stands up *only* if such miraculous gifts are theologically tied *exclusively* to a role of attestation; and that is demonstrably not so. Perhaps Turner is slightly reductionistic on the other side, when he denies any link between miracles and attestation. The expression *signs of an apostle* or the like occurs in a few crucial passages (Acts 2:43; 5:12; 2 Cor. 12:12), and it teaches us not to avoid the link altogether. Even in Jesus' ministry, miraculous signs *do* attest who Jesus is, even if they never *ensure* faith: "Believe me for the works' sake," the Master declares, if not for the teaching itself (John 10:38).[31] But because miraculous signs have a distinctively attesting role in some instances, it does not follow that this is the *only* role they play.

The healing and other miracles of Jesus are explicitly connected not only with the *person* of Jesus, *but also with the new age he is inaugurating.* The evidence is neatly summarized by Turner,[32] building on the works of Richardson, Kallas, and van der Loos.[33] Indeed, as I have argued elsewhere, Matthew 8:16–17 explicitly connects Jesus' mira-

---

30. B. B. Warfield, *Counterfeit Miracles* (1918; reprint ed., London: Banner of Truth Trust, 1972). See similarly John F. MacArthur, Jr., *The Charismatics: A Doctrinal Perspective* (Grand Rapids: Zondervan, 1978), 73ff.; John F. Walvoord, *The Holy Spirit* (Findlay, Ohio: Dunham, 1958), 173ff.; and many others.

31. On this point, see the firm critique of Colin Brown, *Miracles and the Modern Mind* (Grand Rapids: Eerdmans, 1984), by William Lane Craig, "Colin Brown, *Miracles and the Critical Mind:* A Review Article," *Journal of the Evangelical Theological Society* 27 (1984): 473–85.

32. Turner, "Spiritual Gifts Then and Now," 24–26.

33. A. Richardson, *The Miracle Stories of the Gospels* (London: SCM, 1941); J. Kallas, *The Significance of the Synoptic Miracles* (London: SPCK, 1961); H. van der Loos, *The Miracles of Jesus* (Leiden: Brill, 1965).

cles of healing and exorcism with the atonement that had not yet taken place.[34] They serve as foretastes of and are predicated on the cross-work that is their foundation and justification. When a charismatic insists that there is healing in the atonement, he or she is of course right. Biblically speaking, the question is not whether there is healing in the atonement, but what blessings secured by the atonement one can *expect* to receive between the first advent of the Messiah and the second. But of that I shall say more.

Within the biblical-theological framework I have sketched out, the curious differences between tongues in Acts and tongues in 1 Corinthians 12–14 can be more or less happily accommodated. Thus we observe that tongues in Acts occur only in groups, are not said to recur, are public, and may serve various purposes of attestation; while tongues in 1 Corinthians fall to the individual, may be used in private, must be translated if in public, and serve no purpose of attestation. Much of the debate over such differences has proved exceedingly sterile because each position, like each of the "six blind men of Hindustan" who undertook to describe an elephant, not only uses one part of the evidence as a grid to define the other parts, but also actually tends to overlook the whole. So one party tells us tongues must attest the inception of the new age, and therefore they are now obsolete; another advises us they are the criterion of a second definitive enduement of the Spirit, when Luke does not say that and Paul forbids such a view; another makes public edification so central that the attesting role of tongues in Acts 10–11 and the private use of tongues in 1 Corinthians 14 are both consigned to oblivion; and so on. Meanwhile we have lost sight of the centrality of the Spirit as the guarantee of the full inheritance yet to come, the first fruits of the harvest we are yet to enjoy, the way in which or by which we are to walk.[35] The diverse manifestations of the Spirit outlined in my first chapter are *all* ways by which God's people manifest the Spirit's presence. As the χαρίσματα (charismata) as a group have often been overschematized, and as the purpose of miracles has often been overschematized, so this or that particular χάρισμα (charisma) has often been overschematized—not least the χάρισμα (charisma) of tongues. Why should not tongues serve a diversity of functions? There are, of course, as I argued in my third chapter, some important commonalities in the nature of tongues described in

34. D. A. Carson, "Matthew" in *The Expositor's Bible Commentary*, ed. Frank E. Gaebelein, 12 vols. (Grand Rapids: Zondervan, 1984), 8:204–7.

35. See also the stress on "way," *camino*, to be lived, walked, as traced out by M. A. Barriola, *El Espiritu Santo y la Praxis Cristiana: El tema del camino en la teologia de San Pablo* (Montevideo: Instituto Teologico des Uruguay, 1977).

Scripture; but the differences in purpose or role should be embraced, not constrained by the dictates of a reductionistic grid.

Reflections on Second-Blessing Theology

Despite Hollenweger's sixfold typology of the charismatic movement,[36] most of the debates between charismatic Protestants and non-charismatic Protestants revolve around his first type—those who teach a two-stage way of salvation, the first essential to eternal life, the second to Christian victory and effective service. This second-blessing theology, as I shall call it, has a long history in the so-called holiness traditions. The distinctive contribution of much of the charismatic movement to that tradition, however, is the insistence on tongues as the criterion that one has received this second blessing, the blessing itself customarily labeled the "baptism of [or "in" or "with"] the Holy Spirit."

By now it should be clear where at least my superficial difficulties with the charismatic movement lie. First, it is not clear from the biblical texts that we have examined that "baptism in the Holy Spirit" is a technical term referring to a postconversion enduement of the Spirit to be pursued by each believer. Luke's evidence can be made to fit that grid only if it is misapplied, and Paul stands positively against it. Second, even if that grid is adopted, it is hard to see on what basis the gift of tongues is made a *criterion* of the Spirit's baptism. Even if the charismatic exegesis of, say, Acts 8 were right (and in my view it is not), one would still have to integrate that exegesis with other texts. Therefore, it would be necessary to distinguish, as Wiebe points out, a view that makes tongues-speaking evidence that one has been baptized in the Spirit, from a view that makes tongues-speaking the *only* evidence that one has been baptized in the Spirit, from a view that makes tongues-speaking the *conclusive* evidence that one has been baptized in the Spirit, and so forth.[37] The constraints needed for a *criterion* are extremely tight, and the exegetical support is simply not there. I remain persuaded that at this point the majority of modern charismatics are profoundly unbiblical.

But the question of second-blessing theology itself, apart from the question of tongues-speaking, is more difficult, for it extends beyond the purpose of tongues and even beyond the "holiness tradition." One

---

36. See Walter J. Hollenweger, "Charismatic and Pentecostal Movements: A Challenge to the Churches," in *The Holy Spirit*, ed. D. Kirkpatrick (Nashville: Tidings, 1974).

37. Phillip H. Wiebe, "The Pentecostal Initial Evidence Doctrine," *Journal of the Evangelical Theological Society* 27 (1984): 465–72.

stream of Reformed thought has also embraced it, perhaps best known in the modern world through the writings of Lloyd-Jones. He argues, for instance, that the sealing of the Spirit in Ephesians 1:13 is a distinct, postconversion experience of the Spirit;[38] and in his posthumously published series of sermons entitled *Joy Unspeakable*,[39] the doctor seeks to establish the same general point in a variety of ways. Partly as a result, the Reformed movement in Britain is currently somewhat split between those who are sympathetic to certain aspects of the charismatic movement and those who are not—both sides claiming support from Lloyd-Jones, who, unfortunately, can no longer tell us which side is misinterpreting him. More broadly, many charismatics seek to establish their particular brand of second-blessing theology partly on an array of texts I have not mentioned, including John 20:22, Galatians 3:1–5, 14, Hebrews 2:2–3, and a number of others.

I cannot here enter the lists on these texts, but in my judgment, the exegetical evidence does not in any of these passages support any form of structured second-blessing theology.[40]

On the other hand, I am persuaded that Lloyd-Jones and many others both within and without the charismatic movement have put their fingers on something extremely important, even if they have not always developed the point in accord with a firm exegesis of the text. We may sense their point when we remember that many noncharismatics, reacting against the excesses of second-blessing theology, have so resolutely set themselves to be open *only* to the one enduement connected with their conversion that no further pursuit of the Lord or of profound spiritual experience is thought wise or necessary. But there is firm, biblical evidence of New Testament *believers* who seek the Lord in disciplined, self-abased prayer and who consequently come into a distinct, further experience of the Spirit. Paul can exhort believers to be filled with the Spirit (Eph. 5:18); and after noncharismatics have said all they wish about the present imperative meaning "be being filled with the Spirit" or the like, in order to avoid any hint of a *climactic* second filling, the fact remains that the command is

---

38. D. Martyn Lloyd-Jones, *God's Ultimate Purpose: An Exposition of Ephesians 1* (Grand Rapids: Baker, 1979), 243–378.

39. D. Martyn Lloyd-Jones, *Joy Unspeakable: The Baptism of the Holy Spirit* (Eastbourne: Kingsway, 1984).

40. For example, to appeal to the aorist participle πιστεύσαντες *(pisteusantes)* in Eph. 1:13 as if in itself it provides any support for the view that the exercise of faith is anterior to the sealing of the Spirit displays ignorance not only of the Greek verbal system, but also of the fact that adverbial participles modifying finite verbs refer, in many occurrences, to action that is concurrent with that of the finite verb.

empty if Paul does not think it dangerously possible for Christians to be too "empty" of the Spirit. Or again, when the believers in Acts 4 utter their moving prayer (vv. 24–30), Luke reports the result: "After they prayed, the place where they were meeting was shaken. And they were all *filled with the Holy Spirit* and spoke the word of God boldly" (4:31, italics added).

In short, I see biblical support for the thesis that although all true believers have received the Holy Spirit and have been baptized in the Holy Spirit, nevertheless the Holy Spirit is not necessarily poured out on each individual Christian in precisely equivalent quantities (if I may use the language of quantity inherent in the metaphor of "filling"). How else can we explain the peculiar unction that characterizes the service of some relatively unprepossessing ministers? Although I find no biblical support for a second-blessing theology, I do find support for a second-, third-, fourth-, or fifth-blessing theology. Although I find no χάρισμα *(charisma)* biblically established as the criterion of a second enduement of the Spirit, I do find that there are degrees of unction, blessing, service, and holy joy, along with some more currently celebrated gifts, associated with those whose hearts have been specially touched by the sovereign God. Although I think it extremely dangerous to pursue a second blessing attested by tongues, I think it no less dangerous not to pant after God at all, and to be satisfied with a merely creedal Christianity that is kosher but complacent, orthodox but ossified, sound but soundly asleep.[41]

Reflections on Revelation

Doubtless you will recall that in the treatment of prophecy in my third chapter, I largely followed Grudem's excellent study, but expressed dissatisfaction at a couple of crucial points. One of these deserves further exploration. Some take Grudem to be distinguishing between the authority of prophets (such as the Old Testament writing prophets) whose revelation from God extended to the very words and the authority of prophets whose revelation from God consisted in general ideas only. Grudem himself disavows this formulation: but as he

41. Moreover, within this framework it is possible to provide a coherent theological explanation of the charismatic's actual experience: see especially Packer, *Keep in Step with the Spirit*, 219–28. Here, too, we might mention that the Puritans, who saw in the expression *baptism in the Holy Spirit* neither a necessary reference to conversion nor to a postconversion enduement, could use it in prayer for revival: "Baptize us afresh with thy Holy Spirit!" or the like. See Iain Murray, "Baptism with the Spirit: What Is the Scriptural Meaning?" *Banner of Truth* 127 (April 1974): 5–22.

has been misunderstood along these lines, we need to probe the cause of the misunderstanding and seek a way out of the dilemma.

This misunderstanding is unwittingly injurious to the doctrine of Scripture. It is true that Scripture insists that God's superintending inspiration of Scripture extends right down to Scripture's words (as Grudem himself elsewhere argues);[42] but thoughtful expositors of the doctrine have carefully distinguished between the *mode* of inspiration and the *result* of inspiration in order to avoid all mechanical theories of dictation. The *result* of inspiration is a text truly from God, right down to the words, while also being in the words of the human author; but that does not mean the *mode* of inspiration required God to dictate the text. However, by referring to the revelation that the prophet *receives* as either in conceptual categories or in words, this view pushes back from the resulting message or text to the *mode* of inspiration. There is too little evidence that much of Scripture was revealed by this mode, and the problems such a formulation raises are real and intractable.[43]

This raises the possibility, at least, that revelation, whatever the mode, might well *not* be *communicated* accurately unless the *results* are guaranteed. In that case the prophecy that has actually come by revelation might well have to be evaluated, *without reflection on the quality of the revelation itself.*

Some of the debate is hampered by a view of revelation that is narrower than that employed in Scripture. Consider, for instance, these words from Vos:

> The question may be raised, whether within the limits of the principles here laid down, there can be expected still further revelation entitled to a place in the scheme of N[ew] T[estament] Revelation. Unless we adopt the mystical standpoint, which cuts loose the subjective from the objective, the only proper answer to this question is, that new revelation can be added only, in case new objective events of a supernatural character take place, needing for their understanding a new body of interpretation supplied by God. This will actually be the case in the eschatological issue of things. What then occurs will constitute a new epoch in re-

---

42. Wayne A. Grudem, "Scripture's Self-Attestation and the Problem of Formulating a Doctrine of Scripture," in *Scripture and Truth*, ed. D. A. Carson and John D. Woodbridge (Grand Rapids: Zondervan, 1983), 19–39, 359–68.

43. An attempt has been made to discuss the *contemporary* questions surrounding the doctrine of Scripture espoused by the main streams of historic Christianity in D. A. Carson and John D. Woodbridge, eds., *Scripture and Truth* (Grand Rapids: Zondervan, 1983); idem, *Hermeneutics, Authority, and Canon* (Grand Rapids: Zondervan, 1986); D. A. Carson, "Three Books on the Bible: A Critical Review," *Journal of the Evangelical Theological Society* 26 (1983): 337–67.

demption worthy to be placed by the side of the great epochs in the Mosaic age and the age of the first Advent. Hence the Apocalypse mingles with the pictures of the final events transpiring the word of prophecy and of interpretation. We may say, then, that a third epoch of revelation is still outstanding. Strictly speaking, however, this will form less a group by itself than a consummation of the second group. It will belong to N[ew] T[estament] revelation as a final division. Mystical revelation claimed by many in the interim as a personal privilege is out of keeping with the genius of Biblical religion. Mysticism in this detached form is not specifically Christian. It occurs in all types of religion, better or worse. At best it is a manifestation of the religion of nature, subject to all the defects and faults of the latter. As to its content and inherent value it is unverifiable, except on the principle of submitting it to the test of harmony with Scripture. And submitting it to this it ceases to be a separate source of revelation concerning God.[44]

Here we find the neat antithesis, objective revelation or uncontrolled mysticism. But the Bible's use of "revelation" (ἀποκάλυψις, *apokalypsis*) and "to reveal" (ἀποκαλύπτω, *apokalyptō*) reflects a wider range of possibilities. In all of the occurrences, the revelation is granted by God, Jesus Christ, or the Holy Spirit, or brought about directly by them or in connection with them. Especially frequent are the references to the revelation of Jesus Christ at the parousia, or to the gospel itself, including the space-time manifestation of Jesus Messiah. Normally these terms are *not* used when some more specific term is available (such as dream or vision); and, as Grudem himself rightly points out, "revelation" can take place in some surprising contexts.[45]

For instance, when Peter makes his confession at Caesarea Philippi, he has to be *told* that the Father had *revealed* this truth to him (Matt. 16:17 par.): apparently revelation can take place without the individual *knowing* that it is taking place or has taken place. In Galatians 1:16, it pleased God to reveal his Son, Paul says, ἐν ἐμοί *(en emoi)*—literally, "in me," presumably "to me" or even "with reference to me." This of course has reference to Paul's conversion: we are not dealing here with the objective self-disclosure of the Son of God in space-time history, a revelation witnessed widely and now attested by the public record of Scripture, but with the private disclosure of the Son to and in Paul.[46] If someone objects that Paul's conversion is unique, involv-

44. Geerhardus Vos, *Biblical Theology: Old and New Testaments* (Grand Rapids: Eerdmans, 1948), 326–27.

45. Wayne A. Grudem, *The Gift of Prophecy in 1 Corinthians* (Washington, D.C.: University Press of America, 1982), 69–70, 119–36.

46. See further William Baird, "Visions, Revelation, and Ministry: Reflections on 2 Cor 12:1–5 and Gal 1:11–17," *Journal of Biblical Literature* 104 (1985): 651–62.

ing as it did the appearance of the resurrected Christ after his ascension, we may nevertheless compare Matthew 11:27 and 1 Corinthians 2:10. In the former, we are told, "No one knows the Son except the Father, and no one knows the Father except the Son and those to whom the Son chooses to *reveal* him"; in the latter, after being told that God's wisdom has been hidden in the past, and from the rulers of this age, we are assured that "God has *revealed* it to us by his Spirit"—and the contrast with the rulers of the age makes it clear that the referent of this "revelation" is not simply the appearance of Jesus Messiah, but the conversion of some people over against other people. This too is called "revelation," even though unveiling of the Son to the inward eye of faith in a particular individual is not *itself* either the public revelation of the Son in history or the parousia—the two alternatives offered by Vos.

This does not mean that from the point of conversion on, the believer understands all of the Son that has thus been revealed to him or her, or could verbalize the experiences with infallible assertions. More revelation takes place in the believer's life as he or she grows in grace and understanding. Paul can write to converts and explain some foundational Christian truth, and then add, "All of us who are mature should take such a view of things. And if on some point you think differently, that too God *will make clear* [lit., "will reveal"] to you" (Phil. 3:15). A similar understanding of revelation lies behind Ephesians 1:17, and probably also behind some passages where the terms *revelation* and *to reveal* are not actually used (e.g., Eph. 3:14–19). There is no hint in any of these contexts that the "revelation" involved falls into one of Vos's two categories. Apparently, at least some of this revelation came through a quiet (possibly even unrecognized but no less gracious) divine disclosure, part of the Christian's growing grasp of spiritual realities—a growing grasp that can come only by revelation, which is to say it comes by grace.

Thus, when Paul presupposes in 1 Corinthians 14:30 that the gift of prophecy depends on revelation, we are not limited to a form of authoritative revelation that threatens the finality of the canon. To argue in such a way is to confuse the terminology of Protestant systematic theology with the terminology of the Scripture writers. The prophecy Paul has in mind is revelatory and Spirit-prompted, and it may, as Turner and others suggest,[47] deal largely with questions of application of gospel truth (though there is no biblical restriction along such lines). None of this means it is necessarily authoritative, infallible, or canon-threatening. Such prophecies must still be evaluated, and they are

47. Turner, "Spiritual Gifts Then and Now," 46–48.

principially submissive to the apostle and his gospel. To bring such a prophecy "to the test of the harmony of Scripture," to use the language of Vos, may dismiss it as a *separate* source of revelation on an authority scale at par with that of Scripture; but it is difficult to see how such a test dismisses the claim to revelation in the attenuated sense sometimes found within Scripture itself and argued for here.

Not all visions or revelations mediated even by apostles were necessarily above thoughtful examination. The Macedonian call (Acts 16:9), as Bowers has pointed out, took place while Paul had already started the move toward Europe;[48] and once Paul had related the vision to the others in his team, they *collectively* concluded (συμβιβάζοντες, *sumbibazontes*)[49] that it meant they should press on for Macedonia. An apostle was not kept free from error or sin just because he was an apostle. These specially appointed men, however, *did* recognize their own peculiar authority *under* the gospel (Gal. 1:8–9) and *over* the church (e.g., 1 Cor. 4; 14:37–38; 2 Cor. 10–13). How they themselves distinguished binding truth would take us too far afield to explore here; my only purpose in raising these points is to stress that revelation and authority in the New Testament are more nuanced concepts than is sometimes recognized.

Among those who closely observe the phenomenon of alleged contemporary prophecy, there is widespread agreement that the person uttering such prophecy remains in control of his or her own language. Those who have command of two or more languages can switch from one to the other at will, depending on the language of the congregation. As one charismatic explains:

> The language we use in prophecy is under our control. Prophecy comes through a *particular* human being, and it will be expressed in the language of that person. When a highly educated man speaks in prophecy, he will very likely use a different vocabulary than a poorly educated person would use.[50]

The conclusion to be drawn from such observations is that not much can be concluded, so far as the authority status of the contemporary phenomenon is concerned. After all, conservative noncharismatics will be the first to insist that even the Scripture writers use the language, style, and vocabulary native to them; so the fact that the modern

48. W. Paul Bowers, "Paul's Route Through Mysia: A Note on Acts xiv.8," *Journal of Theological Studies* 30 (1979): 507–11.
49. I am grateful to Dr. Peter T. O'Brien for reminding me of this.
50. See Bruce Yocum, *Prophecy: Exercising the Prophetic Gifts of the Spirit in the Church Today* (Ann Arbor: Servant, 1976), 82.

"prophet's" language remains under his or her personal control cannot be used to discredit the phenomenon. Neither can it be taken as evidence that the result is as authoritative as Scripture, for after all, such control is the common experience of almost all human communication.

Before we attempt any summarizing evaluations, perhaps we should cast a cursory eye at the somewhat ambiguous evidence provided by church history.

Reflections on the Evidence of History

There is a considerable historiography that argues that the phenomenon of tongues and other "charismatic" gifts died out fairly early in the history of the church. This varies from Knox's amusing and sometimes savage denunciation of what he calls "enthusiasm"[51] to more pedestrian studies that may admit strange phenomena do recur, but insist that such aberrations are found only in fringe groups, among sectarian heretics.[52] Thus one noncharismatic ends his study of both the Bible and church history with these words: "We conclude by quoting Paul, who said: 'Tongues shall cease' (I Cor. 13:8). They have."[53] There are enough loose pieces to make us fearful that the historical records are being handled (or mishandled) on the basis of a strong commitment to a predetermined conclusion.

Scarcely less committed are the rising number of historical studies by charismatics who appeal to the same evidence to prove that the gift of tongues has always been operative in one wing or another of the church.[54] These works tend to ignore the major doctrinal and other variations that frequently mar the witness of the relatively small numbers who have espoused "charismatic" positions and practices; they tend to milk what evidence there is without evenhanded weighing of the proportion, frequency, theology, and influence of the groups they examine. They rightly point out that, after all, the distinctives of Protestant theology had to be formulated in the face of a "mother church" that largely opposed them; so why should not a new reformation take place today, a charismatic reformation? Popularity or frequency in

51. Ronald Knox, *Enthusiasm* (Oxford: Oxford University Press, 1950).

52. E.g., George W. Dollar, "Church History and the Tongues Movement," *Bibliotheca Sacra* 120 (1963): 309–11; Cleon L. Rogers, Jr., "The Gift of Tongues in the Post Apostolic Church," *Bibliotheca Sacra* 122 (1965): 134–43.

53. Robert G. Gromacki, *The Modern Tongues Movement* (Philadelphia: Presbyterian and Reformed, 1967), 143.

54. E.g., Stanley M. Burgess, *The Spirit and the Church: Antiquity* (Peabody, Mass.: Hendrickson, 1984); Ronald A. N. Kydd, *Charismatic Gifts in the Early Church* (Peabody, Mass.: Hendrickson, 1984).

the history of the church is no necessary criterion of faithful exegesis and of spiritual vitality. Indeed, at the popular level this stance can become virulent enough to produce the following:

> For the church's early rejection of the genuine Baptism With The Holy Spirit, with the visible and audible Biblical evidence of "speaking in other tongues," as the initial and only evidence authenticating reception of this Baptism, IS WITHOUT POSSIBILITY OF CONTRADICTION, THE MOST MONUMENTAL, THE MOST AWESOME, AND THE MOST SINFUL BLUNDER IN ALL OF THE ALMOST TWO MILLENNIA OF CHURCH HISTORY!![55]

It is not possible in this context to pass the evidence in review. There are, however, some remarkably careful and evenhanded studies now available, and a student is well advised to begin with them.[56] So far as the early church is concerned, it appears as if tongues were extremely rare after the beginning of the second century, but prophecy was known and cherished in the church until the rise of Montanism. Forms of "charismatic" behavior recur in various small minorities. These recurring displays are common enough both in Christendom and beyond that an anthropologist such as Christie-Murray can conclude, "It can be stated with some confidence that if an anthropologist were to work systematically through the literature on his subject, he would find glossolalia in one form or another to be almost universal."[57]

What can be safely concluded from the historical evidence? First, there is enough evidence that some form of "charismatic" gifts continued sporadically across the centuries of church history that it is futile to insist on doctrinaire grounds that every report is spurious or the fruit of demonic activity or psychological aberration. Second, from the death of Montanism until the turn of the present century, such phenomena were never part of a major movement. In each instance, the group involved was small and generally on the fringe of Christianity. Third, the great movements of piety and reformation that have in God's mercy occasionally refreshed and renewed the church were

55. From an unsolicited pamphlet sent to me by an organization called Pentecostal Christian Evangelism.

56. E.g., Louis Bouyer, "Some Charismatic Movements in the History of the Church," in *Perspectives on Charismatic Renewal*, ed. Edward D. O'Connor (Notre Dame: University Press, 1975), 113–31; George H. Williams and Edith Waldvogel, "A History of Speaking in Tongues and Related Gifts," in *The Charismatic Movement*, ed. Michael P. Hamilton (Grand Rapids: Eerdmans, 1975), 61–113; W. J. Samarin, *Tongues of Men and Angels: The Religious Language of Pentecostalism* (New York: Macmillan, 1972).

57. David Christie-Murray, *Voices from the Gods: Speaking with Tongues* (London: Routledge and Kegan Paul, 1979).

not demonstrably crippled because their leaders did not, say, speak in tongues. Those who have thoughtfully read the devotional and theological literature of the English Puritans will not be easily convinced that their spirituality was less deep, holy, powerful, Spirit-prompted than what obtains in the contemporary charismatic movement. The transformation of society under the Spirit-anointed preaching of Howell Harris, George Whitefield, John and Charles Wesley, and others finds no parallel in the contemporary charismatic movement.[58] It would be a strange calculus which concluded that a modern charismatic lives on a higher spiritual plane than did, say, Augustine, Balthasar Hubmaier, Jonathan Edwards, Count von Zinzendorf, or Charles Spurgeon, since none of these spoke in tongues. Fourth, very often the groups that did emphasize what today would be called charismatic gifts were either heretical or quickly pushed their "gifts" to such extremes that their praxis proved dangerous to the church. For instance, with varying degrees of rapidity, the leaders of the Evangelical Awakening came to warn people against the dangers of the so-called French Prophets. Even those leaders who at first hoped that they displayed the Spirit's presence eventually concluded that at very least they were so unbalanced in their views, so desperately fixated on their cherished experiences, so profoundly unteachable, that young believers had to be diverted from them. Even Edward Irving (often judged the forerunner of the charismatic movement) despite his immense strengths and gifts adopted a strange Christology, an extraordinarily subjective understanding of the leading of the Lord, a decidedly arrogant posture toward his colleagues. He ultimately fell into a black despair occasioned by his false views on healing. To argue, with one recent charismatic writer, that this man was "the Scottish John the Baptist of the Charismatic Movement" who swept away "the unscriptural hypothetical basis" of the truncation of the Spirit's gifts, and who "produced a coherent theological understanding of the person and power of the Holy Spirit and the operation of His gifts, resulting in a more complete recapture of apostolic patterns,"[59] is simultaneously to misread and

58. One thinks, for instance, of the evidence chronicled by John Wesley Bready, *This Freedom—Whence?* (New York: American Tract Society, 1942—the American edition of *England: Before and After Wesley*); Arnold Dallimore, *George Whitefield*, 2 vols. (Edinburgh: Banner of Truth, 1970, 1979).

59. Paul Elbert, "Calvin and the Spiritual Gifts," in *Essays on Apostolic Themes: Studies in Honor of Howard M. Ervin*, ed. Paul Elbert (Peabody, Mass.: Hendrickson, 1985), 142–43. A more negative though generally evenhanded treatment of Irving is provided by his most recent biographer: Arnold Dallimore, *Forerunner of the Charismatic Movement: The Life of Edward Irving* (Chicago: Moody, 1983).

falsely assess both the modern charismatic movement and Edward Irving, and perhaps also the apostolic patterns and John the Baptist.

Although to my knowledge the theory has not been worked out anywhere in great detail, it is probable that prophecy waned with the rise of Montanism because the church was seeking to protect herself from the extravagant claims of the Montanists. The more the latter claimed to enjoy Spirit-given, prophetic gifts of superlative authority—so sterling an authority, in fact, that much of Scripture could be confidently dismissed—the more the church was bound to respond by stressing the stability and immutability of the apostolic deposit. If prophecy was to be abused in the fashion of the Montanists, prophecy itself would ultimately become suspect. But it must be remembered that this theological stance was an ecclesiastical *reaction*. The fact that the church made room for prophecy until the Montanist abuse strongly suggests that what the church understood by "prophecy" up to that time *did not in any way jeopardize the apostolic deposit*. It was the authority claim of Montanism that was so profoundly dangerous, ultimately threatening numerous cardinal doctrines of the church. Contemporary charismatics and noncharismatics alike ought to recognize that when Montanism first arose, its view of the authority status of prophecy was at that point an aberration—even though something very like that view (though without its entailments) seems to predominate in both charismatic and noncharismatic circles today.

If this historical assessment is correct, then there may be reason to suppose that noncharismatic wings of the contemporary church may still enjoy some use of "prophecy" without calling it that. Calvin seems to be open to this possibility. Commenting on "prophets" in Ephesians 4:11, he suggests they are "those who excelled by special revelation"; and then he adds, "none such now exist, *or they are less manifest*" (italics added).[60] In his commentary on 1 Corinthians 12:28–31, he suggests that "prophets" refers to those who are skillful at making known God's will, primarily by applying prophecies, threats, promises, and the teaching of Scripture. He then goes on to acknowledge he may be wrong, for it is difficult to be certain when such gifts or offices have been kept from the church for so long a time, *except for traces or shades of them still to be found*.[61]

One begins to suspect, then, that prophecy may occur more often than is recognized in noncharismatic circles, and less often than is recognized in charismatic circles. We may happily agree that preaching cannot be identified with prophecy, but what preacher has not had

60. *Institutes* 4.3.4.
61. Calvin, in loc.

the experience, after detailed preparation for public ministry, of being interrupted in the full flow of his delivery with a new thought, fresh and powerful, interrupting him and insinuating itself upon his mind, until he makes room for it and incorporates it into his message—only to find after the service that the insertion was the very bit that seemed to touch the most people, and meet their needs? Most charismatics would label the same experience a "prophecy."

Similar things could be said for many of the other "charismatic" gifts. Healing is not restricted to charismatic circles, (I could mention some remarkable answers to prayers for healing among other groups.) I have myself experienced what would in other circles be called "the gift of faith," in which I was given utter assurance that certain things would take place, even though the prospect flew in the face of normal prognostications and stood removed from the kinds of promises normally associated with the gospel and its demand for faith. The wife of a Baptist minister, a close friend who serves in a noncharismatic environment, has been praying in tongues in her private devotions for years—ever since as a teen-ager she found herself able to do so, without any contact with (what was then) Pentecostalism. With little effort, I could provide many interesting examples of the utilization of "charismatic" gifts in decidedly noncharismatic groups. The words of Turner are wise:

> Worse, the exaggerated personal experiential dualism tends to be projected onto the Charismatic/evangelical divide to create a claimed experiential dualism between relatively powerless evangelicals, lacking charismata, and Charismatics living in victory, power and the plenitude of charismata. It is this last dualism which popularly undergirds the 'practical argument' for pursuing a post-conversion 'Spirit baptism'.
>
> But the problem for the practical argument is that the dualism breaks down when examined. Healing is not a gift confined to 'Charismatics'; even if practised more often by them. Similarly . . . 'words of the Lord' or 'revelations' (in the general New Testament sense, not in the technical Systematic-Theological one) are not just imparted to neo-Pentecostalists. They are widely reported (albeit in other language) in the evangelical literature too. In other words, on closer examination there is no sharp dividing line between evangelical experience and the new-Pentecostalist one. There is no question of 'leaving the realm of natural Christianity' and entering, by the gateway of Spirit-baptism, into 'supernatural Christianity', as it is popularly put; nor of leaving a *charismaless* Christianity for a charismatic one. The basic difference is one of degree and not of kind; one of emphasis, and not absolute.[62]

62. Turner, "Spiritual Gifts Then and Now," 53.

Reflections on the Charismatic Movement

I do not propose to attempt a grand synthesis, but to offer a few personal assessments of the modern charismatic movement, arising out of the study of both Scripture and the contemporary movement itself. The movement is so diverse that it may prove helpful to enumerate negative and positive reflections separately.

At its worst, the charismatic movement needs to rethink several issues.

One such issue is the appeal to tongues as a criterion of anything. The abuse is particularly strong in Protestant charismatic circles; Roman Catholic forms of the charismatic movement have tended to depreciate the criterion value of tongues.[63] That some form of "tongues" is found in every major religious heritage does not disqualify its potential as a God-given gift in the Christian heritage, but it should warn us that for the same reason speaking in tongues is not a reliable indicator of *anything*—not even of being a Christian. If my exegesis is even approximately correct, there is no biblical warrant for treating tongues-speaking as the critical and normative evidence of a certain level of spiritual experience or vitality. This is not to return surreptitiously to an anticharismatic position and automatically rule out every instance of alleged tongues-speaking without further examination or reflection. Rather, assuming the authenticity of some tongues-speaking today, all Christians should insist *"the same emphasis should be given it that the Bible does. We should not neglect what the Bible teaches, nor should we exalt what the Bible does not."*[64] That means we must agree that tongues do not constitute essential evidence of Spirit baptism; they are not intended for every believer; in public they must edify the church, and follow the two or three rules Paul laid down to achieve this end; and in private they are of little concern to the church, provided the individual Christian who is thus exercising his or her gift of tongues is not blowing it out of proportion, using it as a substitute for other forms of piety, or proselytizing fellow believers with it.

Especially naive is the view of tongues that treats the gift as the great unifying point amongst the various branches of Christendom. Certainly much of the division is pointless. Where there are responsible reasons for division, there has often grown remarkable ignorance of the points of continuity, and not a little animosity directed toward the other camps. One must register a mild protest at this testimony from a Protestant charismatic leader whose experience of the "bap-

---

63. See Francis A. Sullivan, "Speaking in Tongues," *Lumen Vitae* 31 (1976): 145–70.
64. Edwin H. Palmer, *The Holy Spirit: His Person and Ministry* (Phillipsburg, N.J.: Presbyterian and Reformed, 1974), 112.

tism" and of "speaking in tongues" led to a dramatic breach in the walls of partition:

> I now loved those whom I had previously rejected. Only when such personal prejudices are removed are we free to see Christ in our brothers. Then the Holy Spirit is able to teach us what he wants to through them. Oh, what an enrichment it has been to meet with Catholics and be introduced to some of the treasures of Catholic life! The Virgin Mary has come alive and I feel I know her now, in the same way as my evangelical heritage helped me to know St. Paul. . . . The sacraments have come alive, too. Not as lifeless mechanical rites, but as "effectual signs," to use the language of the Reformers, as signs that work when there is faith. Holy Communion is for me like an oasis in a parched desert.[65]

This reminds me of certain ecumenical documents where the aim is to phrase all doctrinal matters with such sophisticated ambiguity that no one can disagree, even when there is no real agreement in substance. Even when we recognize the immense pluralism in contemporary Roman Catholicism, it is disconcerting to find Catholicism credited with introducing Mary to this believer, and placing her on a par with Paul. This is strange not only because there is so much less reliable information about her than about Paul, but because traditional Roman Catholicism, Tridentine Catholicism, elevates Mary *above* Paul, making her a co-redemptrix with Christ. Paul is never credited with an immaculate conception, nor has he undergone bodily assumption to heaven. Can it be that this testimony is hiding points of real difference in order to win sympathy, among evangelical and Catholic readers alike, *for the charismatic movement and for the phenomenon of tongues?* The same questions must be asked regarding this witness's experience of the "sacraments." Why must his antecedent experience be stigmatized as "lifeless mechanical rites," and what he has now learned from the Catholic church turn out, *mirabile dictu,* to be what the Reformers taught? Would the witness want to distance himself from the conservative wing of Catholicism that still holds to transubstantiation? Or would he say that such things do not matter, provided one speaks in tongues? Will either a thoughtful Catholic or a thoughtful Protestant be easily convinced that the only test for unity is tongues-speaking? On what biblical basis can tongues become the supreme arbiter, the universal criterion, of all theological and interpretative disputes?

65. Michael Harper, *Three Sisters: A Provocative Look at Evangelicals, Charismatics and Catholic Charismatics and Their Relationship to One Another* (Wheaton: Tyndale, 1979), 49–50. Or does he think that all Catholic charismatics have abandoned some of the traditional distinctives of conservative Catholicism?

Another issue is the thoughtless justification of tongues utterances, prophecies, and visions that are extraordinarily trite, sometimes heretical, rarely examined, only occasionally controlled, or pastorally stupid. Calling an inanity a prophecy does not stop it from being an inanity.

A colleague recently told me of a charismatic preacher in a Latin American country who told his audience, "God has told me that all people here should have refrigerators. How many of you need them?" Naturally, most of the hands went up—despite the fact that half those who had gathered did not even have electricity in their homes, nor access to the fuel that could run gas refrigerators. The appeal was to crass materialism, and in any case did not even analyze the physical needs of the people very astutely. One might well ask if any outsiders fell down on their faces and testified that God was surely present. The same question might be posed of the meeting where a "prophet" got up and announced that someone in the back left-hand corner had a pain in his big toe and needed to be healed.

When I hear a popular charismatic leader on television (who is revered by millions) telling an emotionally and spiritually troubled woman that her problems would have been solved if only she had prayed more frequently in tongues, I am listening to spiritual humbug without a scrap of biblical warrant or a shred of pastoral responsibility. And when a publication offers to give me, free (not counting the "contribution" of $12.00 that I am expected to make), the audio tapes of the testimony of a returned medical missionary who alleges he was caught up into heaven for five and a half days, conversed with Jesus, Paul, Abraham, Elijah, and others, saw "his" mansion seven hundred miles up from the city's foundation, toured the buildings NOW (sic) under construction, and heard Jesus talk about the rapture, Armageddon, and related matters, the kindest interpretation I can offer is that the sponsors of such stuff combine exegetical ignorance and immense gullibility. Have any of them wondered what μονή *(monē)* in John 14—the word the King James Version renders "mansion"—really means? Or whether apocalyptic literature might require a little more subtlety in the expositor who attempts to interpret it?

Once again, I must insist that these frequent failings cannot legitimately be used by the noncharismatic to invalidate all putative tongues, say, today. But if the charismatic movement wishes to establish more credibility, it could begin by exercising more biblical discernment and discretion.

A third issue is the abuse of authority. This failure is far from being universal: some charismatic believers are among the most humble and thoughtful Christians I know. Unfortunately, they are not, by and large, the ones most likely to be in the public eye. I have heard with my own ears enough preachers within charismatic traditions claim for themselves, their interpretations, and their prophecies an authority only barely less than divine. Driving along with one of them some time ago, I was informed that a certain passage in Matthew meant such and such, because the Lord had revealed the meaning to the brother in question. Having recently studied that passage at some length, I perceived that the brother was relying on an extension of a faulty translation. I tried to suggest, as gently as possible, that the Greek original (of which the brother in question was entirely ignorant) could not be taken to support his interpretation. My rebuttal carried no weight: the Lord had told him what the passage meant, and that was the end of the matter so far as he was concerned. His wife reminded me that spiritual things are spiritually discerned—which I could only assume to be their polite way of telling me what they thought of my spiritual status. There was no trace of concern to weigh or test this alleged revelation. Fascinated, I played devil's advocate and said that I was equally convinced that my interpretation was correct, because the Lord had told me so. We drove on for many silent blocks while my colleague, a clergyman, wrestled with that one. He finally replied, "Well, I guess that means the Bible means different things to different people." Of course, he had no idea how he had just invaded the turf of the most liberal exponents of the new hermeneutic, and had abandoned not only the authority of Scripture but also the basis of all rational communication in favor of epistemological solipsism. From all such "revelations," dear Lord, deliver us.

From the point of view of the manipulated, of course, there is an inevitable transfer of biblical authority to that of the interpreter or "prophet." This must lead in time to a spiritual state not even perceived by the manipulated, in which allegiance has been so transferred to particularly loved human authorities that there is no possibility left for the Bible to perform its continuously needed reforming work.

Yet another issue is a deeply ingrained love of sensationalism and triumphalism, and little knowledge of taking up one's cross daily. I do not mean to suggest that any gift of tongues, say, or any "prophecy" as defined here, or any miraculous healing, should be ruled out because it might be thought "sensational." To denigrate the "sensational" in so sweeping a way, a fairly common ploy among noncharismatics, would surely be to indict Jesus and Paul. Rather, the problem lies in love for sensationalism, in the unbiblical and unhealthy focus upon it. Not only in Latin American countries, but elsewhere as well, this fixation on the sensational soon confuses prophecy and pagan divination, miracle and magic, charismatic and spiritistic. It magnifies the importance of what is, biblically speaking, relatively incidental, while ignoring the weightier matters: righteousness, holiness, justice, love, truth, mercy. It is constantly in danger of sacrificing integrity as the rush towards the sensational pelts on: stories of healings are blown out of proportion, so that the genuine instances are lost in exaggeration and distortion; evangelism loses out to manipulated outbursts of emotion ("Let's clap for the Father for a whole minute! Now for the Son! Now for the Holy Spirit! Now Jesus wants to see all of you wave your handkerchiefs back and forth!"); the straightforward and impassioned message of the cross, proclaimed by a Whitefield, is displaced by endless promises to solve personal problems; and only the Christian whose problems have all evaporated and who enjoys perfect health has entered into the fullness of the riches Jesus promises. In the more extreme cases, the triumphalism is carried so far as to promise wealth as well: give your "seed money" to God (i.e., our organization), and watch God multiply it; you are the child of a king—do you not think your heavenly Father wants you to live in royal splendor? Believers who have meditated long on Matthew 10 or John 15:18–16:4, let alone believers in China, will not be impressed by this argument.

Of course, triumphalism is not restricted to charismatic circles and not all charismatic circles stoop to this malevolent evil. But the association is a common one.

The abuse of authority, a love of the sensational, and a fundamental misapprehension of the Bible's restrictions on tongues all come together in the following advice from a charismatic manual:

> A person should claim this gift [tongues] in confidence when he is prayed with to be baptized in the Spirit. . . . Yielding to tongues is an important first step, and it is worth putting effort into encouraging a person to yield to tongues, even to run the risk of being labelled "imbalanced". . . . Often people can be helped to yield to tongues rather easily. After praying with a person to be baptized in the Spirit, the team member should lean over or kneel down and ask the person if he would like to pray in tongues. When he says yes, he should encourage him to speak out, making sounds that are not English. . . . He should then pray with him again. When the person begins to speak in tongues, he should encourage him. . . . After you ask to be baptized in the Holy Spirit and ask for the gift of tongues, then yield to it. Begin by speaking out, if necessary beginning by just making meaningless sounds. The Holy Spirit will form them.[66]

Another issue is that of immense abuses in healing practices. These

66. *The Life in the Spirit Seminars Team Manual* (Notre Dame, Ind.: Charismatic Renewal Services, 1973), 146–51.

abuses are often nothing more than a corollary of the last problem, the love of sensationalism. But the two are differentiable; and either one can be found without the other.

The most common form of abuse is the view that since all illness is directly or indirectly attributable to the devil and his works, and since Christ by his cross has defeated the devil, and by his Spirit has given us the power to overcome him, healing is the inheritance right of all true Christians who call upon the Lord with genuine faith. The entailment, of course, is that if someone is not healed, the failure reflects inadequate faith, since the promises of the Lord are not to be called into doubt. The toll in shattered lives, deeply wounded and defeated Christians, and immense burdens of false guilt is simply incalculable. Almost as distressing is the fact that so much religious energy is expended on the relatively peripheral, at the expense of what is central and focal in all Christian godliness.

Evenhanded biblical exegesis will not support the view that all sickness among Christians will be removed unless there is a personal failure in faith. Some of the argumentation used to advance this position is tortured. No one who approached Jesus for physical healing went away without a cure, we are told; and since Jesus "is the same yesterday and today and forever" (Heb. 13:8), the same must be true today, unless we approach him the wrong way. Observe two failures in the reasoning. First, Hebrews 13:8 is not in context talking about Jesus' healing ministry, and its alleged continuity into the present age. One cannot legitimately conclude that the verse covers *every* facet and feature of Jesus' life, for counterexamples are easy to come by (e.g., Jesus' determined commitment was to obey his Father by going to the cross, and since he is the same yesterday and today and forever it is still his determined commitment to go to the cross). I am not of course arguing that Jesus does *not* heal today, only that the argument as stated is false. And second, if Jesus healed everyone who approached him in the days of his flesh, but not all who call on his name are healed today owing to their false approach, are we therefore to assume that everyone who approached him two thousand years ago had the right approach, but that somehow this right approach was lost to the generations after Pentecost who enjoy the Spirit?

It is also argued that because "there is healing in the atonement," as the slogan puts it, every believer has the right to avail himself or herself of the healing benefit secured by the cross.[67] Sadly, noncharismatics have sometimes reponded to this by *denying* that there is

67. See the references in Walter J. Hollenweger, *The Pentecostals*, trans. R. A. Wilson (London: SCM, 1972), 515, 517.

healing in the atonement—a position that can be defended only by
the most strained exegesis. Of course there is healing in the atonement.
In exactly the same sense, the resurrection body is also in the atonement—even though neither charismatic nor noncharismatic argues
that any Christian has the right to demand a resurrection body *right
now*. The issue is not "what is in the atonement," for surely all Christians would want to say that every blessing that comes to us, now and
in the hereafter, ultimately flows from the redemptive work of Christ.
The issue, rather, is what blessings we have a right to expect as universally given endowments *right now*, what blessings we may expect
only hereafter, and what blessings we may partially or occasionally
enjoy now and in fullness only in the hereafter. As Packer puts it, "That
total healing of the body, with total sinless perfection, are 'in the
atonement,' in the sense that entire personal renewal in Christ's image
flows from the cross (*see* Romans 8:23; Philippians 3:20, 21), is true,
but it is a potentially disastrous mistake to expect on earth what will
only be given in heaven."[68] In other words, this is another form of the
overrealized eschatology so rampant in the church in Corinth.

The apostle Paul experienced illness, illness that was prolonged
enough for him to change his venue (Gal. 4:13–14). This illness may
have been malaria, contracted in the swampy lowlands and prompting
a move north to the high country around Pisidian Antioch (about
thirty-six hundred feet above sea level).[69] But whatever the disease,[70]
Paul does not reflect any guilt because he was not instantly healed:
far from it, he saw it as a providential arrangement to bring him into
the Galatian region where he proceeded to plant churches. Illness
could also afflict members of the apostle's team: according to the pastoral Epistles, Paul had to leave Trophimus behind in Troas to recu-
perate from an illness. One must suppose that Paul prayed for
Trophimus) but his prayer was not answered with healing, at least of
the instant variety (2 Tim. 4:20). Timothy apparently faced frequent
bouts of illness, for which Paul prescribes a little wine, not a healing
miracle (1 Tim. 5:23).[71]

68. Packer, *Keep in Step with the Spirit*, 277 n. 12.
69. See W. M. Ramsay, *St. Paul the Traveller and the Roman Citizen*, 9th ed. (London:
Hodder and Stoughton, 1907), 94–97.
70. For other suggestions, see F. F. Bruce, *The Epistle to the Galatians* (Grand Rapids:
Eerdmans, 1982), 208–9.
71. Some have argued that ἀσθένεια *(astheneia)* here refers to "weakness" rather
than "illness." The word's semantic range certainly includes both; but in this context
it is hard to believe that something other than illness, perhaps a weakening or debili-
tating illness, is meant. In any case, rendering the word *weaknesses* does not remove
the problem, for if the "weaknesses" are physical and frequent, it is hard to imagine
how they differ from illnesses; and if they are moral or spiritual, it is hard to imagine
why Paul would prescribe wine.

Certainly healing was a part of the early church's experience; certainly some illness was connected not merely with the entanglements of a fallen world, but with specific sin (e.g., 1 Cor. 11:30; James 5:15; cf. John 5:14). But as we have seen, not all illness was perceived in this way; and it is not even clear that all healing was instantaneous (do 1 Cor. 12:10; James 5:15; 1 John 5:16–17 require this?).

Occasionally one now finds respected charismatic leaders making the same points, and in language more emotional and more telling than what I am using. For instance, one thinks of the strong protest of Farah,[72] who insists properly that far too many charismatics not only have a defective theology in these areas, but also that this defective theology fosters a fundamental refusal to face facts: people who are *not* healed even when all the "conditions" have been met. He writes:

Bad theology is a cruel taskmaster. As a pastor-shepherd of twenty-eight years [sic] experience, it seems to me that one of our primary responsibilities is to nurse our wounded sheep back to health by a true liberation theology. Shepherds have to bind up the wounds after the traveling teachers and evangelists are gone and the ravaged sheep are left behind. We cannot therefore, do without an adequate Biblical theology of healing. We need a theology that squarely faces facts; I frequently tell my students, "If your theology doesn't fit the facts, change your theology." Jesus is not, after all, a Christian Scientist.[73]

And to this we must add the need for a truly biblical theology of suffering—a subject too vast and complex to be broached here, even though it is obviously related to the subject. But the silence of most charismatics on the subject must be greeted with some dismay.

More difficult to assess is the movement identified with John Wimber and his associated "Vineyard" ministries, sometimes called the "signs and wonders" movement. Assessment is difficult because documentation is sparse and mostly partisan (both for and against); but because the movement is currently generating considerable discussion, a few tentative remarks may not be out of place.

By all accounts, John Wimber, who self-deprecatingly refers to himself as an ex-hippie, is an engaging, humble, bright, and responsible leader. In the movement that has grown up around him, tongues is simply not an issue. He has been influenced by the view that understands Jesus' ministry to be an inbreaking of the kingdom in advance of its consummation, so that Jesus' work can rightly be interpreted,

72. Charles Farah, Jr., "A Critical Analysis: The 'Roots and Fruits' of Faith-Formula Theology," *Pneuma* 3/1 (1981): 3–21.
73. Ibid., 4–5.

in large part, as a confrontation of powers or authorities. The ruler of this world brings about "natural" catastrophes, illness, demonic attacks, bondage to sin, death; Jesus responded by stilling storms, healing the sick, casting out demons, freeing people from the tyranny of sin, raising the dead. Christ's followers have received Christ's authority, and must proclaim the kingdom and exercise that authority in his name. In this context, sickness and suffering (with the notable exception of the aging process) are to be resisted as evil and rebuked.

Wimber himself operates out of a largely Reformed framework. He attempts to honor divine sovereignty, insists that Christians receive the Holy Spirit fully at conversion (in other words, he rejects classical "second-blessing" theology), and by all accounts has weathered the international fame (not to say adulation) that has come his way during the last five or six years. Invited by Peter Wagner of the School of World Mission at Fuller Theological Seminary to teach a course, he did so with such integrity and disarming appeal that his course became the most popular in the seminary. The last third of each three-hour class session was a "laboratory session" in which not only were there healings and various "manifestations," but in which students were also encouraged to observe closely what was going on, and to question closely those who were thus involved in this "charismatic" ministry.

Many students began the course either for or against, either very open or somewhat skeptical. The majority came away far more open than they had been at the beginning. Even if some "healings" could be dismissed on psychological or other grounds, at least some were so transparently miraculous as to convince most critics who were present. Eventually, however, things got out of hand, at least in the opinion of the Board; and the course was cancelled. Some deep divisions continue; Wimber himself, by all accounts, has responded without malice.

This movement clearly stands apart from the charismatic movement, classically considered, and must be evaluated separately. At the risk of premature judgments, my impression is that it is hard to fault the broad sweep of the theology of the movement (at least as it has been reported to me). Moreover, as I shall say in offering a list of the positive contributions of the charismatic movement, Wimber's ministry and the charismatic movement alike have contributed to a certain "consciousness raising," challenging the evangelical world to expect a little more divine intervention than customary wisdom allows. Nevertheless, a few cautions must be articulated.

First, Wimber himself may be unusually endowed, and may serve with maturity and good judgment—I am too far away to want to suggest otherwise. But the same cannot be said for some of his protégés. For instance, at a seminary near Chicago (not the one at which I teach), one such speaker interrupted his address, which was an explanation of the "signs and wonders" movement and theology, to offer an authoritative "word from the Lord": "There is someone here by the name of Bill[74] with a backache, and you need healing. Stand up, for the Lord is going to heal you!" When this authoritative word elicited no response, it was repeated with even greater gusto, and then repeated again. Finally, a student stood up and confessed he had a backache, but said that his name was Mike. "Close enough," the speaker judged, and proceeded with the "healing." Such nonsense ought to be dismissed for what it is.

Second, the movement at Fuller apparently became exploitative and uncontrolled. Some of the students set out to raise from the dead a recently deceased evangelical leader who had died prematurely; and some of the more bizarre features of this failed endeavor constituted some of the final straws that broke the back of the proverbial camel, and brought about the cancellation of Wimber's course.

Third, there is an important lesson to be learned both from 1 Corinthians 12–14 and from certain major movements in the history of the church. In the early days of the Evangelical Awakening, as I have mentioned, both Wesley and (to a lesser extent) Whitefield were open to the contribution of the "French Prophets." But it was not long before both leaders found it necessary to restrain the more uncontrolled manifestations, and to distance themselves from the movement. Paul's approach in 1 Corinthians is similar: he does not want to stifle the Spirit, but the burden of his appeal is to control the extremes and to focus attention where it properly belongs. From this and many other examples, we may distill some advice. When God graciously manifests himself in abnormal and even spectacular ways, the wisest step that the leaders participating in such a movement may take is to curb the excesses, focus attention on the center—on Christ, on loving discipleship, on self-sacrificing service and obedience, on God himself—and not on the phenomena themselves, and still less on a theology or course that attempts to institutionalize the pheonomena. Such discipline will prove far more convincing to noncharismatics (to use a generic expression) than anything else. But where those involved focus on what is distinctive, either they or their less mature followers will quickly distort the movement, sending it careening into irresponsible extremes fundamentally corrosive of mature Christian experience. Sadly, at that point the noncharismatics will respond with a self-justifying theology of their own.

74. The names and one or two details have been changed to protect the guilty.

A final issue is profound misunderstanding of the nature of God's sovereignty. The subject is too complex to be treated here; but it is related to Paul's insistence that although the best gifts are to be sought, the Lord is the one who sovereignly dispenses his grace gifts as he sees fit. How those two perspectives are simultaneously true, and how each is to be applied to our lives, are complex questions; but it is a wholly inadequate approach that treats God as the great potential benefactor whose lavish bounty is held up only by our refusal to go through certain formulaic steps. At the practical level, we must ask if God may be more pleased when we are deeply interested in *him* and not in certain manifestations; when we learn, like Paul, to live with a "thorn in the flesh" if only it will abase us and enable us to drink deeply from his enabling grace; when we grow in confidence in the wisdom of our God, wisdom that sometimes withholds blessings or decides to work with a modern Job.

At its best, however, the charismatic movement has been a blessing to the church. It is unfair to assess the movement and its fruit only at its worst, as if the prolonged recitation of evils vitiates the need to weigh evenhandedly the immense blessings that have come to us through this means.

Above all, the charismatic movement has challenged the church to expect more from God, to expect God to pour out his Spirit upon us in ways that break our traditional molds, to call into question a theology that without sufficient exegetical warrant rejects all possibility of the miraculous except for regeneration.[75] Of course, this is not the case with respect to *all* noncharismatics. On one hand, we are familiar with spiritual leaders outside the charismatic tradition whose gift of faith, say, was thoroughly exceptional, such as George Müller of Bristol.[76] On the other hand, we are also familiar with those who have been repulsed by the charismatic movement's excesses. But it is surely no misjudgment to say that in general Christians have become more open to the possibility of divine, supernatural intervention in their lives than they were before.

75. One of the weakest arguments advanced in favor of the view that the more spectacular χαρίσματα *(charismata)* were withdrawn at the end of the apostolic age depends on the observation that when the lists of the grace gifts (mentioned in the first chapter) are arranged in the chronological order in which they were given there is a decreasing emphasis on the supernatural members. See Ronald E. Baxter, *Gifts of the Spirit* (Grand Rapids: Kregel, 1983), 83–84; Gromacki, *The Modern Tongues Movement*, 125ff. To establish theology on trajectories plotted out in *occasional* documents, when the documents themselves do not reflect such a theological conclusion in the text itself, is always a hermeneutically dubious endeavor—as witness not a few discussions on Christology or on *Frükatholizismus*.

76. See Arthur T. Pierson, *George Müller of Bristol* (Westwood, N.J.: Revell, n.d.).

Part of the problem in making such an assessment is that positions have in many quarters become so polarized that a sympathetic weighing of the evidence is very difficult. My noncharismatic brother in Christ may hear this assessment, and in consternation inquire as to whether I have taken leave of my senses. Close examination of the reasons for this reaction often reveals that he or she is comparing the *worst* of the charismatic movement, which can be very bad indeed, with the *best* of noncharismatic witness, which can be very good indeed. But this, of course, is not quite fair. My charismatic brother or sister in Christ may proceed along precisely opposite lines of comparison. But in this first assessment, I am not suggesting simply that the best be compared with the best and the worst with the worst, for in my experience at least, the resulting comparisons yield very little difference. Rather, I am giving my perceptions of the charismatic movement as a whole versus the noncharismatic evangelical world as a whole; and in such a comparison, my experience has been that the former group is in general more commonly characterized by a greater openness to God's intervention in their lives than I find in the latter group. This witness is spilling out beyond the borders of the charismatic movement itself; and that can only be a good thing. Wimber is right at the principial level: the kingdom has dawned, and all authority has already been given to Christ to reign in the church and over the entire cosmos.

The charismatic movement has been aggressively evangelistic. It is no response to cite the instances where the movement's growth has been due to sheep stealing, for in the first place there are too many counterexamples, and in the second place many noncharismatic congregations boast of many members who abandoned the charismatic circles in which they were converted but in which they were not being fed. I know of no accurate figures, but I suspect that the exchange of members and adherents between charismatic and noncharismatic traditions has in many parts of the world been characterized by fair reciprocity. Meanwhile, however, the charismatic movement has been growing. Anyone familiar with the church in Latin America knows how much of the evangelistic outreach has been borne by the charismatics. In North America and in Britain evangelical groups are by and large holding their own percentage of the population, give or take a bit; the charismatic wing exceeds that rate dramatically.[77] The num-

77. There are of course exceptional pockets—on both sides. For instance, in French Canada numerous branches of evangelicalism are growing rapidly, not just the charismatic wing.

bers alone demonstrate that the growth of the movement cannot be derided as mere sheep stealing.

Nor will it do to question how many of the converts are Christians at all, for that is a factor that has to be faced by all movements where rapid growth takes place. My own experiences of ministering in charismatic circles do not encourage me to think there is a higher proportion of spurious conversions in charismatic groups than in other groups in the same society. But the reasons for their more rapid growth are complex. The growth is not because they have been endued with the Spirit and very few others have been, as charismatics seem to think. I suspect it is more connected with the fact that charismatics are, in general, quicker to talk about their experiences with God, their faith, the way God has worked in their lives. Effective evangelism depends on many people gossiping the gospel.

It is wholly inadequate to complain that the gospel preached by many charismatics is too self-oriented, or too individualistic, or too unbalanced, or too anything else for that matter, if the critics can in turn be charged with a gospel that is too cerebral, too restrictively theoretical, insufficiently evangelistic, and so forth. There are countless exceptions that break *both* stereotypes; but meanwhile, in more places than not, it is the charismatic wing that is growing. Noncharismatics would be better served by recognizing that an open enthusiasm for Christ, a frank willingness to talk about the Lord anywhere, is the matrix out of which effective evangelism is born.

Related to this, but distinguishable from it, is the fact that the charismatic movement has by and large done better at mobilizing lay people than have most other segments of evangelical witness. In part this is a reflection of the movement's youth, vitality, shortage of academically trained leaders, and triumphalism; in part it is a reflection of the movement's insistence that all believers *ought* to be displaying the power of the Spirit. In too many noncharismatic circles, the latter point is creedally observed and related to the priesthood of all believers, but not integrated into life, thought, structure, and witness.

At the exegetical level, the charismatic movement is surely right to argue that the χαρίσματα *(charismata)*, including the more spectacular of them, have not been permanently withdrawn.[78] Critics may rightly insist that in many (though certainly not all) charismatic circles, too much attention is devoted to too few gifts, and almost always the

---

78. Again, I would make an exception of the gift of apostleship in the narrow sense defined in the third chapter—not because it is a peculiar χάρισμα *(charisma)*, but on the ground that this gift is so bound up with personal acquaintance of the resurrected Lord, in his resurrection body (and for the Twelve further bound up with knowing Jesus in the days of his flesh), that it cannot be thought to continue.

spectacular ones. Critics may also rightly question the linkage that is often made between tongues and second-blessing theology. But in my judgment there is no substantial exegetical or theological impediment to recognizing the continued existence of the gift of, say, tongues. Some of the gifts need to be carefully circumscribed so far as their authority status is concerned, and all need to be tested. Moreover, in a thoroughly mature church, it is doubtful that much attention would be focused on such matters. Nor is it necessary to argue that, say, the gift of tongues must be present in *every* church for that church to be complete: there is no warrant for that, either, and ample evidence that the Lord of the church dispenses and withdraws some of his gracious gifts at various times and for various purposes. But when all the caveats are in, there is no biblical warrant for ruling out *all* manifestations of contemporary tongues, on the ground that the gift was withdrawn in the subapostolic period. And it is the charismatic movement that has stimulated the church to rethink these issues and to study afresh the biblical passages on which so many of these issues turn.[79]

Reflections of a Pastoral Nature

Despite some protestations to the contrary,[80] there is no solid evidence that speaking in tongues is characteristically psychologically damaging. Up until about 1966 it was common for psychological studies to treat the phenomenon as fundamentally escapist;[81] but in retrospect one suspects that such judgments were made because the majority of participants belonged to various minority groups—usually the underprivileged. Once Pentecostalism blossomed into the charismatic movement, however, and virtually every stratum of society was affected in some way or other, the old analysis was exposed as inadequate.

Today other approaches predominate. Some have suggested that the tongues movement is a kind of antidote to the influences of an increasingly secular society.[82] Some of the studies are more interested

79. See most recently Watson E. Mills, *A Theological/Exegetical Approach to Glossolalia* (Lanham, Md.: University Press of America, 1985), 114ff.

80. E.g., W. M. Horn, "Speaking in Tongues: A Restrospective Appraisal," *Lutheran Quarterly* 17 (1965): 316–29. See also Richard A. Hutch, "The Personal Ritual of Glossolalia," *Journal for the Scientific Study of Religion* 19 (1980): 255–66.

81. See the observations of Kilian McDonnell, *Charismatic Renewal and the Churches* (New York: Seabury, 1976); Yves M. J. Congar, *I Believe in the Holy Spirit*, trans. David Smit, 3 vols. (New York: Seabury; London: Geoffrey Chapman, 1983), 2:176–77.

82. E.g., Flora M. J. Pierce, "Glossolalia," *Journal of Religion and Psychical Research* 4 (1981): 168–78.

in physiological and cultural rather than psychological factors: "I want to propose," writes one author, "that glossolalia should be defined as a vocalization pattern, a speech automatism, that is produced on the substratum of hyperarousal dissociation, reflecting directly, in its segmental and suprasegmental structure, neurophysiologic processes present in this mental state."[83] But most studies recognize that tongues speaking, which is usually recognized as learned behavior, often conveys a mild sense of well-being, integration, and power. It is not dangerous in itself, but can be psychologically damaging in some of the *uses* to which it is put (for instance, when it is used as the battering ram that disrupts a community). Tongues-speakers are not demonstrably less well-adjusted than others. They have a slightly greater tendency to follow models, whether leaders or groups; and their experience tends to be for most of them somewhat liberating.[84]

Not a little pastoral concern arises from the perceived tension between institutional office and spiritual gift. How, we may ask, does Christ operate in his church? Does he work primarily through the official teachers, structures, and patterns, or primarily through unexpected disclosures, primarily through "gifted" people?[85]

The literature on the subject is large, and takes us far beyond the confines of debate over the charismatic movement. We cannot probe these questions here, but largely following Fung,[86] perhaps this much may be said. First, there is ample evidence that the church recognized certain offices/functions at a very early period, notably elders/overseers (bishops)/pastors on the one hand, and deacons on the other; but those who performed in such posts were expected to be endowed by the Spirit to do so. After all, there is no intrinsic incongruity or incompatibility between structure and giftedness, between office and spiritual gift. But second, the early church by no means confined spiritual

83. Felicitas D. Goodman, *Speaking in Tongues: A Cross-Cultural Study of Glossolalia* (Chicago: University of Chicago Press, 1972), 124.

84. See further John P. Kildahl, "Psychological Observations," in *The Charismatic Movement*, ed. Michael P. Hamilton (Grand Rapids: Eerdmans, 1975), 124–42; Christie-Murray, *Voices*, 199–228; Gerd Thiessen, *Psychologische Aspecte paulinischer Theologie* (Göttingen: Vandenhoeck und Ruprecht, 1983), 66–112, 269–340; and especially H. Newton Maloney and A. Adams Lovekin, Jr., *Glossolalia: Behavioral Science Perspectives on Speaking in Tongues* (New York and Oxford: Oxford University Press, 1985). Their typology, however (260ff.), borrowed from Ernst Troeltsch, is impossibly reductionistic.

85. The problem is nicely set out by Avery Dulles, "Earthen Vessels; Institution and Charism in the Church" in *Above Every Name: The Lordship of Christ and Social Systems*, ed. Thomas E. Clark (New York: Paulist, 1980), 156ff.

86. See Ronald Y. K. Fung, especially his "Ministry in the New Testament," in *The Church in the Bible and the World*, ed. D. A. Carson (Exeter: Paternoster, 1987).

gift to ecclesiastical office. After all, *every* Christian was believed to have some gift, and some gifts associated with a particular office (e.g., teaching and the eldership) were doubtless discharged in some contexts on an informal and ecclesiastically unrecognized fashion. Office without appropriate grace-gift is sterile and even dangerous; but grace-gift without office is merely commonplace. Third, the more public the gift, the more the church must discharge its responsibility to test the gift and, where appropriate, confirm the person so gifted in office. And it is precisely this corporate responsibility that should, ideally, limit the right of the person who feels gifted to challenge the office without the sanction of the church. But the ideal breaks down when the office is held by those who have not been endowed with the requisite grace-gifts, or when the church fails to discharge its responsibility to test and hold accountable those who serve as leaders. Fourth, the majority of grace-gifts, so far as we can tell, were never associated with a particular office. This is true not only for such χαρίσματα *(charismata)* as encouraging, giving, and speaking in tongues, but also for prophecy. Interestingly, some African denominations today recognize a place for prophets in the life of the church who have no necessary connection with the church leadership. These prophets commonly convey messages of encouragement, rebuke, or exhortation.

Perhaps I should end on a more personal note. For many young clergy from noncharismatic traditions, one of their first major crises will develop when some strong voices in the church call for freedom to speak in tongues in public services, or start to proselytize members in home Bible studies. Precisely this situation has generated the polarizations that have split countless churches. What should be done?

In some instances, of course, the split may be unavoidable. But as I faced precisely this situation, in a fairly mild form, when I was in pastoral ministry sixteen years ago, perhaps I can pass on some lessons I learned at that time.

Our church was divided between a few procharismatics and several anticharismatics, with the majority fairly confused between the two, and asking for leadership. Neither of the extremes was virulent, but it was obvious the situation could have rapidly degenerated. I asked for prayer and time: prayer to hold us together and do what was right, and time to survey in weekly meetings what the Bible had to say about the Holy Spirit. I asked for six months, and the last two months or so of that Wednesday night series were devoted to much the same sort of material here put together in more sophisticated fashion. I have changed my mind on a number of minor points since then, and on several issues where I was less clear about what the Scripture said, I acknowledged my confusion and ignorance and tried to convey what I *thought* was being said, while still surveying other interpretative options.

Toward the end of the series, I tried to summarize what I judged to be true points that fair, biblical exegesis could affirm with confidence. The first and most important of these was that tongues cannot possibly serve as a criterion of anything; the second was that I could not find any unequivocal criterion for ruling out *all* contemporary tongues-speaking, even though I thought much of what I had seen was suspect or was manifested outside the stipulations Paul had laid down. I think everyone in the church came to accept these two points, and as a result, 80 percent of our problem was solved. So much of the divisiveness of tongues-speaking turns very little on the tongues phenomenon itself, but on what it allegedly attests. It so easily promotes pride in those who think that it confirms they have a measure of the Spirit not enjoyed by others; and for the same reason it evokes resentment, jealousy, and defensiveness among many noncharismatics who feel they are being relegated to second-class status in the church. Moreover, because we did not conclude that all contemporary tongues must automatically be dismissed as illegitimate, the few who were practicing tongues in private did not feel threatened or begin to hurl accusations that the leadership did not really believe the Bible and was not open to the Spirit.

We then took two more steps. The first was to invite anyone who had attended the series of addresses to testify as to his or her experience on these matters, and to seek to evaluate that experience on the basis of what had been learned from the series. This proved fascinating. In the mercy of God, enough trust had been established to allow us to listen to remarkably diverse points of view, and without rancor. A few testified how they felt they had been helped by their gift of tongues, but were quite willing to admit that they had unwittingly elevated it to the level of criterion, a step they were prepared to abandon. One person, a highly respected deacon, told of his own experiences in the charismatic movement, and how he had left it because he had come to think that its claims were commonly false. Another deacon who, I knew, had been converted in Pentecostal circles, at first said nothing. I did not know what he would say, but I elicited from him his own testimony, not wanting anything to be bottled up. He cheerfully acknowledged, with gratitude to God, the context of his conversion as a young patrolman in the Royal Canadian Mounted Police. In the long watches of the night, when he sat in his car by the hour in a fairly remote part of the Rocky Mountains, he used some of his time praying in tongues, and he felt that the experience had made him profoundly aware of God's presence and had helped to ground his fledgling faith. I asked him if he still, twenty years later, spoke in tongues, and he replied, "No, I don't." I asked him why not; and he answered, with innocent candor, "I guess it's because I don't need it now. I think that was for when I was a baby Christian."

That judgment, of course, needed to be assessed against the testimony of Paul, who, certainly no baby Christian, could testify that he spoke in tongues more than any of the Corinthians. But the direction of the discussion, including the witness of that police officer, was profoundly right in another sense: without suggesting that all experiences of tongues-speaking are spurious, the general effect was to downplay the importance of the phenomenon. That is surely in line with one of Paul's aims in 1 Corinthians 12–14, and the effect in our church was to draw the sting out of further discussion.

I took one more step. I asked for another week to survey New Testament teaching on church discipline before offering any recommendation; and the congregation kindly agreed. At that last Wednesday evening, I tried to outline the three areas that could lead to the supreme sanction, excommunication: flagrantly immoral life, major doctrinal aberration, and a loveless, fundamentally divisive spirit. It was the last one, of course, that was so important in our context: "Warn a divisive person once, and then warn him a second time. After that, have nothing to do with him" (Titus 3:10). This strong response is a reflection of the New Testament's profound commitment to the *unity* of the church. The question, then, was this: In the light of what we had learned of tongues and related gifts in the New Testament, and in the light of the emphasis on loving unity in the body, what stance should we as a church adopt?

The conclusion was that we would not foster tongues-speaking in public meetings, but we would not oppose them if they occurred, provided they fell within the Pauline stipulations. However, those who felt they had the gift were encouraged to practice it in private, rather than in public assembly where those who were still suspicious of all instances of the phenomenon would have been more than a little uncomfortable. We also agreed in the strongest terms that if a charismatic began to use his or her gift to proselytize, or if a noncharismatic began to agitate to squeeze the charismatics out, action would immediately be taken by the church leaders to warn against the divisiveness bound up with such conduct.

In the Lord's mercy, we did not lose anyone, and in six months, the issue was dead. In retrospect, it is clearer to me now than it was then that many things could have gone much worse than they did, if we had not enjoyed the mix of people who were there. Doubtless in a slightly different mix, or in a different ecclesiastical tradition, exactly the same sorts of arguments might have led to occasional use of tongues in public assembly. But of the thrust of the steps taken, and of the relative valuation of church unity and the place of tongues-speaking, I would not change one iota if placed in a similar situation today.

In short, the church must hunger for personal and corporate submission to the lordship of Christ. We must desire to know more of God's presence in our lives, and pray for a display of unleashed, reforming, revivifying power among us, dreading all steps that aim to domesticate God. But such prayer and hunger must always be tempered with joyful submission to the constraints of biblical discipline.

Select Bibliography

Included are works cited in this book, plus a small number of others, technical and semipopular, representing the spectrum of opinion on the charismatic movement. One or two entries in this list I was not able to obtain until after I had sent the manuscript to press—in particular the dissertation by F. Grau and the volume *Charisma und Agape* edited by P. Benoit et al., though from the latter I did obtain an offprint of the essay by James D. G. Dunn and the responses to it. Commentaries are referred to in the text by the last name(s) of the author(s); exact page references for commentaries are unnecessary.

Commentaries, Other Books, and Unpublished Dissertations

Adinolfi, Marco. *Il femminismo della Bibbia*. Rome: R. Ambrosini, 1981.

Adler, Nikolaus. *Das erste christliche Pfingstfest: Sinn und Bedeutung des Pfingstberichtes Apg 2,1–13*. Münster: Aschendorffsche Verlagsbuchhandlung, 1938.

Agrimson, J. Elmo, ed. *Gifts of the Spirit and the Body of Christ*. Minneapolis: Augsburg, 1974.

Allo, E.-B. *Première épître aux Corinthiens*. 2d ed. Paris: Gabalda, 1956.

Anderson, Robert Mopes. *Vision of the Disinherited: The Making of American Pentecostalism*. New York and Oxford: Oxford University Press, 1979.

Arrington, F. L. *Paul's Aeon Theology in 1 Corinthians*. Washington, D.C.: University Press of America, 1978.

Aune, David E. *Prophecy in Early Christianity and the Ancient Mediterranean World*. Grand Rapids: Eerdmans, 1983.

Bachmann, Philipp. *Der erste Brief des Paulus an die Korinther*. 4th ed. Leipzig: A. Deichertsche Verlagsbuchhandlung, 1936.

Baird, William. *The Corinthian Church—A Biblical Approach to Urban Culture*. New York: Abingdon, 1964.

Banks, Robert. *Paul's Idea of Community*. Grand Rapids: Eerdmans, 1980.

Barclay, William. *The Letters to the Corinthians*. Philadelphia: Westminster, 1956.

Barrett, C. K. *The First Epistle to the Corinthians*. 2d ed. London: Black, 1971.

Barriola, M. A. *El Espiritu Santo y la Praxis Cristiana: El tema del camino en la teologia de San Pablo*. Montevideo: Instituto Teologico del Uruguay, 1977.

Barth, Karl. *Church Dogmatics*. Vols. 3/4 and 4/2. Edinburgh: T. and T. Clark, 1966.

————. *The Resurrection of the Dead*. Translated by H. J. Stenning. Reprint. New York: Arno, 1977.

Baxter, Ronald E. *Gifts of the Spirit*. Grand Rapids: Kregel, 1983.

Beet, Joseph Agar. *A Commentary on St. Paul's Epistles to the Corinthians*. 4th ed. London: Hodder and Stoughton, 1839.

Best, Ernest. *One Body in Christ*. London: SPCK, 1955.

Betz, Hans Dieter. *Lukian von Samosata und das Neue Testament: Religionsgeschichtliche und Paränetische Parallelen*. Texte und Untersuchungen zur Geschicte der altchristlichen Literatur, vol. 76. Berlin: Akademie-Verlag, 1961.

Bilezekian, Gilbert. *Beyond Sex Roles: A Guide for the Study of Female Roles in the Bible*. Grand Rapids: Baker, 1985.

Bittlinger, A. *Die Bedeutung der Gnadengaben für die Gemeinde Jesu Christi*. Marburg: Ökumenischer Verlag, 1971.

————. *Gifts and Graces: A Commentary on 1 Cor 12–14*. Translated by H. Klassen. London: Hodder and Stoughton; Grand Rapids: Eerdmans, 1967, 1968.

————. *Gifts and Ministries*. Grand Rapids: Eerdmans, 1973.

Boldrey, Richard, and Joyce Boldrey. *Chauvinist or Feminist? Paul's View of Women*. Grand Rapids: Baker, 1976.

Bornkamm, Günther. *Early Christian Experience*. Translated by Paul L. Hammer. London: SCM, 1969.

Bready, John Wesley. *This Freedom—Whence?* New York: American Tract Society, 1942.

Breckenridge, James F. *The Theological Self-Understanding of the Catholic Charismatic Movement*. Washington, D.C.: University Press of America, 1980.

Brockhaus, U. *Charisma und Amt*. 2d ed. Wuppertal: Brockhaus, 1975.

Brosch, Joseph. *Charismen und Ämter in der Urkirche.* Bonn: Peter Hanstein, 1951.

Brown, Colin. *Miracles and the Modern Mind.* Grand Rapids: Eerdmans, 1984.

Bruce, F. F. *1 and 2 Corinthians.* New Century Bible. London: Marshall, Morgan and Scott, 1971.

Brumback, Carl. *What Meaneth This? A Pentecostal Answer to a Pentecostal Question.* Springfield, Mo.: Gospel Publishing, 1947.

Bruner, Frederick Dale. *A Theology of the Holy Spirit: The Pentecostal Experience and the New Testament.* Grand Rapids: Eerdmans, 1970

Burgess, Stanley M. *The Spirit and the Church: Antiquity.* Peabody, Mass.: Hendrickson, 1984.

Calvin, John. *The First Epistle of Paul the Apostle to the Corinthians.* Edited by David W. Torrance and Thomas F. Torrance. Translated by J. W. Fraser. Grand Rapids: Eerdmans, 1960.

Carson, D. A. *Divine Sovereignty and Human Responsibility: Biblical Perspectives in Tension.* Atlanta: John Knox, 1981.

————. *Exegetical Fallacies.* Grand Rapids: Baker, 1984.

————. *From Triumphalism to Maturity: An Exposition of 2 Corinthians 10–13.* Grand Rapids: Baker, 1984.

————. "Matthew." In *The Expositor's Bible Commentary,* edited by Frank E. Gaebelein. Vol. 8. Grand Rapids: Zondervan, 1984.

Carson, D. A., and John D. Woodbridge, eds. *Hermeneutics, Authority, and Canon.* Grand Rapids: Zondervan, 1986.

————, eds. *Scripture and Truth.* Grand Rapids: Zondervan, 1983.

Cerfaux, Lucien. *The Church in the Theology of Saint Paul.* Translated by Geoffrey Webb and Adrian Walker. New York: Herder and Herder, 1959.

Chevallier, Max-Alain. *Esprit de Dieu, Paroles d'Hommes.* Neuchâtel: Delachaux et Niestlé, 1966.

Christensen, Larry. *Speaking in Tongues and Its Significance for the Church.* Minneapolis: Bethany, 1968.

Christie-Murray, David. *Voices from the Gods: Speaking with Tongues.* London: Routledge and Kegan Paul, 1979.

Clark, Stephen B. *Man and Woman in Christ: An Examination of the Roles of Men and Women in Light of Scripture and the Social Sciences.* Ann Arbor: Servant: 1980.

Clarke, W. K. Lowther. *New Testament Problems.* New York: Macmillan, 1929.

Congar, Yves M. J. *I Believe in the Holy Spirit.* Translated by David Smit. Vol. 2. New York: Seabury; London: Geoffrey Chapman, 1983.

Conzelmann, Hans. *First Corinthians: A Critical and Historical Commentary on the Bible.* Edited by George W. MacRae. Translated by James W. Leitch. Hermeneia series. Philadelphia: Fortress, 1974.

Coppes, Leonard J. *Whatever Happened to Biblical Tongues?* Phillipsburg, N.J.: Pilgrim, 1977.

Crone, T. M. *Early Christian Prophecy: A Study of Its Origin and Function.* Baltimore: St. Mary's University Press, 1973.

Culpepper, Robert H. *Evaluating the Charismatic Movement: A Theological and Biblical Appraisal.* Valley Forge: Judson, 1977.

Cutten, G. B. *Speaking with Tongues, Historically and Psychologically Considered.* New Haven: Yale University Press, 1927.

Dallimore, Arnold. *Forerunner of the Charismatic Movement: The Life of Edward Irving.* Chicago: Moody, 1983.

————. *George Whitefield.* 2 vols. Edinburgh: Banner of Truth, 1970, 1979.

Dautzenberg, Gerhard. *Urchristliche Prophetie: Ihre Erforschung, ihre Voraussetzungen im Judentum und ihre Struktur im ersten Korintherbrief.* Stuttgart: Kohlhammer, 1975.

DeWitt, Norman Wentworth. *St. Paul and Epicurus.* Minneapolis: University of Minnesota, 1954.

Dietrich, Gabriele. *Would That All God's People Were Prophets: Six Biblical Studies Delivered at the 27th General Assembly, World Student Christian Federation.* Hong Kong: WSCF Asia Region, 1977.

Drummond, Henry. *The Greatest Thing in the World.* Old Tappan, N.J.: Revell, 1956.

Dumbrell, W. J. *Covenant and Creation: An Old Testament Covenantal Theology.* Exeter: Paternoster, 1984.

Duncan, D. *Love, The Word That Heals: Reflections on 1st Corinthians, Chapter 13.* Evesham: A. James, 1981.

Dunn, James D. G. *Baptism in the Holy Spirit.* Studies in Biblical Theology, vol. 15. London: SCM, 1970.

————. *Jesus and the Spirit.* Philadelphia: Westminster, 1975.

du Plessis, D. J. *The Spirit Bade Me Go.* Dallas: privately published, 1961.

Dupont, Jacques. *Gnosis: La connaissance religieuse dans les épitres de Saint Paul.* Louvain: E. Nauwelaerts; Paris: J. Gabalda, 1949.

Edgar, Thomas R. *Miraculous Gifts: Are They for Today?* Neptune, N.J.: Loizeaux, 1983.

Edwards, Jonathan. *Charity and Its Fruits.* Edited by Tryon Edwards. 1852. Reprint. Edinburgh: Banner of Truth Trust, 1969.

Edwards, Thomas Charles. *A Commentary on the First Epistle to the Corinthians.* 4th ed. London: Hodder and Stoughton, 1903.

Eichholz, Georg. *Tradition und Interpretation: Studien zum Neuen Testament und zur Hermeneutik.* München: Chr. Kaiser, 1965.

————. *Was heißt charismatische Gemeinde? 1. Korinther 12.* München: Chr. Kaiser, 1960.

Ellis, E. Earle. *Prophecy and Hermeneutic.* Grand Rapids: Eerdmans, 1978.

Engelsen, Nils Ivar Johan. "Glossolalia and Other Forms of Inspired Speech According to I Corinthians 12–14." Ph.D. dissertation, Yale University, 1970.

Ervin, Howard M. *Conversion-Initiation and the Baptism of the Holy Spirit: A Critique of James D. G. Dunn, "Baptism in the Holy Spirit."* Peabody, Mass.: Hendrickson, 1984.

Evans, C. T. *Love Is an Everyday Thing.* Old Tappan, N.J.: Revell, 1974.

Evans, Mary J. *Woman in the Bible.* Downers Grove: Inter-Varsity, 1983.

Ewert, David. *The Holy Spirit in the New Testament.* Scottdale, Penn.: Herald, 1983.

Findlay, George Gillanders. "St. Paul's First Epistle to the Corinthians." Cols. 727–953 in *The Expositor's Greek Testament.* Edited by W. Robert Nicoll. Vol. 2. London: Hodder and Stoughton, 1897–1910.

Fitzer, Gottfried. *"Das Weib schweige in der Gemeinde": Über den unpaulinischen Charakter der mulier-taceat-Verse in 1. Korinther 14.* Theologische Existenze Heute, vol. 10. München: Chr. Kaiser, 1963.

Fontenrose, J. *The Delphic Oracle.* Berkeley: University of California, 1978.

Gaffin, Richard B., Jr. *Perspectives on Pentecost: New Testament Teaching on Gifts of the Holy Spirit.* Phillipsburg, N.J.: Presbyterian and Reformed, 1979.

Gilquist, Peter. *Let's Quit Fighting About the Holy Spirit.* Grand Rapids: Zondervan, 1974.

Godet, Frédéric. *Commentaire sur la première épitre aux Corinthiens.* 2d ed. 2 vols. Reprint ed. Neuchâtel: L'Imprimerie Nouvelle L.-A. Monnier, 1965.

Goldingay, John. *The Church and the Gifts of the Spirit.* Bramcote: Grove, 1972.

Gonsalvez, H. E. "The Theology and Psychology of Glossolalia." Ph.D. dissertation, Northwestern University, 1978.

Goodman, Felicitas D. *Speaking in Tongues: A Cross-Cultural Study of Glossolalia.* Chicago: University of Chicago Press, 1972.

Grau, F. "Der neutestamentliche Begriff χάρισμα." Ph.D. dissertation, Tübingen University, 1946.

Green, Michael. *I Believe in the Holy Spirit.* Grand Rapids: Eerdmans, 1975.

Gromacki, Robert G. *The Modern Tongues Movement.* Philadelphia: Presbyterian and Reformed, 1967.

Grosheide, F. W. *Commentary on the First Epistle to the Corinthians.* Grand Rapids: Eerdmans, 1953.

Grossmann, S. *Genade-gaven in evenwicht: van charismatische beweging tot charismatische gemeentevernieuwing.* Kampen: Nieuw Leven, 1980.

Grudem, Wayne A. *The Gift of Prophecy in 1 Corinthians.* Washington, D.C.: University Press of America, 1982.

Guy, H. A. *New Testament Prophecy: Its Origin and Significance.* London: Epworth, 1947.

Hamilton, Michael P. *The Charismatic Movement.* Grand Rapids: Eerdmans, 1975.

Harbsmeier, Götz. *Das Hohelied der Liebe.* Neukirchen: Verlag der Buchhandlung des Erziehungsvereins, 1952.

Harper, Michael. *Three Sisters: A Provocative Look at Evangelicals, Charismatics and Catholic Charismatics and Their Relationship to One Another.* Wheaton: Tyndale, 1979.

Harrington, Daniel J. *The Light of All Nations: Essays on the Church in New Testament Research.* Wilmington: Glazier, 1982.

Harris, W. B. *The First Epistle of St Paul to the Corinthians.* Madras, India: Serampore College, 1958.

Hart, Mattie Elizabeth. "Speaking in Tongues and Prophecy as Understood by Paul and at Corinth, with Reference to Early Christian Usage." Ph.D. dissertation, University of Durham, 1975.

Heading, J. *First Epistle to the Corinthians.* Kilmarnock: Ritchie, 1967.

Heim, Karl. *Die Gemeinde des Auferstandenen: Tübingen Vorlesungen über den 1. Korintherbrief.* München: Neubau-Verlag, 1949.

Heinrici, C. F. G. *Der erste Brief an die Korinther.* 8th ed. Göttingen: Vandenhoeck und Ruprecht, 1896.

Hemphill, K. S. "The Pauline Concept of Charisma: A Situational and Developmental Approach." Ph.D dissertation, Cambridge University, 1976.

Héring, Jean. *The First Epistle of Saint Paul to the Corinthians.* 2d ed. Translated by R. W. Heathcote and A. J. Allcock. London: Epworth, 1962.

Hermann, Ingo. *Kurios und Pneuma: Studien zur Christologie der paulinischen Hauptbriefe.* München: Kösel-Verlag, 1961.

Hill, David. *New Testament Prophecy.* Atlanta: John Knox, 1980.

Hodge, Charles. *I and II Corinthians.* 1857, 1859. Reprint. Edinburgh: Banner of Truth Trust, 1974.

Hoekema, Anthony A. *Holy Spirit Baptism.* Grand Rapids: Eerdmans, 1972.

————. *What About Tongues-Speaking?* Grand Rapids: Eerdmans, 1966.

Hollenweger, Walter J. *Conflict in Corinth—Memoirs of an Old Man: Two Stories That Illuminate the Way the Bible Came to Be Written.* New York: Paulist, 1982. English translation of "Konflikt in Korinth: Moiren eines alten Mannes (1 Kor. 12–14)." *Kaiser Traktat* 31 (1978): 5–92.

————. *The Pentecostals.* Translated by R. A. Wilson. London: SCM, 1972.

Horton, H. *The Gifts of the Spirit.* Springfield, Mo.: Gospel Publishing, 1975.

Horton, Stanley M. *What the Bible Says About the Holy Spirit.* Springfield, Mo.: Gospel Publishing, 1976.

Hugedé, Norbert. *La Métaphore du Miroir dans les Epîtres de saint Paul aux Corinthiens.* Neuchâtel: Delachaux et Niestlé, 1957.

Hummel, Charles E. *Fire in the Fireplace: Contemporary Charismatic Renewal.* Downers Grove: Inter-Varsity, 1978.

Hunter, Harold D. *Spirit-Baptism: A Pentecostal Alternative.* Lanham, Md.: University Press of America, 1983.

Hurd, John C. *The Origin of 1 Corinthians.* New York: Seabury, 1965.

Jervell, Jacob. *The Unknown Paul: Essays on Luke-Acts and Early Christian History.* Minneapolis: Augsburg, 1984.

Joly, Robert. *Le vocabulaire chrétien de l'amour est-il original?* Φιλεῖν et Ἀγαπᾶν dans le grec antique. Bruxelles: Presses Universitaires, 1968.

Judisch, Douglas. *An Evaluation of Claims to the Charismatic Gifts.* Grand Rapids: Baker, 1978.

Jungkuntz, Theodore R. *Confirmation and the Charismata.* Lanham, Md.: University Press of America, 1983.

Kähler, E. *Die Frau in den paulinischen Briefen.* Zürich: Gotthelf-Verlag, 1960.

Kallas, J. *The Significance of the Synoptic Miracles.* London: SPCK, 1961.

Käsemann, Ernst. *Essays on New Testament Themes.* Translated by W. J. Montague. Philadelphia: Fortress, 1982.

————. *Exegetische Versuche und Besinnungen.* 2d ed. 2 vols. Göttingen: Vandenhoeck und Ruprecht, 1960–65.

————. *Leib und Leib Christi.* Tübingen: J. C. B. Mohr, 1933.

————. *New Testament Questions of Today.* Translated by W. J. Montague. London: SCM, 1969.

Kertelge, Karl. *Gemeinde und Amt im Neuen Testament.* München: Kösel-Verlag, 1972.

Kieffer, René. *Le primat de l'Amour: commentaire épistémologique de 1 Cor 13.* Paris: du Cerf, 1975.

Kildahl, John P. *The Psychology of Speaking in Tongues.* New York: Harper and Row, 1972.

Kim, Seyoon. *The Origin of Paul's Gospel.* Tübingen: J. C. B. Mohr; Grand Rapids: Eerdmans, 1981.

Kinghorn, Kenneth Cain. *Gifts of the Spirit.* Nashville: Abingdon, 1976.

Knox, Ronald. *Enthusiasm.* Oxford: Oxford University Press, 1950.

Knox, Wilfrid L. *St Paul and the Church of the Gentiles.* Cambridge: Cambridge University Press, 1961.

Koenig, John. *Charismata: God's Gifts for God's People.* Philadelphia: Westminster, 1978.

Krajewski, Ekkehard. *Geistesgaben: Eine Bibelarbeit über 1. Korinther 12–14.* Kösel: J. G. Oncken, 1963.

Kremer, J. *Pfingstbericht und Pfingstgeschehen: Eine exegetische Untersuchung zu Apg.2.1–13.* Stuttgart: KBW, 1973.

Kruse, Colin G. *New Testament Models for Ministry: Jesus and Paul.* Nashville: Nelson, 1983.

Kuyper, Abraham. *The Work of the Holy Spirit.* Translated by Henri de Vries. 1900. Reprint. Grand Rapids: Eerdmans, 1975.

Kydd, Ronald A. N. *Charismatic Gifts in the Early Church.* Peabody, Mass.: Hendrickson, 1984.

Lang, Mabel. *Cure and Cult in Ancient Corinth: A Guide to the Asklepion.* Princeton: American School of Classical Studies at Athens, 1977.

Laurentin, René. *Catholic Pentecostalism.* London: Darton, Longman and Todd, 1977.

Lias, J. J. *The First Epistle to the Corinthians.* Cambridge: Cambridge University Press, 1907.

Lietzmann, Hans, and Werner Georg Kümmel. *An die Korinther I. II.* Handbuch zum Neuen Testament, vol. 9. Tübingen: J. C. B. Mohr, 1969.

Lincoln, Andrew T. *Paradise Now and Not Yet.* Cambridge: Cambridge University Press, 1981.

Livingstone, A. C. *The Miracle of Love.* Boston: G. K. Hall, 1973.

Lloyd-Jones, D. M. *God's Ultimate Purpose: An Exposition of Ephesians 1:1–23.* Grand Rapids: Baker, 1979.

————. *Joy Unspeakable: The Baptism of the Holy Spirit.* Eastbourne: Kingsway, 1984.

Lührmann, Dieter. *Das Offenbarungsverständnis bei Paulus und in den paulinischen Gemeinden.* Neukirchen-Vluyn: Neukirchener Verlag, 1965.

MacArthur, John F., Jr. *The Charismatics: A Doctrinal Perspective.* Grand Rapids: Zondervan, 1978.

————. *1 Corinthians.* Chicago: Moody, 1984.

MacGorman, Jack W. *The Gifts of the Spirit: An Exposition of 1 Corinthians 12–14.* Nashville: Broadman, 1974.

Mallone, George. *Those Controversial Gifts.* Downers Grove: Inter-Varsity, 1983.

Maloney, H. Newton, and A. Adams Lovekin, Jr. *Glossolalia: Behavioral Science Perspectives on Speaking in Tongues.* New York and Oxford: Oxford University Press, 1985.

Mare, W. Harold. "1 Corinthians." In *The Expositor's Bible Commentary,* edited by Frank E. Gaebelein, vol. 10. Grand Rapids: Zondervan, 1976.

Marshall, I. Howard. *Acts.* Leicester: Inter-Varsity, 1980.

Marston, George. *Tongues, Then and Now.* Phillipsburg, N.J.: Presbyterian and Reformed, 1983.

Martin, Ralph P. *The Spirit and the Congregation: Studies in 1 Corinthians 12–15.* Grand Rapids: Eerdmans, 1984.

————. *The Worship of God: Some Theological, Pastoral, and Practical Reflections.* Grand Rapids: Eerdmans, 1982.

Mather, Anne. "Theology of the Charismatic Movement in Britain from 1964 to the Present Day." Ph.D. dissertation, University College of North Wales, 1982.

McDonnell, Kilian. *Charismatic Renewal and the Churches.* New York: Seabury, 1976.

Meeks, Wayne A. *The First Urban Christians: The Social World of the Apostle Paul.* New Haven: Yale University Press, 1983.

Menoud, Philippe H. *Jésus-Christ et la Foi: Recherches néo-testamentaires.* Neuchâtel: Delachaux et Niestlé, 1975.

Metzger, Bruce M. *A Textual Commentary on the Greek New Testament.* London: United Bible Society, 1971.

Meyer, Heinrich August Wilhelm. *Critical and Exegetical Hand-Book to the Epistles to the Corinthians.* Translated by D. Douglas Bannerman. 1884. Reprint. Winona Lake: Alpha, 1979.

Millon, G. *Les grâces de service. La manifestation de l'Esprit pour l'utilité: charismes, diaconies et opérations selon 1 Corinthiens 12:4–7.* Mulhouse: Centre de Culture Chrétienne, 1976.

Mills, Watson E. *A Theological/Exegetical Approach to Glossolalia.* Lanham, Md.: University Press of America, 1985.

Minear, Paul S. *Images of the Church in the New Testament.* Philadelphia: Westminster, 1960.

Moffatt, J. *The First Epistle of Paul to the Corinthians.* London: Hodder and Stoughton, 1934.

Moltmann, Jürgen. *The Church in the Power of the Spirit: A Contribution to Messianic Ecclesiology.* Translated by Margaret Kohl. San Francisco: Harper and Row, 1977.

Montague, George T. *The Holy Spirit: Growth of a Biblical Tradition.* New York: Paulist, 1976.

————. *Riding the Wind: Learning the Ways of the Spirit.* Ann Arbor: Servant, 1974.

Morris, Leon. *The First Epistle of Paul to the Corinthians.* Grand Rapids: Eerdmans, 1958.

————. *Testaments of Love.* Grand Rapids: Eerdmans, 1981.

Mühlberger, S. *Mitarbeiter Gottes: Ein Arbeitsheft zum 1. Korintherbrief.* Klosterneuburg: Osterreichisches Katholisches Bibelwerk, 1978.

Mühlen, Heribert. *A Charismatic Theology: Initiation in the Spirit.* London: Burns and Oates; New York: Paulist, 1978.

Müller, U. B. *Prophetie und Predigt im Neuen Testament.* Gütersloh: Gütersloher Verlagshaus Mohn, 1975.

Murphy-O'Connor, J. *St. Paul's Corinth: Texts and Archaeology.* Wilmington: Glazier, 1983.

Mussner, Franz. *Christus, das All und die Kirche: Studien zur Theologie des Epheserbriefes.* 2d ed. Trier: Paulinus, 1955.

Nygren, Anders. *Agape and Eros: A Study of the Christian Idea of Love.* 3 vols. London: SPCK, 1932–39.

Olshausen, Hermann. *A Commentary on Paul's First and Second Epistles to the Corinthians.* 1855. Reprint. Minneapolis: Klock and Klock, 1984.

Opsahl, Paul D., ed. *The Holy Spirit in the Life of the Church: From Biblical Times to the Present.* Minneapolis: Augsburg, 1978.

Orr, William F., and James Arthur Walther. *1 Corinthians.* Anchor Bible, vol. 32. Garden City, N.Y.: Doubleday, 1976.

Packer, J. I. *Keep in Step with the Spirit.* Leicester: Inter-Varsity; Old Tappan, N.J.: Revell, 1984.

Palmer, Edwin H. *The Holy Spirit: His Person and Ministry.* Phillipsburg, N.J.: Presbyterian and Reformed, 1974.

Panagopoulos, J. Ἡ Ἐκκλησία τῶν προφητῶν. Τὸ προφητικὸν Χάρισμα ἐν τῇ Ἐκκλησίᾳ τῶν δύο πρώτων αἰώνων. Athens: Historical Publications, Stefanos Basilopoulos, 1979.

————, ed. *Prophetic Vocation in the New Testament and Today. Novum Testamentum* Supplements, vol. 45. Leiden: Brill, 1977.

Parry, David. *Not Mad, Most Noble Festus: This Charismatic Thing, What Is It All About?* Huntingdon, Ind.: Our Sunday Visitor, 1980.

Pearson, Birger Albert. *The Pneumatikos-Psychikos Terminology.* Missoula, Mont.: Scholars, 1973.

Prior, David. *The Message of 1 Corinthians: Life in the Local Church.* Leicester and Downers Grove: Inter-Varsity, 1985.

Quebedeaux, Richard. *The New Charismatics II: How a Christian Renewal Movement Became a Part of the American Religious Mainstream.* New York: Harper and Row, 1983.

Reiling, J. *Hermas and Christian Prophecy: A Study of the Eleventh Mandate. Novum Testamentum* Supplements, vol. 37. Leiden: Brill, 1973.

Richardson, A. *The Miracle Stories of the Gospels.* London: SCM, 1941.

Riggs, Ralph M. *The Holy Spirit Himself.* Springfield, Mo.: Gospel Publishing, 1949.

Robbins, John W. *Scripture Twisting in the Seminaries. Part I: Feminism.* Jefferson, Md.: Trinity Foundation, 1985.

Robertson, Archibald, and Alfred Plummer. *A Critical and Exegetical Commentary on the First Epistle of St Paul to the Corinthians.* 2d ed. Edinburgh: T. and T. Clark, 1914.

Robertson, Pat. *My Prayer for You.* Old Tappan, N.J.: Revell, 1977.

Robinson, John A. T. *The Body.* London: SCM, 1952.

Roloff, Jürgen. *Apostolat-Verkündigung Kirche: Ursprung, Inhalt und Funktion des kirchlichen Apostelamtes nach Paulus, Lukas und den Pastoralbriefe.* Gütersloh: Gerd Mohn, 1965.

Ruef, John. *Paul's First Letter to Corinth.* London: SCM, 1977.

Samarin, W. J. *Tongues of Men and Angels: The Religious Language of Pentecostalism.* New York: Macmillan, 1972.

———. *Variation and Variables in Religious Glossolalia: Language in Society.* London: Cambridge University Press, 1972.

Schlatter, Adolf. *Paulus—Der Bote Jesu: Eine Deutung seiner Briefe an die Korinther.* 3d ed. Stuttgart: Calwer, 1962.

Schlier, Heinrich. *Nun aber bleiben diese Drei: Grundriss des christlichen Lebensvollzuges.* 2d ed. Einseideln: Johannes Verlag, 1972.

———. *Die Zeit der Kirche: Exegetische Aufsätze und Vorträge.* 4th ed. Freiberg: Herder, 1966.

Schlink, Basilea. *Ruled by the Spirit.* Translated by John and Mary Foote and Michael Harper. Minneapolis: Bethany, 1969.

Schmithals, Walther. *Gnosticism in Corinth: An Investigation of the Letters to the Corinthians.* Translated by John E. Steely. Nashville: Abingdon, 1971.

———. *Paul and the Gnostics.* Translated by John E. Steely. Nashville: Abingdon, 1972.

Schnackenburg, Rudolf. *Baptism in the Thought of St. Paul: A Study in Pauline Theology.* Translated by G. R. Beasley-Murray. New York: Herder and Herder, 1964.

Schütz, John Howard. *Paul and the Anatomy of Apostolic Authority.* Cambridge: Cambridge University Press, 1975.

Schweizer, Eduard. *Church Order in the New Testament.* Translated by Frank Clarke. Studies in Biblical Theology, vol. 32. London: SCM, 1971.

———. *The Holy Spirit.* Translated by Reginald and Ilse Fuller. Philadelphia: Fortress, 1978.

Scroggie, W. Graham. *The Love Life: A Study of I Corinthians xiii.* London: Pickering and Inglis, n.d.

Senft, C. *La première épître de saint Paul aux Corinthiens.* Neuchâtel: Delachaux et Niestlé, 1979.

Sevenster, J. N. *Paul and Seneca. Novum Testamentum* Supplements, vol. 4. Leiden: Brill, 1961.

Seyer, H. D. *The Stewardship of Spiritual Gifts: A Study of First Corinthians, Chapters Twelve, Thirteen, and Fourteen, and the Charismatic Movement.* Madison: Fleetwood, 1974.

Shallis, Ralph. *Le miracle de l'Esprit: Les sept opérations initiales du Saint-Esprit.* Fontenay-sous-Bois, France: Editions Telos, 1977.

Smedes, Lewis B. *Love Within Limits: Realizing Selfless Love in a Selfish World.* Grand Rapids: Eerdmans, 1978.

Smith, Charles R. *Tongues in Biblical Perspective: A Summary of Biblical Conclusions Concerning Tongues.* 2d ed. Winona Lake, Ind.: BMH, 1973.

Sneck, William Joseph. *Charismatic Spiritual Gifts: A Phenomenological Analysis.* Washington, D.C.: University Press of America, 1981.

Soiron, Thaddäus. *Die Kirche als der Leib Christi.* Düsseldorf: Patmos, 1951.

Spicq, Ceslaus. *Agapé dans le Nouveau Testament.* 3 vols. Paris: Gabalda, 1958–59.

Spittler, Russell P. *Perspectives on the New Pentecostalism.* Grand Rapids: Baker, 1976.

Stalder, Kurt. *Das Werk des Geistes in der Heiligung bei Paulus.* Zürich: EVZ-Verlag, 1962.

Stendahl, Krister. *Paul Among Jews and Gentiles.* London: SCM, 1977.

Stott, John R. W. *The Baptism and Fullness of the Holy Spirit.* Chicago: Inter-Varsity, 1964.

Stronstad, Roger. *The Charismatic Theology of Luke.* Peabody, Mass.: Hendrickson, 1984.

Suenens, Léon-Joseph. *A New Pentecost?* New York: Seabury, 1974.

Sullivan, Francis A., S.J. *Charisms and Charismatic Renewal: A Biblical and Theological Study.* Ann Arbor: Servant: 1982.

Swete, Henry Barclay. *The Holy Spirit in the New Testament.* 1910. Reprint. Grand Rapids: Baker, 1976.

Thiessen, Gerd. *Psychologische Aspekte paulinischer Theologie.* Göttingen: Vandenhoeck und Ruprecht, 1983.

————. *The Social Setting of Pauline Christianity: Essays on Corinth.* Philadelphia: Fortress, 1982.

Thomas, Robert L. *Understanding Spiritual Gifts: The Christian's Special Gifts in the Light of 1 Corinthians 12–14.* Chicago: Moody, 1978.

Thrall, M. E. *I and II Corinthians.* Cambridge: Cambridge University Press, 1965.

Tillard, J.-M. R. *Il y a charisme et charisme: la vie religieuse.* Brussels: Lumen Vitae, 1977.

Turner, M. M. B. "Luke and the Spirit: Studies in the Significance of Receiving the Spirit in Luke-Acts." Ph.D. dissertation, Cambridge University, 1980.

van der Loos, H. *The Miracles of Jesus.* Leiden: Brill, 1965.

van der Mensbrugghe, François. *Le mouvement charismatique: retour de l'Esprit? retour de Dionysos?* Genève: Labor et Fides, 1981.

Volz, P. *Die Eschatologie der jüdischen Gemeinde im neutestamentlichen Zeitalter.* Tübingen: J. C. B. Mohr, 1934.

Vorster, W. S., ed. *The Spirit in Biblical Perspective.* Pretoria: University of South Africa, 1980.

Vos, Geerhardus. *Biblical Theology: Old and New Testaments.* Grand Rapids: Eerdmans, 1948.

Walvoord, John F. *The Holy Spirit.* Findlay, Ohio; Dunham, 1958.

Warfield, B. B. *Counterfeit Miracles.* 1918. Reprint. London: Banner of Truth Trust, 1972.

Watney, Paul B. "Ministry Gifts: God's Provision for Effective Mission." Ph.D. dissertation, Fuller Theological Seminary, 1979.

Weiss, Johannes. *Der erste Korintherbrief.* 10th ed. Göttingen: Vandenhoeck und Ruprecht, 1897.

Wendland, Heinz-Dietrich. *Die Briefe an die Korinther.* Das Neue Testament Deutsch, vol. 7. 13th ed. 1936. Göttingen: Vandenhoeck und Ruprecht, 1972.

Wilkinson, John. *Health and Healing: Studies in New Testament Principles and Practice.* Edinburgh: Handsel, 1980.

Williams, Cyril G. *Tongues of the Spirit: A Study of Pentecostal Glossolalia and Related Phenomena.* Cardiff: University of Wales, 1981.

Williams, J. Rodman. *The Gift of the Holy Spirit Today.* Plainfield, N.J.: Logos, 1980.

Wischmeyer, Oda. *Der höchste Weg. Das 13. Kapitel des 1. Korintherbriefes.* Gütersloh: Gerd Mohn, 1981.

Wolff, C. *Der erste Brief des Paulus an die Korinther. Zweiter Teil: Auslegung der Kapitel 9–16.* Berlin: Evangelische Verlagsanstalt, 1982.

Yocum, Bruce. *Prophecy: Exercising the Prophetic Gifts of the Spirit in the Church Today.* Ann Arbor: Servant, 1976.

Zuntz, G. *The Text of the Epistles: A Disquisition upon the Corpus Paulinum.* London: British Academy, 1953.

Articles

Aalen, S. "A Rabbinic Formula in 1 Cor 14,34." *Studia Evangelica II* (1964): 513–25.

Adolfini, M. "Il silenzio della dona in 1 Cor. 14, 33b–36." *Bibbia e Oriente* 19 (1975): 121–28.

Albright, W. F., and C. S. Mann. "Two Texts in I Corinthians." *New Testament Studies* 16 (1969–70): 271–76.

Almlie, G. L. "Women's Church and Communion Participation: Apostolic Practice or Innovative Twist?" *Christian Brethren Review* 33 (1982): 41–55.

Aune, David E. "Magic in Early Christianity." In *Aufstieg und Niedergang der römischen Welt* II.2 (Berlin: de Gruyter, 1980): 1507–57.

――――. "The Use of προφήτης in Josephus." *Journal of Biblical Literature* 101 (1982): 419–21.

Baker, David L. "The Interpretation of 1 Cor 12–14." *Evangelical Quarterly* 46 (1974): 224–34.

Baird, William. "Visions, Revelation, and Ministry: Reflections on 2 Cor 12:1–5 and Gal 1:11–17." *Journal of Biblical Literature* 104 (1985): 651–62.

Banks, R. "Paul and Women's Liberation." *Interchange* 18 (1976): 81–105.

Banks, Robert, and Geoffrey Moon. "Speaking in Tongues: A Survey of the New Testament Evidence." *Churchman* 80 (1966): 278–94.

Barr, Allan. "Love in the Church." *Scottish Journal of Theology* 3 (1950): 416–25.

Barrett, C. K. "Apollos and the Twelve Disciples of Ephesus." In *The New Testament Age: Studies in Honor of Bo Reicke*, 2 vols., edited by William C. Weinrich, 1:29–32. Macon, Ga.: Mercer University Press, 1984.

Barth, Markus. "A Chapter on the Church—the Body of Christ: Interpretation of I Corinthians 12." *Interpretation* 12 (1958): 131–56.

Bartling, Walter J. "The Congregation of Christ—A Charismatic Body. An Exegetical Study of 1 Corinthians 12." *Concordia Theological Monthly* 40 (1969): 67–80.

Bassler, J. M. "1 Cor 12:3—Curse and Confession in Context." *Journal of Biblical Literature* 101 (1982): 415–18.

Beare, F. W. "Speaking with Tongues." *Journal of Biblical Literature* 83 (1964): 229–46.

Behm, Johannes. "γλῶσσα, ἑτερόγλωσσος." In *TDNT*, 1:719–27.

Best, E. "The Interpretation of Tongues." *Scottish Journal of Theology* 28 (1975): 45–69.

Bittlinger, Arnold. "Die charismatische Erneuerung der Kirchen: Aufbruch urchristlicher Geisterfahrung." In *Erfahrung und Theologie der Heiligen Geistes*, edited by Claus Heitmann and Heribert Mühlen, 19–35. Hamburg: Agentur des Rauhen Hauses; München: Kösel, 1974.

Blair, H. J. "First Corinthians 13 and the Disunity at Corinth." *Theological Educator* 14 (1983): 69–77.

Bouttier, M. "Complexio oppositorum. Sur les formules de 1 Cor. 12,13; Gal. 3, 26–28; Col. 3, 11–12." *New Testament Studies* 23 (1976): 1–19.

Bouyer, Louis. "Some Charismatic Movements in the History of the Church." In *Perspectives on Charismatic Renewal*, edited by Edward D. O'Connor, 113–31. Notre Dame: University Press, 1975.

Bowers, W. Paul. "Paul's Route Through Mysia: A Note on Acts xiv.8." *Journal of Theological Studies* 30 (1979): 507–11.

Bowman, John Wick. "The Three Imperishables—A Meditation on I Corinthians 13." *Interpretation* 13 (1959): 433–43.

Boyd, Donald G. "Spirit and Church in I Corinthians 12–14 and the Acts of the Apostles." In *Spirit Within Structure: Studies in Honor of George Johnston*, edited by E. J. Furcha, 55–66. Allison Park: Pickwick, 1983.

Brattgard, Helge. "Den nytestamentliga pneumatologin och det karismatika." *Tidsskrift for Teologi og Kirke* 51 (1980): 177–88.

Braun, H. "περπερεύομαι ." In *TDNT*, 6:93–95.

Brennan, James. "The Exegesis of I Corinthians 13." *Irish Theological Quarterly* 21 (1954): 270–78.

Brown, Schuyler. "Apostleship in the New Testament as an Historical and Theological Problem." *New Testament Studies* 30 (1984): 474–80.

Brox, Norbert. "ΑΝΑΘΕΜΑ 'ΙΗΣΟΥΣ (1 Kor 12,3)." *Biblische Zeitschrift* 12 (1968): 103–11.

Bultmann, Rudolf. "πιστεύω." In *TDNT*, 6:174–228.

Caddeo, Silvio. "L'Opera dello Spirito." *Ricerche Bibliche e Religiose* 8 (1973): 59–89.

Callan, Terrance. "Prophecy and Ecstasy in Greco-Roman Religion and in 1 Corinthians." *Novum Testamentum* 27 (1985): 125–40.

Carson, D. A. "Three Books on the Bible: A Critical Review." *Journal of the Evangelical Theological Society* 26 (1983): 337–67.

Chenu, Bruno. "Prophétisme et Eglise." *Les Echos de Saint Maurice* 1 (1981): 25–42.

Cirignano, Giulio. "Carismi e ministeri in 1 e 2 Corinzi." *Parole di Vita* 26 (1981): 109–22.

Clark, Gillian. "The Women in Corinth." *Theology* 85 (1982): 256–62.

Cleary, F. X. "Women in the New Testament: St. Paul and the Early Pauline Tradition." *Biblical Theology Bulletin* 10 (1980): 78–82.

Congar, Yves M. J. "Renouveau charismatique et théologie du Saint-Esprit." *La Vie Spirituelle* 135 (1981): 735–49.

Conring, Warner. "Auslegung eines biblischen Textes: 1 Korinther 14." In *Glaube und Öffentliche Meinung: Der Beitrag christlicher Verbände zum politischen Entscheidungsprozeß*, edited by Horst Bannach, 72–78. Stuttgart: Radius Verlag, 1970.

Cothenet, E. "Les prophètes chrétiens comme exégètes charismatiques de l'Ecriture." In *Prophetic Vocation in the New Testament and Today*, edited by J. Panagopoulos. *Novum Testamentum* Supplements, vol. 45. Leiden: Brill, 1977.

Cottle, R. E. "All Were Baptized." *Journal of the Evangelical Theological Society* 17 (1974): 75–80.

Craig, William Lane. "Colin Brown, *Miracles and the Critical Mind:* A Review Article." *Journal of the Evangelical Theological Society* 27 (1984): 473–85.

Cuming, G. J. "ἐποτίσθημεν (I Corinthians 12,13)." *New Testament Studies* 27 (1981): 283–85.

Currie, S. D. " 'Speaking in Tongues': Early Evidence Outside the New Testament Bearing on 'Glossais Lalein.' " *Interpretation* 19 (1965): 274–92.

Dacquino, P. "La chiesa 'corpo del Cristo.' " *Revista Biblica* 29 (1981): 315–30.

_____. "L'autentica carita cristiana (1 Cor 13,3)." *Bibbia e Oriente* 19 (1977): 41–44.

Daines, Brian. "Paul's Use of the Analogy of the Body of Christ—With Special Reference to 1 Corinthians 12." *Evangelical Quarterly* 50 (1978): 71–78.

Danker, Frederick W. "Postscript on 1 Corinthians 13,12." *Catholic Biblical Quarterly* 26 (1964): 248.

Dautzenberg, Gerhard. "Glossolalie." In *Reallexikon für Antike und Christentum* 11 Lf. 82 (1979): 225–46.

_____. "Tradition, paulinische Bearbeitung und Redaktion in 1 Kor 14,26–40." In *Tradition und Wirklichkeit*, 17–29. Frankfurt and Bern: Peter Lang, 1974.

_____. "Zum religionsgeschichtlichen Hintergrund der διάκρισις πνευμάτων (1 Kor 12,10)." *Biblische Zeitschrift* 15 (1971): 93–104.

_____. "Zur urchristlichen Prophetie." *Biblische Zeitschrift* 22 (1978): 125–32.

Davies, J. G. "Pentecost and Glossolalia." *Journal of Theological Studies* 3 (1952): 228–31.

de Broglie, G. "Le texte fondamentale de Saint Paul contre la foi naturelle." *Recherches de Science Religieuse* 39 (1951): 253–66.

Denton, D. R. "Hope and Perseverance." *Scottish Journal of Theology* 34 (1981): 313–20.

Derrett, J. Duncan M. "Cursing Jesus (1 Cor. XII.3): The Jews as Religious 'Persecutors.'" *New Testament Studies* 21 (1974–75): 544–54.

Dollar, G. W. "Church History and the Tongues Movement." *Bibliotheca Sacra* 120 (1963): 309–11.

Dominy, B. "Paul and Spiritual Gifts: Reflections on 1 Corinthians 12–14." *Southwestern Journal of Theology* 26 (1983): 49–68.

Doughty, D. J. "Women and Liberation in the Churches of Paul and the Pauline Tradition." *Drew Gateway* 50 (1979): 1–21.

Downing, F. G. "Reflecting the First Century: 1 Corinthians 15:12." *Expository Times* 95 (1984): 176–77.

Dreyfus, François. "Maintenant la foi, l'espérance et la charité demeurent toutes les trois (1 Cor 13,13)." In *Studiorum Paulinorum*, 2 vols., 1:403–12. Analecta Biblica, vol. 17–18. Rome: Pontifical Biblical Institute, 1963.

Dufort, Jean-Marc. "Comportements et attitudes dans les groupes charismatiques: une lecture herméneutique." *Science et Esprit* 30 (1978): 255–78.

Dulles, Avery. "Earthen Vessels; Institution and Charism in the Church." In *Above Every Name: The Lordship of Christ and Social Systems*, edited by Thomas E. Clark, 155–87. New York: Paulist, 1980.

Dumbrell, W. J. "The Role of Women—A Reconsideration of the Biblical Evidence." *Interchange* 21 (1977): 14–22.

Dunn, James D. G. "Discernment of Spirits: A Neglected Gift." In *Witness to the Spirit: Essays on Revelation, Spirit, Redemption,* edited by W. Harrington, 79–96. Dublin: Irish Biblical Association, 1979.

————. "The Responsible Congregation (1 Co 14,26–40)." In *Charisma und Agape (1 Ko 12–14),* edited by P. Benoit etal., 201–69. Rome: St. Paul vor den Mauern, 1983.

Dupont, Jacques. "La Mission de Paul d'après Actes 26.13–23 et la Mission des Apôtres d'après Luc 24.44–49 et Actes 1.8." In *Paul and Paulinism: Studies in Honor of C. K. Barrett,* edited by Morna D. Hooker and Stephen G. Wilson, 290–99. London: SPCK, 1982.

du Toit, A. B. "Die Charismata—'n Voortsetting van die gesprek. Pauliniese Kriteria ten opsigte can die beoefening van die individuele Charismata volgens 1 Kor. 12–14." *Nederduitse Gereformeerde Teologiese Tydskrif* 20 (1979): 189–200.

Eggenberger, O. "Die neue Zungenbewegung in Amerika." *Theologische Zeitschrift* 21 (1965): 427–46.

Elbert, Paul. "Calvin and Spiritual Gifts." *Journal of the Evangelical Society* 22 (1979): 235–56. Revised under the title "Calvin and the Spiritual Gifts," in *Essays on Apostolic Themes: Studies in Honor of Howard M. Ervin,* edited by Paul Elbert, 115–43. Peabody, Mass.: Hendrickson, 1985.

Elliott, J. K. "In Favour of καυθήσομαι at I Corinthians 13[3]." *Zeitschrift für die neutestamentliche Wissenschaft* 62 (1971): 297–98.

Ellis, E. Earle. "Christ and Spirit in I Corinthians." *Christ and Spirit in the New Testament: Studies in Honour of C. F. D. Moule,* edited by Barnabas Lindars and Stephen S. Smalley, 269–77. Cambridge: Cambridge University Press, 1973.

————. "Prophecy in the New Testament and Today." In *Prophetic Vocation in the New Testament and Today,* edited by J. Panagopoulos, 46–57. *Novum Testamentum* Supplements, vol. 45. Leiden: Brill, 1977.

————. "The Role of the Christian Prophet in Acts." In *Apostolic History and the Gospel: Studies in Honour of F. F. Bruce,* edited by W. Ward Gasque and Ralph P. Martin, 55–67. Exeter: Paternoster, 1970.

————. "The Silenced Wives of Corinth (1 Cor. 14:34–35)." In *New Testament Textual Criticism: Its Significance for Exegesis: Studies in Honor of Bruce M. Metzger,* edited by Eldon J. Epp and Gordon D. Fee, 213–20. Oxford: Clarendon, 1981.

Ervin, Howard M. "As the Spirit Gives Utterance." *Christianity Today* 13 (1969): 623–26.

Evans, Craig A. "The Prophetic Setting of the Pentecost Sermon." *Zeitschrift für die neutestamentliche Wissenschaft* 74 (1983): 148–50.

Farah, Charles, Jr. "A Critical Analysis: The 'Roots and Fruits' of Faith-Formula Theology." *Pneuma* 3/1 (1981): 3–21.

Fee, Gordon D. "Hermeneutics and Historical Precedent—a Major Problem in

Pentecostal Hermeneutics." In *Perspectives on the New Pentecostalism*, edited by Russell P. Spittler, 118–32. Grand Rapids: Baker, 1976.

————. "Tongues—Least of the Gifts? Some Exegetical Observations on 1 Corinthians 12–14." *Pneuma* 2/2 (1980): 3–14.

Fernandez, Pedro. "El bautismo en el Espiritu Santo: Hermeneutica catolica de la renovacion carismatica." *Ciencia Tomista* 108 (1981): 277–325.

Fiorenza, Elisabeth Schlüsser. "Women in the Pre-Pauline and Pauline Churches." *Union Seminary Quarterly Review* 33 (1978): 153–66.

Flanagan, Neil M. "Did Paul Put Down Women in 1 Cor. 14:34–36?" *Biblical Theology Bulletin* 11 (1981): 10–12.

Flood, E. "Christian Love: Some Pauline Reflections." *Clergy Review* 69 (1984): 233–37.

Forbes, Christopher. "Glossolalia in Early Christianity." Unpublished paper. Macquarie University, 1985.

Ford, J. M. "Toward a Theology of 'Speaking in Tongues.'" *Theological Studies* 32 (1971): 15–16.

Foster, John. "The Harp at Ephesus." *The Expository Times* 74 (1962–63): 156.

Fraiken, Daniel. "'Charismes et Ministères,' à la lumière de 1 Cor 12–14." *Eglise et Théologie* 9 (1978): 455–63.

Frohlich, Karlfried. "Charismatic Manifestations and the Lutheran Incarnational Stance." In *The Holy Spirit in the Life of the Church*, edited by Paul D. Opsahl, 136–57. Minneapolis: Augsburg, 1978.

Fuller, R. H. "Tongues in the New Testament." *American Church Quarterly* 3 (1963): 162–68.

Fung, Ronald Y. K. "Charismatic versus Organized Ministry? An Examination of an Alleged Antithesis." *Evangelical Quarterly* 52 (1980): 195–214.

————. "Ministry, Community and Spiritual Gifts." *Evangelical Quarterly* 56 (1984): 3–20.

————. "Ministry in the New Testament." In *The Church in the Bible and the World*, edited by D. A. Carson. Exeter: Paternoster, 1987.

————. "Some Pauline Pictures of the Church." *Evangelical Quarterly* 53 (1981): 89–107.

Garner, G. G. "The Temple of Asklepius at Corinth and Paul's Teaching." *Buried History* (Melbourne) 18 (1982): 52–58.

Gerhardsson, B. "1 Kor 13—Zur Frage von Paulus' rabbinischem Hintergrund." In *Donum Gentilicium: New Testament Studies: Studies in Honour of D. Daube*, edited by E. Bammel, 185–209. London: Clarendon, 1978.

Giles, Kevin. "Prophecy in the Bible and in the Church Today." *Interchange* 26 (1980): 75–89.

Gill, David H. "Through a Glass Darkly: A Note on 1 Corinthians 13,12." *Catholic Biblical Quarterly* 25 (1963): 427–29.

Gillespie, Thomas W. "A Pattern of Prophetic Speech in First Corinthians." *Journal of Biblical Literature* 97 (1978): 74–95.

Gnilka, Joachim. "Geistliches Amt und Gemeinde nach Paulus." In *Foi et Salut selon S. Paul,* edited by D. G. B. Franzoni et al., 233–53. Analecta Biblica, vol. 42. Rome: Pontifical Biblical Institute, 1970.

Graham R. W. "Paul's Pastorate in Corinth: A Keyhole View of His Ministry." *Lexington Theological Quarterly* 17 (1982): 45–58.

Grant, Robert M. " 'Holy Law' in Paul and Ignatius." In *The Living Text: Studies in Honor of Ernest W. Saunders,* edited by Dennis E. Groh and Paul K. Jewett, 65–71. Lanham, Md.: University Press of America, 1985.

Grasso, Domenico. "I carismi nella Chiesa antica." *Augustinianum* (Rome) 20 (1980): 671–86.

Greeven, H. "Propheten, Lehrer, Vorsteher bei Paulus: Zur Frage der 'Amter' in Urchristentum." *Zeitschrift für die neutestamentliche Wissenschaft* 44 (1952–53): 1–43.

Gruber, Winfried. "Charismatische Bewegung des Geistes." *Theologisch-praktisch Quartalschrift* 129 (1981): 262–73.

Grudem, Wayne. "A Response to Gerhard Dautzenberg on 1 Cor. 12:10." *Biblische Zeitschrift* 22 (1978): 253–70.

————. "1 Corinthians 14, 20–25: Prophecy and Tongues as Signs of God's Attitude." *Westminster Theological Journal* 41 (1979): 381–96.

————. "Scripture's Self-Attestation and the Problem of Formulating a Doctrine of Scripture." In *Scripture and Truth,* edited by D. A. Carson and John D. Woodbridge, 19–39; 359–68. Grand Rapids: Zondervan, 1984.

Guillet, Jacques. "Paul on the Discernment of Spirits." In *A Companion to Paul,* edited by Michael J. Taylor, 165–73. New York: Alba House, 1975.

Gundry, R. H. " 'Ecstatic Utterance' (N.E.B.)?" *Journal of Theological Studies* 17 (1966): 299–307.

Haacker, Klaus. "Das Pfingstwunder als exegetisches Problem." In *Verborum Veritas: Festschrift für G. Stählin,* edited by Otto Böcher and Klaus Haacker, 125–31. Wuppertal: Brockhaus, 1970.

Hanimann, Joseph. "Nous avons été abreuvés d'un seul Esprit." *Nouvelle Revue Théologique* 94 (1972): 400–405.

Harpur, T. W. "The Gift of Tongues and Interpretation." *Canadian Journal of Theology* 12 (1966): 164–71.

Harris, W. " 'Sounding Brass' and Hellenistic Technology." *Biblical Archaeology Review* 8 (1982): 38–41.

Harrisville, R. A. "Speaking in Tongues: A Lexicographical Study." *Catholic Biblical Quarterly* 38 (1976): 35–48.

Havet, J. "Christ collectif ou Christ individuel en I Cor., XII,12?" *Ephemerides Theologicae Lovaniensis* 23 (1947): 499–529.

Heine, Ronald E. "The Structure and Meaning of 1 Cor. 13,3–13." In *Increase in Learning: Studies in Honor of James G. Van Buren*, edited by R. J. Owens, Jr., and B. Hamm, 63–72. Manhattan, Kans.: Christian College, 1979.

Herron, Robert W., Jr. "The Origin of the New Testament Apostolate." *Westminster Theological Journal* 45 (1983): 101–31.

Hill, Andrew E. "The Temple of Asclepius: An Alternate Source for Paul's Body Theology." *Journal of Biblical Literature* 99 (1980): 437–39.

Hine, Virginia H. "Pentecostal Glossolalia: Toward a Functional Interpretation." *Journal for the Scientific Study of Religion* 8 (1969): 211–26.

Hodges, Zane C. "The Purpose of Tongues." *Bibliotheca Sacra* 120 (1963): 226–33.

Hoffmann, Ernst. "Pauli Hymnus auf die Liebe." *Deutsche Vierteljahrsschrift für Literaturwissenschaft und Geistesgeschichte* 4 (1926): 58–73.

Hollenweger, Walter J. "After Twenty Years' Research on Pentecostalism." *Theology* 87 (1984): 403–12.

————. "Charismatic and Pentecostal Movements: A Challenge to the Churches." In *The Holy Spirit*, edited by D. Kirkpatrick. Nashville: Tidings, 1974.

————. "Narrativité et théologie interculturelle. Un aspect néglige dé 1 Co 14." *Revue de Théologie et de Philosophie* 110 (1978): 209–23.

Horn, W. M. "Speaking in Tongues: A Restrospective Appraisal." *Lutheran Quarterly* 17 (1965): 316–29.

House, H. W. "Tongues and the Mystery Religions of Corinth." *Bibliotheca Sacra* 140 (1983): 134–50.

Howard, J. Kier. "Neither Male nor Female: An Examination of the Status of Women in the New Testament." *Evangelical Quarterly* 55 (1983): 31–42.

Hunter, Harold. "Tongues-Speech: A Patristic Analysis." *Journal of the Evangelical Theological Society* 23 (1980): 125–37.

Hurley, James B. "Did Paul Require Veils or the Silence of Women? A Consideration of I Cor. 11:2–16 and I Cor. 14:33b–36." *Westminster Theological Journal* 35 (1972–73): 190–220.

Hutch, Richard A. "The Personal Ritual of Glossolalia." *Journal for the Scientific Study of Religion* 19 (1980): 255–66.

Iber, Gerhard. "Zum Verständnis von I Cor.12:31." *Zeitschrift für die neutestamentliche Wissenschaft* 54 (1963): 43–52.

Jacob, René. "Pluralisme et Unité: 1 Co 12,12–30." *Assemblées du Seigneur* 34 (1973): 54–59.

Jaquette, J. R. "Toward a Typology of Formal Communicative Behaviors: Glossolalia." *Anthropological Linguistics* 9 (1967): 1–8.

Jensen, Peter F. "Calvin, Charismatics and Miracles." *Evangelical Quarterly* 51 (1979): 131–44.

Jeremias, Joachim. "ΟΜΩΣ (I Cor 14,7; Gal 3,15)." *Zeitschrift für die neutestamentliche Wissenschaft* 52 (1961): 127–28.

Johanson, B. C. "Tongues, a Sign for Unbelievers? A Structural and Exegetical Study of 1 Corinthians XIV. 20–25." *New Testament Studies* 25 (1978–79): 180–203.

Johansson, Nils. "I Cor. xiii and I Cor. xiv." *New Testament Studies* 10 (1963–64): 383–92.

Johnston, Raymond. "Creation, Culture and Charismatics." *The Scottish Bulletin of Evangelical Theology* 2 (1984): 23–31.

Johnston, Robert K. "Pentecostalism and Theological Hermeneutics: Some Evangelical Options." *Covenant Quarterly* 42 (1984): 3–16.

Jones, Hywel. "Are There Apostles Today?" *Foundations* 13 (Autumn 1984): 16–25.

Jones, Peter. "Y a-t-il deux types de prophéties dans le NT?" *Revue Réformée* 31 (1980): 303–17.

Kantzer, Kenneth S. "The Charismatic Movement." Unpublished class notes. Trinity Evangelical Divinity School, 1985–86.

Karris, Robert J. "Women in the Pauline Assembly: To prophesy (1 Cor 11,5) but not to speak (14,34)?" In *Women Priests: A Catholic Commentary on the Vatican Declaration*, edited by Leonard Swidler and Arlene Swidler, 205–8. New York: Paulist, 1977.

Kelleher, S. "Charisms in the Pauline Writings." *Biblebhashyam* 2 (1976): 196–204.

Kendal, E. Lorna. "Speaking with Tongues." *The Church Quarterly Review* (1967): 11–19.

Keydell, Rudolf. "ΟΜΩΣ." *Zeitschrift für die neutestamentliche Wissenschaft* 54 (1963): 145–46.

Kieffer, René. " 'Afin que je sois brûlé' ou bien 'afin que j'en tire orgueil'? (1 Cor XIII.3)." *New Testament Studies* 22 (1975–76): 95–97.

Kildahl, John P. "Psychological Observations." In *The Charismatic Movement*, edited by Michael P. Hamilton, 124–42. Grand Rapids: Eerdmans, 1975.

Klauck, H.-J. "Der Gottesdienst in der Gemeinde von Korinth." *Pastoralblatt* (Cologne) 36 (1984): 11–20.

Klein, George. "Christian Love According to 1 Cor. 13." *Concordia Theological Monthly* 30 (1959): 432–45.

Knoch, O. " 'Jeder trage etwas bei' (1 Kor 14,26): die Mitgestaltung des Gemeindegottesdienstes durch Gemeindeglieder." In *Gemeinde im Herrenmahl: Zur Praxis der Messfeier: Festschrift für Mgr. Emil Lengeling*, edited by T. Maas-Ewerd and K. Richter, 61–72. Frankfurt: Benziger, 1976.

Koenig, John. "From Mystery to Ministry: Paul as Interpreter of Charismatic Gifts." *Union Seminary Quarterly Review* 33 (1978): 167–74.

Kraft, H. "Vom Ende der urchristlichen Prophetie." In *Prophetic Vocation in the New Testament and Today*, edited by J. Panagopoulos, 162–285. *Novum Testamentum* Supplements, vol. 45. Leiden: Brill, 1977.

Kraus, Hans J. "Charisma prophetikon: eine Studie zum Verständnis der neutestamentlichen Geistesgabe bei Zwingli und Calvin." In *Wort und Gemeinde: Probleme und Aufgaben der praktischen Theologie: Festschrift für E. Thurneysen*, edited by R. Bohren and M. Geiger. Zürich: EVZ-Verlag, 1968.

Kremer, Jacob. " 'Eifert aber um die grösseren Charismen!' (1 Kor 12,31a)." *Theologisch-Praktische Quartalschrift* 128 (1980): 321–35.

Kuss, O. "Enthusiasmus und Realismus bei Paulus." *Auslegung und Verkündigung* 1 (1963): 260–70.

Lacan, Marc-François. "Le mystère de la charité: 1 Co 12,31–13,13." *Assemblées du Seigneur* 35 (1973): 56–61.

——————. "Les trois qui demeurent: I Cor. 13,13." *Recherches de Science Religieuse* 46 (1958): 321–43.

Lampe, G. W. H. "The Testimony of Jesus Is the Spirit of Prophecy (Rev 19:10)." In *The New Testament Age: Studies in Honor of Bo Reicke*, 2 vols., edited by William C. Weinrich, 1:245–58. Macon: Mercer University Press, 1984.

Lienhard, Joseph T. "On 'Discernment of Spirits' in the Early Church." *Theological Studies* 41 (1980): 505–29.

Lund, Nils W. "The Literary Structure of Paul's Hymn to Love." *Journal of Biblical Literature* 50 (1931): 266–76.

Lyonnet, Stanislas. "Agape et charismes selon 1 Co 12,31." In *Paul de Tarse: apôtre de notre temps*, edited by L. De Lorenzi, 509–27. Rome: Abbaye de S. Paul h.l.m., 1979.

MacDonald, W. G. "Glossolalia in the New Testament." *Bulletin of the Evangelical Theological Society* 7 (1964). 39–68.

MacGorman, J. W. "Glossolalic Error and Its Corrections: 1 Corinthians 12–14." *Review and Expositor* 80 (1983): 389–400.

Malan, F. S. "The Use of the Old Testament in 1 Corinthians." *Neotestamentica* 14 (1981): 134–70.

Malony, H. Newton. "Debunking Some of the Myths About Glossolalia." *Journal of the American Scientific Affiliation* 34 (1982): 144–48.

Maly, K. "1 Kor. 12,1–3: Eine Regel zur Unterscheidung der Geister?" *Biblische Zeitschrift* 10 (1966): 82–95.

Manus, Chris Ukachukwu. "The Subordination of Women in the Church. 1 Co 14:33b–36 Reconsidered." *Revue Africaine de Théologie* 8 (1984): 183–95.

Martin, Francis. "Le baptème dans l'Esprit: Tradition du Nouveau Testament et vie de l'Eglise." *Nouvelle Revue Théologique* 106 (1984): 23–58.

Martin, Ira Jay. "I Corinthians 13 Interpreted by Its Context." *Journal of Bible and Religion* 18 (1950): 101–5.

Martin, Ralph P. "A Suggested Exegesis of I Corinthians 13:13." *Expository Times* 82 (1970–71): 119–20.

Martucci, Jean. "Diakriseis Pneumaton (1 Cor. 12:10)." *Eglise et Theologie* 9 (1978): 465–71.

Marxsen, Willi. "Das 'Bleiben' in 1. Kor 13, 13." In *Neues Testament und Geschichte: Festschrift für O. Cullmann*, edited by Heinrich Baltensweiler and Bo Reicke, 233–39. Zürich: Theologischer Verlag; Tübingen: J. C. D. Mohr, 1972.

Mather, Anne. "Talking Points: The Charismatic Movement." *Themelios* 9/3 (April 1984): 12–21.

McRay, J. R. "*To Teleion* in 1 Cor 13,10." *Restoration Quarterly* 14 (1971): 168–83.

Mehat, André. "L'Enseignement sur 'les choses de l'Esprit' (1 Corinthiens 12,1–3)." *Revue d'Histoire et de Philosophie Religieuses* 63 (1983): 395–415.

Menzies, William W. "The Holy Spirit in Christian Theology." In *Perspectives in Evangelical Theology*, edited by Kenneth S. Kantzer and Stanley N. Gundry, 67–69. Grand Rapids: Baker, 1979.

Meyer, Paul W. "The Holy Spirit in the Pauline Letters: A Contextual Exploration." *Interpretation* 33 (1979): 3–18.

Mickelsen, Berkeley, and Alvera Mickelson. "Does Male Dominance Tarnish Our Translations?" *Christianity Today* 22 (1979): 1313–18.

Miguens, Emanuel. "1 Cor 13,8–13 Reconsidered." *Catholic Biblical Quarterly* 37 (1975): 76–97.

Milliken, Jimmy A. "The Nature of the Corinthian Glossolalia." *Mid-America Theological Journal* 8 (1984): 81–107.

Moo, Douglas J. "1 Timothy 2.11–15. Meaning and Significance." *Trinity Journal* 1 (1980): 62–83.

———. "The Interpretation of 1 Timothy 2:11–15: A Rejoinder." *Trinity Journal* 2 (1981): 198–222.

Moss, John. "I Corinthians xiii.13." *Expository Times* 73 (1962): 253.

Moss, Vernon F. "I Corinthians xiii.13." *Expository Times* 73 (1961): 93.

Mowry, M. L. "Charismatic Gifts in Paul." In *Bible Studies in Contemporary Thought*, edited by M. Ward. Burlington, Vt.: n.p., 1975.

Mueller, Theodore. "A Linguistic Analysis of Glossolalia." *Concordia Theological Quarterly* 45 (1981): 185–91.

Murphy-O'Connor, J. "Interpolations in 1 Corinthians." *Catholic Biblical Quarterly* 48 (1986): 81–94.

Murray, Iain. "Baptism with the Spirit: What Is the Scriptural Meaning?" *Banner of Truth* 127 (April 1974): 5–22.

Neirynck, F. "De grote drie bij een niewe vertaling van I Cor., XIII, 13." *Ephemerides Theologicae Lovaniensis* 39 (1963): 595–615.

O'Brien, Peter T. "The Church as a Heavenly and Eschatological Entity." In *The Church in the Bible and the World*, edited by D. A. Carson. Exeter: Paternoster, 1987.

Odell-Scott, D. W. "Let the Women Speak in Church: An Egalitarian Interpretation of 1 Cor 14:33b–36." *Biblical Theology Bulletin* 13 (1983): 90–93.

Osborn, E. "Christology and Pietism." *Australian Biblical Review* 32 (1984): 1–17.

———. "Spirit and Charisma." *Colloquium* (Australia and New Zealand) 7 (1974): 30–41.

Osborne, G. R. "Hermeneutics and Women in the Church." *Journal of the Evangelical Theological Society* 20 (1977): 337–52.

Packer, J. I. "Theological Reflection on the Charismatic Movement." *Churchman* 94 (1980): 7–25, 103–25.

Painter, John. "Paul and the πνευματικοί at Corinth." In *Paul and Paulinism: Studies in Honour of C. K. Barrett*, edited by Morna D. Hooker and Stephen G. Wilson, 237–50. London: SPCK, 1982.

Panagopoulos, J. "Die urchristliche Prophetie: Ihr Charakter und ihre Funktion." In *Prophetic Vocation in the New Testament and Today*, edited by J. Panagopoulos, 1–32. *Novum Testamentum* Supplements, vol. 45. Leiden: Brill, 1977.

Pearson, Birger Albert. "Did the Gnostics Curse Jesus?" *Journal of Biblical Literature* 86 (1967): 301–5.

Perrot, C. "Carisme et institution chez Saint Paul." *Recherches de Science Religieuse* 71 (1983): 81–92.

Pierce, Flora M. J. "Glossolalia." *Journal of Religion and Psychical Research* 4 (1981): 168–78.

Poythress, Vern S. "Linguistic and Sociological Analyses of Modern Tongues-Speaking: Their Contributions and Limitations." *Westminster Theological Journal* 42 (1979): 367–98.

———. "The Nature of Corinthian Glossolalia: Possible Options." *Westminster Theological Journal* 40 (1977): 130–35.

Pritchard, N. M. "Profession of Faith and Admission to Communion in the Light of 1 Corinthians 11 and Other Passages." *Scottish Journal of Theology* 33 (1980): 55–70.

Ratzinger, Joseph. "Bemerkungen zur Frage der Charismen in der Kirche." In *Die Zeit Jesu: Festschrift für Heinrich Schlier*, edited by Günther Bornkamm and Karl Rahner, 257–72. Freiburg: Herder, 1970.

Reiling, J. "Prophecy, the Spirit and the Church." In *Prophetic Vocation in the New Testament and Today*, edited by J. Panagopoulos, 58–76. *Novum Testamentum* Supplements, vol. 45. Leiden: Brill, 1977.

Richards, J. R. "Romans and I Corinthians: Their Chronological Relationship and Comparative Dates." *New Testament Studies* 13 (1966–67): 14–30.

Riesenfeld, Harald. "Vorbildliches Martyrium: Zur Frage der Lesarten im 1 Kor 13,3." In *Donum Gentilicium: Festschrift für D. Daube*, edited by E. Bammel, 210–14. London: Clarendon, 1978.

Robeck, Cecil, Jr. "The Decade in Pentecostal-Charismatic Literature (1973–82): A Bibliographical Essay." *TSF Bulletin* 8/5 (May-June 1985): 23–26.

Roberts, P. "A Sign—Christian or Pagan?" *Expository Times* 90 (1978): 199–203.

Robertson, O. Palmer. "Tongues: Sign of Covenantal Curse and Blessing." *Westminster Theological Journal* 38 (1975): 43–53.

Robinson, D. W. B. "Charismata versus Pneumatika: Paul's Method of Discussion." *Reformed Theological Review* 31 (1972): 49–55.

Rogers, Cleon L., Jr. "The Gift of Tongues in the Post Apostolic Church." *Bibliotheca Sacra* 122 (1965): 134–43.

Rogers, E. R. "ΕΠΟΤΙΣΘΗΜΕΝ Again." *New Testament Studies* 29 (1983): 139–42.

Samarin, William J. "Variation and Variables in Religious Glossolalia." *Language in Society* 1 (1972): 121–30.

Sanders, Jack T. "First Corinthians 13." *Interpretation* 20 (1966): 159–87.

Schelkle, K. H. "Im Leib oder außer des Leibes: Paulus als Mystiker." *Tübinger Theologische Quartalschrift* 158 (1978): 285–93.

Schindler, Alfred. "Charis oder Charisma? Zur Entstehung einer bedenklichen theologischen Alternative in der Alten Kirche." *Evangelische Theologie* 41 (1981): 235–43.

Schlosser, Jacques. "Le corps en 1 Co 12,12–31." In *Le corps et le corps du Christ dans la première épître aux Corinthiens*, edited by Victor Guénel. Paris: du Cerf, 1983

Schmidt, K. L. "κύμβαλον." In *TDNT*, 3:1037–39.

Schnackenburg, Rudolf. "Apostles Before and During Paul's Time." In *Apostolic History and the Gospel: Studies in Honor of F. F. Bruce*, edited by W. Ward Gasque and Ralph P. Martin, 287–303. Exeter: Paternoster, 1970.

—————. "Christus, Geist und Gemeinde (Eph. 4:1–16)." In *Christ and Spirit in the New Testament: Studies in Honour of C. F. D. Moule*, edited by Barnabas Lindars and Stephen S. Smalley, 279–96. Cambridge: Cambridge University Press, 1973.

Schneeberger, V. D. "Charisma und Agape." *Communio Viatorum* 19 (1976): 151–56.

Schrenk, Gottlob. "Geist und Enthusiasmus: Eine Erläuterung zur paulinischen Theologie." In *Wort und Geist: Festschrift für Karl Heim*, edited by Adolf Röberle and Otto Schmiz, 75–97. Berlin: Furche-Verlag, 1934.

Schulz, Siegfried. "Die Charismenlehre des Paulus: Bilanz der Probleme und Ergebnisse." In *Rechtfertigung: Festschrift für Ernst Käsemann*, edited by

Johannes Friedrich, Wolfgang Pöhlmann, and Peter Stuhlmacher, 443–60. Tübingen: J. C. B. Mohr; Göttingen: Vandenhoeck und Ruprecht, 1976.

Schütz, John H. "Charisma, New Testament." In *Theologische Realenzyklopädie* 7 (Berlin, 1981): 688–93.

Schweizer, Eduard. "The Service of Worship: An Exposition of I Corinthians 14." *Interpretation* 13 (1959): 400–408.

————. "Worship in the New Testament." *The Reformed and Presbyterian World* 24 (1957): 196–205. Reprint in *Neotestamentica: German and English Essays 1951–63*, 333–43. Zürich: Zwingli, 1963.

Scroggs, R. "The Next Step: A Common Humanity." *Theology Today* 34 (1978): 395–401.

————. "Paul and the Eschatological Woman." *Journal of the American Academy of Religion* 40 (1972): 283–303.

Seaford, R. "1 Corinthians XIII.12." *Journal of Theological Studies* 35 (1984): 117–20.

Sigountos, J. C., and M. Shank. "Public Roles for Women in the Pauline Church: A Reappraisal of the Evidence." *Journal of the Evangelical Theological Society* 26 (1983): 283–95.

Sisti, P. A. "Unità nella varietà (1 Cor. 12,1–11)." *Bibbia e Oriente* 7 (1965): 187–95.

Sjöberg, Erik. "Herrens bud 1 kor. 14.37." *Svensk Exegesk Arsbok* 22–23 (1957–58): 168–71.

Smith, D. Moody. "Glossolalia and Other Spiritual Gifts in a New Testament Perspective." *Interpretation* 28 (1974): 307–20.

Snyder, H. "The Church as Holy and Charismatic." *Evangelical Review of Theology* 6 (1983): 307–20.

Spicq, C. "L'ἀγάπη de I Cor., XIII. Un example de contribution de la sémantique à l'exégèse néo-testamentaire." *Ephemerides Theologicae Lovaniensis* 31 (1955): 357–70.

Stendahl, Krister. "Glossolalia and the Charismatic Movement." In *God's Christ and His People: Studies in Honor of Nils Alstrup Dahl*, edited by J. Jervell and W. Meeks. Oslo: University Press, 1977.

————. "The New Testament Evidence." In *The Charismatic Movement*, edited by Michael P. Hamilton, 49–60. Grand Rapids: Eerdmans, 1975.

Strathmann, H. "μάρτυς κτλ." In *TDNT*, 4: 474–514.

Sullivan, Francis A. "Speaking in Tongues." *Lumen Vitae* 31 (1976): 21–46.

Sweet, J. P. M. "A Sign for Unbelievers: Paul's Attitude Toward Glossolalia." *New Testament Studies* 13 (1966–67): 240–57.

Sweetman, Leonard, Jr. "Gifts of the Spirit: A Study of Calvin's Comments on 1 Cor 12:8–10, 18; Romans 12:6–8; Ephesians 4:11." In *Exploring the Heritage of John Calvin*, edited by D. H. Holwerda, 273–303. Grand Rapids: Baker, 1976.

Talbert, Charles H. "Paul's Understanding of the Holy Spirit: The Evidence of 1 Corinthians 12–14." In *Perspectives on the New Testament: Studies in Honor of Frank Stagg*, edited by Charles H. Talbert, 95–108. Macon, Ga.: Mercer University Press, 1985.

Thiselton, A. C. "The 'Interpretation' of Tongues: A New Suggestion in the Light of Greek Usage in Philo and Josephus." *Journal of Theological Studies* 30 (1979): 15–36.

————. "Realized Eschatology at Corinth." *New Testament Studies* 24 (1978): 510–26.

Thomas, R. L. "Tongues Will Cease." *Journal of the Evangelical Theological Society* 17 (1974): 81–89.

Titus, Eric L. "Did Paul Write I Corinthians 13?" *Journal of Bible and Religion* 27 (1959): 299–302.

Toews, J. E. "The Role of Women in the Church: The Pauline Perspective." *Direction* 9 (1980): 25–35.

Tolbert, M. O. "The Place of Spiritual Gifts in Ministry." *Theological Educator* 14 (1983): 53–63.

Toussaint, S. D. "First Corinthians Thirteen and the Tongues Question." *Bibliotheca Sacra* 120 (1963): 311–16.

Trompf, G. W. "On Attitudes Toward Women in Paul and Paulinist Literature: 1 Corinthians 11:3–16 and Its Context." *Catholic Biblical Quarterly* 42 (1980): 196–215.

Trummer, P. "Charismatischer Gottesdienst. Liturgische Impulse aus 1 Cor 12 und 14." *Bibel und Liturgie* 54 (1981): 173–78.

Tuckett, C. M. "1 Corinthians and Q." *Journal of Biblical Literature* 102 (1983): 607–19.

Tulane, Carl G. "The Confusion About Tongues." *Christianity Today* 13 (1968): 7–9.

Turner, M. M. B. "The Concept of Receiving the Spirit in John's Gospel." *Vox Evangelica* 10 (1977): 24–42.

————. "Jesus and the Spirit in Lucan Perspectives." *Tyndale Bulletin* 32 (1981): 3–42.

————. "The Significance of Receiving the Spirit in Luke-Acts: A Summary of Modern Scholarship." *Trinity Journal* 2 (1981): 131–58.

————. "Spirit Endowment in Luke-Acts: Some Linguistic Considerations." *Vox Evangelica* 12 (1981): 45–63.

————. "Spiritual Gifts Then and Now." *Vox Evangelica* 15 (1985): 7–64.

Van Elderen, B. "Glossolalia in the New Testament." *Bulletin of the Evangelical Theological Society* 7 (1964): 53–58.

van Unnik, W. C. "Jesus: Anathema or Kyrios (I Cor. 12:3)." In *Christ and Spirit in the New Testament: Studies in Honour of C. F. D. Moule*, edited by Barnabas

Lindars and Stephen S. Smalley, 113–26. Cambridge: Cambridge University Press, 1973.

Vella, A. G. "Agapé in I Corinthians XIII." *Melita Theologica* 18 (1966): 22–31, 57–66.

von Rad, Gerhard. "Die Vorgeschichte der Gattung von 1 Cor. 13,4–7." In *Geschichte und Altes Testament: Festschrift für A. Alt*, 153–68. Tübingen: J. C. B. Mohr, 1953. Translated under the title *The Problem of the Hexateuch and Other Essays*, 301–17. Edinburgh: Oliver and Boyd, 1965.

Walker, W. O. "The 'Theology of Women's Place' and the 'Paulinist' Tradition." *Semeia* 28 (1983): 101–12.

Weeks, Noel. "On Silence and Head Covering." *Westminster Theological Journal* 35 (1972): 21–27.

Wiebe, Phillip H. "The Pentecostal Initial Evidence Doctrine." *Journal of the Evangelical Theological Society* 27 (1984): 465–72.

Wilkinson, T. L. "Tongues and Prophecy in Acts and 1st Corinthians." *Vox Reformata* 31 (1978): 1–20.

Williams, Cyril G. "Glossolalia as a Religious Phenomenon: 'Tongues' at Corinth and Pentecost." *Journal of Religion and Religions* 5 (1975): 16–32.

Williams, George H., and Edith Waldvogel. "A History of Speaking in Tongues and Related Gifts." In *The Charismatic Movement*, edited by Michael P. Hamilton, 61–113. Grand Rapids: Eerdmans, 1975.

Wischmeyer, O. "Traditionsgeschichtliche Untersuchung der paulinischen Aussagen über die Liebe (ἀγάπη)." *Zeitschrift für die neutestamentliche Wissenschaft* 74 (1983): 222–36.

Wright, G. "Diversity in the Church." *Theological Educator* 14 (1983): 64–68.

Zens, Jon. "Aspects of Female Priesthood: A Focus on 1 Cor. 11:2–16 and 1 Cor. 14:34–35." *Baptist Reformation Review* 10/3 (1981): 3–18.

————. "Building up the Body—One Man or One Another?" *Baptist Reformation Review* 10/2 (1981): 10–29.

Index of Subjects

217

103–4; private use of, 35, 104–5, 143,
157, 169; and prophecy, 100–3, 117–
21, 121–31; speaking in, 18, 36, 58–
61, 70, 76, 77–87, 134, 138–39, 157–
60, 165–66, 170–71; and unbelievers,
108–17, 147; xenoglossia, 79, 138. *See
also* Language, known

Visions, 35, 141, 164. *See also*
Revelations

Wisdom, word of, 38, 135
Wonders of God, 138, 142
Women, 16, 121–31
Worship: pagan, 25; order in Christian,
117–31

Zēloō, 53–58

Index of Names

Index of Scripture

225